10

4 sons
3 daus

olin
889–92)

Mary
(*b* 1895)
= Tom Strickland
(*d* 1938)
= Major John Lyon
(*b* 1901)

Ivo
(1896–1915)

Irene
(*b* 1902)
= 2nd Earl of
Plymouth
(1889–1943)

sons

Mary
(1919–62)
= Roderic Thesiger
(*b* 1915)
= Nigel Grey
(1891–1974)

Hugo
(1922–70)
= Virginia
Forbes Adam
(*b* 1922)

Francis
(*b* 1951)
= Frances-Jane
Harper

Richard
(1949–51)

Frances
(*b* 1950)

Jane
(*b* 1953)

Perdita
(*b* 1955)
= Jeremy Beckett
(*b* 1952)

James
(*b* 1958)

LAUGHTER FROM A CLOUD

LAUGHTER FROM A CLOUD

Laura,
Duchess of Marlborough

For Linda & Bob
With Much
Appriation & Thanks
Laura Marlborough

27 May 1980

WEIDENFELD AND NICOLSON
LONDON

ISBN 0 297 77739 4

Printed and bound in Great Britain by
Butler & Tanner Ltd
Frome and London

CONTENTS

The title of this book is taken from a passage written by my grandmother, Lady Wemyss, quoting her friend, Professor Sir Walter Raleigh (1861–1922):

I wish my children and grandchildren to remember me when they are happy and glad, and to be glad and happy when they remember me. I like to think, as dear 'Professor' Raleigh said, that when they read these lines they may think they hear the echo of my 'laughter from a cloud'.

ILLUSTRATIONS

The publishers would like to thank the author for kindly lending us all the photographs except number 22.

ACKNOWLEDGEMENTS

I am grateful to the following for granting me permission to quote copyright material: Mr Winston S. Churchill (the letters of his father, the late Randolph S. Churchill), Mr Cole Lesley ('Mongoose Annee' by the late Sir Noël Coward), Mr Anthony Pelissier (his poem 'Lady Boy'), and Mrs Hugo Charteris (my late brother's letters).

The family trees were compiled by Hugo Vickers.

L.M.

For Michael
(1926–69)

I

Childhood

The progress of the Duke of Norfolk since he underwent an operation has been steady and continuous ... Miss Asquith is now well on the road to complete recovery, and has been able to go out for a motor drive ... Mrs Sheppard, owing to an attack of neuritis was unable to have the honour of dining with Their Majesties at Windsor Castle on Tuesday evening ... The Hon. Mrs Guy Charteris gave birth to a daughter on Tuesday at 26, Catherine Street, Westminster.

Thus did *The Times* Court page greet the news of my birth in August 1915, while the Great War raged on, a war in which three of my uncles died in common with very many of their generation. Apparently – horrifying to contemplate – I nearly killed my mother as I weighed twelve pounds, and the doctors and nurses were so busy trying to save her life that I was given to 'Percey', my Tennant grandmother's ladies' maid, who told me years later that she was terrified of the responsibility. Anyhow, I am here to tell the tale. I must have been meant to survive as I even rose above being sat upon (literally) by my aunt Kakoo (the Duchess of Rutland), on my mother's bed shortly after I was born.

It is true to say that I was born into what is known as the privileged class. I prefer the word 'aristocracy'. It used to mean something, and certainly one took one's place in it for granted, but at the same time I was quite pleased about the fact when I was old enough to appreciate it. Now there are so many Peers it is becoming a bit of a joke.

My father was the only surviving son of the eleventh Earl of Wemyss, and my mother was a Tennant, so I am the product of the union of two distinctive and interesting Scottish families. The Wemysses go back into the mists of time. An early ancestor escorted Margaret, the Maid of Norway, to Scotland in 1290. Another was killed at the battle of Flodden. But I have always had a soft spot for a less admirable predecessor, about whom my grandfather used to tell me as a child. This was the notorious Colonel Francis Charteris who succeeded in being drummed out of three regiments in his lifetime for cheating at cards, theft and embezzlement. Later he took to gambling and money-lending, on which he founded his vast fortune. His character did not improve in his later years, and at the age of fifty-five he was put in prison for raping his maidservant – a recurrent vice of his. When he died in 1732 his body was savagely mutilated by the mob on the way to his funeral. Of the Colonel it has been said: 'Without the excuse of low environment he demeaned himself more indecently and immorally than the lowest denizen of the London which his presence disgraced. He was so bad a man that even the title of a rake, as we accept it, is degraded by its association with his person and his ways.' (E. Beresford Chancellor, *Lives of the Rakes*, Philip Allen and Co., 1925, III, p. 166.)

In contrast to the Wemysses and Charterises, the Tennants had their origins as crofters in Ayrshire in the seventeenth century, rising to riches and power through the Industrial Revolution. There was a famous Glasgow landmark known as Tennant's Stalk (pronounced 'stack' in Scotland), a chimney three times the height of Nelson's Column, which dominated the chemical factory created by Charles Tennant after he had revolutionized the industrial world with his patented bleaching powder and other products. The Tennant story is one of those romances of industry, spreading eventually into gold, copper and sulphur mines, steelmaking and shipbuilding. It makes me sad in a way as I have always considered the Industrial Revolution to have been a disaster for this country, but that was how the fortune of one side of my family was made. I can only add that not a penny of it came my way!

The Victorian entrepreneur of the family was my great-grandfather, Sir Charles Tennant, who was born in 1823 and lived into this century. He was a Liberal Member of Parliament and married twice, producing sixteen children. The most famous of his daughters was Margot, who made her mark as the wife of Asquith, the Prime Minister. Then there were two daughters noted for their beauty, both of whom died young, Charty (Lady

Ribblesdale) and Laura Lyttelton, after whom I am named. By all accounts Laura was very lovable and inspired devotion in all who knew her. When she died in childbirth aged twenty-three, she was deeply mourned. By his second marriage at the age of seventy-five Sir Charles had four more daughters, and because of the great age span between the sixteen children, I still have two great-aunts living today, Peggy (Dame Margaret Wakehurst), and Kay (Baroness Elliot of Harwood).

I have no preference for either side of my family, having been tossed between my four grandparents during half my childhood years. Their houses and lives were very different, both representing the rich and fashionable life of their epoch but in absolutely opposite ways. As a child of a Tennant–Charteris marriage, brought up amongst these families in their different homes, my early days were far removed from what is generally understood as normal childhood. Surrounded by grandparents and several generations of eccentric aunts and uncles, there was an ever-present link with the influences of the past. However unhappy or lonely I have been later in life, this accident of birth has always saved me from what I most dread, monotony and boredom.

I was christened Frances Laura, though, according to the files of Somerset House, I was born Jean Charteris, a name I have little liking for. In later life I used to ask my father about this, but got no more satisfactory answer than 'It's quite impossible.' So I shall have to leave 'Jean' as one of the mysteries of life and forget her.

My earliest recollections are of total adoration of my mother, who died young. She must have been a heavenly person – so many people who knew her have told me this – and it more than explains how I felt about her as a small child.

My parents had four children – Ann, then me, then another daughter, Mary Rose, the youngest being my only brother, Hugo. I loved my elder sister very much as a child and still do, but we are very different. My younger sister I never liked much but my brother I loved deeply. My father played little part in my life until I was somewhat older. Then I enjoyed his company enormously, but not really as a father. He was talented in many ways. I believe he had some kind of work at a place called the 'Investment Registry', but I would say he was an inefficient and uninterested man of business. He loved the country and was a great ornithologist and, suitably enough, he was a 'cuckoo' as far as his children were concerned. He was a shy and sensitive man, so when I think of him as I knew him in my childhood I always try to allow for the shock and misery he must have suffered, finding himself alone with four young children. I suppose he didn't know what to do and so, not unnaturally, did nothing, leaving our upbringing to our grandparents, aunts and uncles. He seemed at his happiest when poised intently over his birds egg collection. Eventually, twenty years after my mother's death, he married my step-mother, Violet Porter from Dundee.

My birthplace was a house in an unspoilt street in Westminster, 26 Catherine Street, which my Tennant grandparents had built for my mother as a wedding present. There we spent our winters. The street was rather poor and quiet, except that it had many public houses on the corners of adjoining streets like Buckingham Street, now called Buckingham Place. Our house happened also to be a corner house. It was quite large and commodious but not grand like the houses of many of the children with whom we did our various lessons or went to tea. In those days girls very rarely went away to school; they attended day schools. Nor did we ever have a butler or housekeeper, though there was a cook and plenty of maids. Compared to our relations who had a full staff, we felt quite poor.

There was a small house opposite the schoolroom windows, shared by George Gage and 'Chips' Channon. Neither was married at that time and we used to call them Mr and Mrs Chips or Lord and Lady Gage. One Christmas Chips presented me with an enormous teddy-bear. The reason for this unexpected generosity was that he was courting my youngest aunt, 'Bibs' (Lady Irene Charteris), at the time. His ploy failed however, for in 1921 she married Lord Windsor, later the Earl of Plymouth. Also nearby lived an attractive blonde called Edyth Baker, who was a well-known pianist and to whom we listened in grateful relief from our own hopeless piano lessons. Just round the corner at 10 Buckingham Street lived Lord and Lady Lytton. Pamela Lytton was a famous beauty who lived till the age of ninety-seven. She had captured the heart of Winston Churchill in India in the 1890s and he described her as the most beautiful girl he had ever seen. He must have continued to think that, for much later his son Randolph told me that they lunched together at the Savoy on their respective birthdays well into old age, much to the annoyance of Clemmie.

There was little traffic so we could roller-skate in the middle of the road. Those were happy days and many memories remain vivid – street cries, small pony-drawn carts selling their various wares, and the rather elegant and acrobatic fellow who whirled round our street lighting the gas standards, treating his bicycle as a polo pony, a long rod in his hand with which he poked the gas into life at dusk, hardly pausing at each lamp-post, never dismounting, never missing his target, whistling all the while and leaving a warm glowing trail. I loved to watch for him as evening came. All these phantoms have faded away into the twilight; there is no time or space for them in the neon-lit London of today. The barrel-organ grinder and his monkey Tick were another great feature of our street; even before my mother died they were one of the few things I liked about London. I certainly hated the dreary walks in Hyde Park. St James's Park wasn't so bad, for there at least we could feed the many wonderful-looking species of ducks and the pelicans which were black from London soot. I thought it foolish to go to the parks, all dressed up and clean to please our nanny who, in turn, wanted to show off to other nannies. My sister Ann was pushed by Nanny Oger and I was trundled along by the nursery maid. It should have been the other way round, as I was the younger, but I don't look back in anger over that. Nanny Oger came from the unkind version of the breed. Once she kicked my brother across the nursery on his china potty, which broke; he always said he would carry the scars till the day he died. My sister Ann was her favourite.

In the summer, we rented various houses in the country. 'Taken' houses are seldom memorable or attractive, but I do remember proper teas being laid out on a table on the lawn, and it seemed warmer than our summers are now. Also, tea as a real meal isn't made much of nowadays. We children were allowed to take part in these grown-up feasts as long as we put on clean, rather starched cotton frocks, particularly if our parents had friends to stay. Some days we had picnics. Most people love picnics but I have always disliked them and still do. They are invariably uncomfortable and more fun for the mosquitoes than the guests. The days we went in the pony cart were not so bad. I had secret talks with the pony; I always loved all animals.

I haven't yet said anything about the way I looked. Well, it wasn't too good. I was much too fat and something funny had happened to my legs; I was knock-kneed, and still am; also bow-legged. I had horrid great splints strapped on at bedtime. I hated the splints and I've been self-conscious about my legs ever since, although they are not so bad now that I am thin, but if I stand naturally I still look as though I had been born on a horse. My face was greenish-white, but I did have rather nice brown eyes. I learnt more about them later in life. Randolph Churchill always called my eyes and lashes my 'shutters'. I often felt sick, in fact I often was sick. I used to overhear discussions as to whether I really was ill or whether it was because my mother was going away and I wanted to go too. But I didn't do it on purpose; I just felt sick.

My first ten years of life were nonetheless very happy. Winters in London, summers in rented country houses, holidays divided between grandparents, sometimes a short unpleasant two weeks of 'sea air' at lodging houses with Nanny. Of all the places we went to in order to benefit our health, I hated Broadstairs most; perhaps that is why I have such an antipathy to Mr Edward Heath. My mind goes back to paddling in icy water and making dull and ludicrous sandcastles, occasional rides on poor old sea-side ponies, trying to make them jump the breakwaters to relieve the general dullness of a holiday by the sea.

One summer we had a house near Cobham in Surrey. I had my first pony. I don't suppose she was much to look at, but I thought she was the most beautiful thoroughbred in the world. I spent hours grooming her and attending to her smallest needs. I called her Greta Garbo. Papa spent his time bird-nesting, always dressed in dirty old clothes, with just his bottom showing out of some hedge, the rest of his body invisible as he stole eggs from some poor bird for his collection. At this house we had a new nursery governess. One day we were returning from a walk with her, when my Papa hove into sight, looking his usual scruffy self. This governess, having never met him, was horrified when we ran towards him. 'Come here, children,' she screamed. 'Keep away from that dirty tramp.' Normally our governesses were young and they came and went at a great rate. Most of them were hysterically inclined and seemed to cry very easily when we put frogs and worms in their beds to precipitate their departure. Many of them were French, so they were probably homesick. Later on we had older governesses, made of sterner stuff, particularly one called Mlle Angerhoff. She seemed to stay for ever but I was quite fond of her. Despite the fact they fought like fiends my brother also liked her and kept in touch with her till her death.

Life drifted on. I realize now how happy I was that last summer we were all together. How often one doesn't fully appreciate one's good fortune and just takes it for granted until some twist of fate unexpectedly takes it away, and one's life is smashed till one starts again. One August when we were staying with my Wemyss grandparents at Gosford in East Lothian, my mother went for a walk with the agent, Mr Connor. On her return she looked sad. I asked where she had been and she replied gently and naturally: 'I have been to choose the place where I shall be buried when I die.' Suddenly I felt quite cold; it was no longer a glowing summer morning full of fun and excitement. I asked no more – which was unlike me – but from that moment I could hardly bear to let my mother out of my sight; I felt how necessary and precious she was to me. I shall never forget that day, or indeed the autumn of 1925.

I was just ten years old. We returned to London in late September to the usual round of classes and lessons in the schoolroom. We had been to various day schools but this year it was home tuition. Later on I went to Miss Wolf's famous little day school, famous really for letting us do nothing. Although my mother seemed well, I was unhappy all that October, haunted by what she had told me in Scotland. Then on 5 November 1925, my small world crashed around me. My mother was my entire life, perhaps to an unusual extent, but that's how it was. All morning during the dreary lessons in the schoolroom, which was on the ground floor, I had a frightening feeling that *something* had gone wrong – that something was that my mother had died. She had been to Stanway, my Wemyss grandparents' Gloucestershire house, for the weekend. She had returned, exhausted, on Sunday evening to enter a Park Lane nursing home to undergo a minor gynaecological operation. We visited her on the Sunday evening before bedtime. On the Monday morning I pretended to do some simple arithmetic, doubled up over a copy book. My one recurrent thought was 'It can't happen – but if it does, what then?' Big tears splashed down on the copy book. A little later Ann and I were told that our mother was dead. There were no tears then for me, just dry wide-open eyes staring ahead into an endless future of utter misery. Why had I been born? What was the point? Endless questions with nobody to answer them.

It was a typical November day with little light, cold and raw. I looked out on the slightly foggy street; the odd leaves that had escaped being swept and burnt danced about people's feet. The barrel organ arrived outside our house. The grinder, our old friend, with his monkey Tick started turning the handle; the tune of some well-loved hackneyed music filled the sad air and he looked at our windows, smiling and waving with his free hand, expecting the usual happy faces, accompanied by a shower of pennies. How could he know? Not yet, anyway. I tried to wave, but it was impossible. I was really quite numb. Also, a strange fury was mounting inside me against the whole human race. I kept thinking, 'How can I love anyone ever again?' Toby, my mother's dog, was beside me. I leant down and buried my face in his thick ruff of a neck. I found some comfort from his sooty old coat. He too was to have a broken heart, but clever as the dog was he hadn't yet realized and was therefore able to wag his tail, a plume of London grime. I thought to myself: 'You need a bath, but what does that or anything else matter now?'

It was Guy Fawkes night and fireworks started. I have hated Guy Fawkes night ever since. I went upstairs to the nursery. My brother, Hugo, was too young to understand the tragedy that pervaded the house. My younger sister had already been taken away to our Asquith cousins, to a 'Peter Pan' world from which she never really recovered. I do not know where my sister Ann was, perhaps with poor numb Papa. Again I went to the window, subconsciously looking for hope. This time I could look over many rooftops. The bangs and sparks that always set the scene for 5 November seemed ear-splitting, wrong and terrible. I had no personal experience of the war beyond vague recollections of being carried down to the kitchen during so-called air-raids, but these were rather gay occasions for a baby, relieving the monotony of the night, for even at that age I was almost an insomniac. Later, of course, I saw many photographs which brought home to me the full horror of the First World War. So, on this never-to-be-forgotten evening, I thought: 'London looks as though it is under shell-fire.' I felt so hurt and miserable that I almost wished London *was* on fire and that other people would be suffering as I was. I have noticed since then that some unhappy people become remarkably self-centred and selfish, so my bitter thoughts as a child of ten are perhaps understandable.

Soon the house seemed crowded with our close relations. To me it was just a kaleidoscope of white, tear-stained faces trying to give me comfort, something they didn't realize was impossible. On my way through the front hall I noticed the family doctor's top hat. So Dr Parkinson, known as 'Parki', was here, helping, I presumed, to make arrangements for my mother's body to be brought home. Indeed she soon was brought home and she lay in the drawing-room, looking young and beautiful, surrounded by red roses and lilies of the valley. As I looked at her, my childish mind kept questioning – was she really dead? Or was it all some nightmare that I would soon awake from? (I thought of this some years later when my younger sister Mary Rose found my grandmother's dog apparently asleep, though in fact it was stiff and lifeless. She said: 'I thought only flowers died.') I remember vividly the tranquil beauty of my mother's face, giving me no fear of death, just filling me with great surges of lonely unhappiness that I was left behind. Since then I have seen many people dying and dead, on bombed streets and in hospital beds, but only once again have I seen the inner radiance and tranquillity that I saw on that cruel November day.

I am not religious in the conventional sense. I practically never go to church, although I have often gone when duty bound, and always went as a child. However, I often say a prayer or two when I am walking the dogs or gardening. I'm pretty sure there is another life when we die – but I feel it cannot be anything to do with life as we live it here; it would all be too much of a muddle. Clearly, we on earth do not know the answer.

Memories of my mother make her into a kind of saint, always gay, always there when needed. She always had *time*, she always understood. She gave out too much of herself, more than her rather fragile body could spare, or she would have survived the anaesthetic which killed her. Or maybe she was needed in some other place; who knows? Many years later my aunt suddenly

produced an obituary which had been written in *The Times* by
Cyril Asquith in which he wrote:

She never disapproved or interfered, never pretended or posed or
preached. Indeed, her most salient trait, at first sight, was a rippling,
unforced gaiety, as fresh and healing as a lark song, and seemingly as
inexhaustible ... Cast in an heroic mould, her mind and heart were,
but not her physical frame. It took little enough to snap the link,
already worn thin in the service of those she loved, that held her to
them.

We did not go to my mother's funeral at Aberlady in Scotland,
on the piece of sea-battered land she had chosen for a grave. It
is a beautiful place, though sad and cold, whereas she was gay
and warm. Following the funeral my grandmother Wemyss
wrote:

To [us] who were there that day the sight and the sound of the far
flying geese will always have a sacred significance. They seemed to
speak of liberation into the wide, wild spaces, far from the dust and
din, the tiredness and turmoil of our earth. They seemed to speak of
strength and sweetness, of new courage and fresh enterprise, they
seemed to glide with transcendental rhythm, through Halcyon Zephyrs
to find Elysian pastures, filled with God's own peace.

My mother's death marked what seemed to be the end of
childhood. For a time I cared about nothing and nobody and
turned instead to animals for the giving and taking of love. The
immediate future looked as bleak and grim as that November
day. Little black and white suits were bought at Harrods for
Ann and myself, and on them we had to wear black arm-bands.
How I hated those ill-fitting garments, and the arm-bands seemed
an insult to my mother's memory and everything she would
have hated for her children. I still think it wrong to have dressed
us in that way.

2

Stanway

My life now changed its pattern. My sisters, brother and I spent
the rest of our childhood divided between Wemyss and Tennant
grandparents, with a short winter in London with my father who
moved from Catherine Street to a house in Oxford Square. My
grandfather Wemyss became my idol and I spent much time in
his enchanting company at Stanway, his Gloucestershire home.
Accompanied by nannies and governesses we would leave
Oxford Square to catch the 4.45 Pullman from Paddington to
Moreton-in-the-Marsh. We had tea on the train and invariably
met people we knew. Quite a lot of luggage travelled with us but
we didn't have to bother about it. At the other end, the porters
carried it to the one or perhaps two cars that never failed to meet
us. From Moreton-in-the-Marsh it was a further three-quarters
of an hour's drive to Stanway.

This lovely house, once the summer residence of the Abbots
of Tewkesbury, sat comfortably at the foot of the North Cotswold Hills, and was golden in colour and hewn from local stone.
One entrance was the beautiful Inigo Jones gatehouse decorated
with shells and the arms of the Tracys. Inside that there was
another archway which led to an inner courtyard, on the right of
which was the front door and a magnificent oriel window which
lit the long hall with many different shades of light, the mullioned
glass so ancient that each pane appeared to glint with a different
colour, whether it was sunny or cloudy outside. Also on this side
of the house were four wide sixteenth-century stone mullioned
windows. Facing the front door on the other side of the courtyard
was a private entrance to the churchyard. The church looked
mellow and in keeping with the house, peaceful amongst its

tombstones. My sister Ann used to like to sit on one of the stones writing poems; I used to find her there and tease her by saying: 'What a melancholy waste of time.'

The kitchen yard and domestic quarters were also on the right, beyond the second archway, and further along in another yard were the stables and old coach houses. On the left there was a path bordered by flowering ornamental trees, which led to the tithe barn, said to be the largest in England. We loved it and so did the villagers who held many dances there. Here too was a vast expanse of lawn on which grew a huge Wellingtonia tree, in whose branches we built our tree houses. On one side of Stanway was a village with a sparkling brook, and on the other a steep hill with another huge lawn cut in it. On its top there was a strange edifice consisting of one small room with pointed roof, reaching to the sky. This 'folly' was known as The Pyramid. Inside Stanway, the hall and passages were bitterly cold. L.P. Hartley, one of my aunt Cynthia Asquith's greatest friends, wrote that it had 'the odd mixture of the Spartan and the splendid which belongs to the English aristocracy'. As a child great courage was needed to run to the loo at night, and the freezing temperature ensured that one's visit there was as brief as possible.

When we arrived at the house, my grandfather immediately came out of his sitting-room to greet us. Sometimes I went straight to the nursery, past the portraits of the Tracy family, from whom the Wemysses inherited Stanway in the female line. At other times, if the house party bored my grandfather, he would have me brought down to dinner and I would sit next to him. He was a very human man with wit, charm and many un-developed talents; he liked to play at life and encouraged me to think of everything as one huge roulette table. He spent many hours playing games of chance and skill and if I mastered them too well, he cheated to win. This cheating, no doubt inherited from the notorious Colonel, came into force in *L'Attaque* where he would place me in front of a mirror so that he could spy on the identities of my men. Even so he often lost and not only to me. In his early life a great fortune passed from his hands in the casinos of the South of France. My grandfather also shared the Colonel's fondness for maidservants – not that he raped them. Instead of a valet he employed a maidservant, so that at shooting parties people were amused to hear a voice call for 'Lord

Wemyss's maid' to hasten to his lordship's bedroom. Later on in life I compared all men to my grandfather Wemyss and it was not fair to them. When I was fifteen he once said to me, 'You make me want to be young again.' His current mistress, Lady Angela Forbes, heard the remark and was furious. I understood the 'dew drop' (as compliments were called) and was delighted, thinking secretly, 'Whatever age you are, I love you best,' although by then I was very attracted by one of my uncles and a groom called Bert.

My father's eldest brother Ego was killed before I was born, but he had married and had two boys, one the present Wemyss and the other his brother Martin who is now Lord Charteris of Amisfield. Martin was the favourite out of my multitude of cousins and in fact, by the age of fourteen, he and another cousin, Michael Asquith, had made me realize the power of what we called 'S.A.' – sex appeal. They said I 'bitched them up'. I knew vaguely by instinct what they meant so it became an enjoyable and harmless game, except that it enraged them and taught me early in life the power of woman over man. Martin devoted his life to the Court and was for many years the Queen's private secretary, both as Princess Elizabeth and later. When we were children I never dreamt that this would be his role, guessing that his only path to a royal palace would be as 'lover' or 'court jester', both of which are now out of date and out of fashion. Now he is Provost of Eton College, where presumably he will have more time for sculpture, at which he excels. It was my cousin Michael Asquith who brought me to terms with a traumatic experience which caught me unawares. I got the 'curse' as we called that ghastly period in the month and I had a lot of pain and felt like hell. I screamed with horror and thought I was going to bleed to death. Ann was more comfort than my governess who made matters worse by saying: 'For one week in every month you will stay in bed for a day and then no riding or physical exercise for the rest of the week.' As you may imagine, with no further explanation, I thought the world had gone mad. Michael Asquith was more practical. He simply said, 'No more tomboy nonsense from you when you have the "curse". I'm going to tell the others you're "in China", in other words breakable and delicate like china or porcelain' – rather a good expression, and it certainly helped to rationalize this new horror of growing up.

Stanway was a happy, if somewhat divided house. My grand-mother Wemyss, known as 'Grumps', had her own friends. I remember watching her play croquet with Lord Balfour and James Barrie, the playwright. Even now his *Peter Pan* is an annual Christmas event in London and the proceeds go to the Great Ormond Street Hospital for children; all other rights in his works went to my aunt Cynthia Asquith, who was his secretary companion for most of his life in England. I can see him now making us work on the plays he wrote for us. It was hard work, all done very seriously; one had to be word-perfect by a certain hour. Then Barrie would appear, his perpetual pipe and tartan rug wrapped round his knees against the cruel cold of the great hall at Stanway. In one of the fantasies he created for us, I recall, there was a ghost-like wheel through which some of us emerged as Shakespearean characters, some very improbably, as for instance, me as Juliet! For my 'balcony' I appeared out of the top of a large door at the end of the hall; in fact I was stand-ing on a ladder held by the groom. My Romeo was Simon Asquith, son of my aunt Cynthia, who did the Nurse's voice. Looking back, I cannot see why it was all taken so seriously. I think this was Barrie's influence, for the strength of his fantasy, as of his affinity with children, lay in this quality of seriousness. But out of his sight I was often in fits of laughter so that I burst out of my dress at the back, which then had to be done up again by the unseen groom.

A frequent visitor to Stanway was Barrie's great friend, G.K. Chesterton. He had a vast body and tiny feet, about which he was most self-conscious. D.H. Lawrence used to come but made little impact on me. H.G. Wells was sometimes there and I loved listening to him conversing with 'Grumps'. We called Lord Balfour 'Nuncky'. I do not know what kind of friendship he and my grandmother had for each other; my own family maintain he was just a great friend. She did have one great love during her marriage, the poet Wilfrid Blunt, and my grandfather told me he was the father of one of my aunts. At the time Grandpapa was having a love affair with the beautiful Duchess of Leinster, whose photograph he always had by his bed. While this affair was going on 'Grumps' was in Egypt with Wilfrid Blunt and, realizing that she was pregnant, she telegraphed my grandfather that she was coming home. I suppose she thought it prudent to

return. My grandfather, on receiving the news, replied by tele-
graph: 'Do not worry, I too am having a baby.' I tell this to show
how divided their life was. But their houses were large and their
outlook Edwardian, so life and marriage continued in a civilized
way.

My sister Ann was mostly in Grumps's 'pencil and paper'
games part of the house. From the age of about ten I stuck to
my grandfather. If he was away, I spent much time in the stables,
kitchen, servants' hall, housekeeper's room and, best of all, in
the stillroom with a wonderful Scottish stillroom maid called
Katie. She taught me the art of making bread and many other
good things. She was always warm and comforting, like the
delicious fresh rolls she made for breakfast to go with all her
home-made jams and marmalades, The schoolroom at Stanway
had an old cracked-up gramophone on which favourite songs
were repeated endlessly, such as 'Life is Just a Bowl of Cherries'
– I wish it were! The servants' hall also had an old gramophone
and there was plenty of fun and dancing. I suppose a rather
flirtatious relationship with the male staff was not realized at the
time, but our nursery maid used to 'carry on' with the chauffeur
– with the result that she got fat and, to my great sadness, left
under rather a large cloud. I guessed what had happened because
it was always happening to my white mice.

I received little proper education, but at Stanway we did have
a considerable amount of 'reading aloud'. My father, grandmother and aunt Cynthia loved the sound of their own voices.
Dickens, Walter Scott and Jane Austen were read aloud as part
of everyday life. At least it gave us a taste for literature. *Alice in
Wonderland* I enjoyed, but did not really appreciate until later
in life. Now I often have it by my bed. As a child I read *Black
Beauty* constantly and cried a thousand tears each time I read it.
The Wind in the Willows was superficially understood, but at
least made each 'toad' have personality. I adored animals and
when I had a bad cold I used to look at my dog, Russell, and
think how stupid doctors were to fail to find a cure for the common cold in the head, after all those dreadful and often unnecessary experiments made on dogs – and anyway, a dog never has
a runny nose. They just sneeze and it's all over.

Besides Stanway, we spent some of our time in Scotland. I used
to play two rounds of golf with my grandfather Tennant, from

North Berwick down to Muirfield. On that coast there were at least ten or more first-class courses, some of them owned by my Wemyss grandparents. There was a lovely little course called Kilspindle, though playing golf there wasn't easy as so many gulls' feathers looked like one's ball. Here they had a small house, Harefield, where they lived when they rented Gosford in two parts to very rich people like Mrs Sassoon. The billiards room was the dividing line which broke this very large house into two halves. I have a picture of my great-grandfather called 'Four Generations', taken in the marble hall. My great-grandfather was known as the 'Brigadier', and his father, my great-great-grandfather was known as the 'Hunting Earl'. His memory still lingers in East Lothian and Berwickshire. Surtees dedicated *Mr Sponge's Sporting Tour* to 'The Right Honourable Lord Elcho, in gratitude for many seasons of excellent sport with his hounds on the border'. I think I must have inherited my love of hunting from the 'Hunting Earl', because none of the rest of the family liked horses or were any good in the hunting field. There are pictures by Raeburn and Hurleston that used to hang in the billiards room, together with a portrait by Sargent of the 'Brigadier'. Sargent also painted a lovely picture of 'Grumps' and her two sisters, called 'The Three Graces'. The 'Hunting Earl' is mentioned in *Handley Cross*: when asked for his qualifications for the post of huntsman, James Pigg's reply to Jorrocks was, 'I could be huntsman to the great Lord Wemyss himself.' There was also a fascinating painting of him by Ferneley at Melton Mowbray in a pink coat on a chestnut horse. The 'Hunting Earl' was sometimes known as 'Le Venerable', but he cheated at whist worse than my grandfather did at bridge; it apparently gave him great pleasure and sent him chuckling to bed. 'Le Venerable' was also very popular with those he employed. He had tombstones like this erected to some favourite servants:

> Here lies within this tomb confined
> Virtue and probity combined,
> An honest cook who many a year
> To her employers found good cheer.
>
> Hannah Gillam, who died May III 1803, aged 50.

I often played golf, and very well in those days, with both my grandfathers. I remember their funny-looking old-world clubs made with hickory-wood shafts, extraordinary-looking putters with huge heads, but in the end it was on the greens that they beat me. As my shots got longer from the tee, their game grew shorter with age. I remember one very funny scene when my great-uncle, Evan Charteris, joined us. My grandfather Wemyss made him pay a green fee on his own golf course, at which they had a sharp, childish quarrel with one another. My grandfather went very bald early in life and great-uncle Evan was also bald, but he had one long piece of hair which he curled round the top of his head like a toupé. The two brothers were standing glaring at each other when suddenly my grandfather said, 'At least my hair prefers death to dishonour.' End of conversation for that round of golf. My great-uncle Evan was a wonderful man, fastidious, charming, with a great taste for all the arts. He was a KC knighted for his work. He married late in life, and by then he owned a lovely collection of pictures with which he surrounded himself at his house in Eaton Square, and it was there I have my last memories of him.

We also spent much time with our Tennant grandparents. I have given the impression that the Charterises were more interesting and intellectual than the Tennants. Actually both families had mutual links, long before the marriage of my parents. Both 'Grumps' and my Wemyss grandfather were considered 'Souls' – that brilliant and beautiful group who thought themselves the stars of the social world of the day. Another 'Soul' was my Tennant great-aunt, Margot Asquith. She was scarcely good-looking (a description I hate when applied to a woman) but she was more than adequately compensated with brains, high spirits, wit and a formidable character. Her *bons mots* were famous. For example, of F.E. Smith (later Lord Birkenhead) she said: 'He has one trouble. His brains have gone to his head.' And in a heated discussion about spiritualism she declared: 'The conversation of the living is boring enough but it is nothing to the conversation of the dead.' Many of my cousins were afraid of her sharp tongue and personal remarks, but I was devoted to her, being well accustomed to her type of conversation from Stanway. She once told me she would have been much more attractive but for an unfortunate accident. When out hunting she had caught one of her nostrils on a tree. According to her she hung there for some time until rescued by some gallant gentleman. In those days there was little plastic surgery but, observing her large nose, I must say both sides looked the same to me.

The Tennants had a house in London and a villa in North Berwick, then fashionable for golfing fanatics and for those who found the climate agreeable. It was called Hyndford House, just along the coast from the Wemyss mansion, Gosford House. From there we continued north to Morayshire to their house Innes, for more golf at Lossiemouth, where Ramsay MacDonald, the first Labour Prime Minister, came from.

It was my Tennant grandmother who saw to all the practicalities of life. She made sure we were properly dressed and went to the dentist. None of this sort of thing happened at Stanway. I loved her but she wasn't an easy person. She was a fine-looking woman with beautiful eyes and impeccable taste in houses and gardens. I enjoyed learning many things from her, although after I married she wrote me some pretty cruel letters, probably deserved. She had a wonderful cook called Mrs Sinclair and the food was delicious. Altogether it was a very different life from Stanway. The visitors were mostly family and the conversation was neither as amusing nor as intellectual. At Innes I had a pony called Fatty Arbuckle, named after the film star, a fat, funny man who was quite well known in those days. This pony had a donkey as a companion and the donkey, like me, thought the pony fat and funny. A great number of peacocks that my grandmother loved strutted around the house and garden but on no account could we bring their beautiful bright-eyed feathers into the house as this was considered unlucky. I have continued to feel this way about peacocks' feathers indoors ever since. My Tennant grandmother liked her food. All the garden fruit was put in her little flower-room and before she handed it over to the cook and butler she would have a good guzzle on her own. Also, she arranged on one table hundreds of lovely sweet-peas of different colours, an idea I copied from her and have carried out in various houses of my own. Ann didn't like Innes; she was far happier at Stanway. But I was happy in both grandparents' establishments once I got over my mother's death.

3

David Long

The official ending of childhood and my debut into the outer world was marked by my first presentation at Court. Before the Second World War presentations were glittering and memorable sights as queues of lit-up cars containing mothers and daughters, and a mass of white feathers and diamonds, made their slow progression up the Mall to Buckingham Palace. Having no mother, my aunt Letty (Lady Violet Benson, Martin's mother) performed this duty of accompanying me to the Palace. Dressed in white with three snow-white feathers attached at the back of my head, I thought I looked demure even if I wasn't. The procession interested me as the route was crammed with waving onlookers, eager for a glimpse of those making their way to the Court of King George v and Queen Mary.

On arrival in the inner courtyard of the Palace, there was a red carpet and many 'flunkies' to open the car doors. Aunt Letty and I were ushered inside and up to the Ballroom where we sat amongst rows of beautiful women in tiaras, accompanying young girls in white. Appearances obviously varied, but though the girls had youth on their side they compared poorly with the magnificence and loveliness of the older women, who had come to present them. At the end of the room the King and Queen sat enthroned amongst members of the royal family, and scattered about were many uniformed and bemedalled men of the Court circle, some of whom I knew or recognized. The whole scene had a profound impact on me. With this shimmering, glittering sight ahead, it seemed that a curtain had lifted to reveal a new world previously hidden from me. My eyes filled with tears and I forgot to worry about whether or not I would be able to curtsey as elegantly as I had planned and practised. The time came for me to make my first salutation to the reigning monarch and his Queen. My aunt and I were escorted to a position near the thrones; her name was called and then mine. I curtsied so deeply that for a moment I wondered if I would arise as elegantly as I had descended! I happened to catch the King's eye and detected an endearing twinkle. I wondered if he was thinking of something Portia Stanley repeated to me when I was staying with her at Holwood: 'I'm always nice to young girls. You never know who they may marry.'

Having been presented, I was free to take my place in society. One day in 1933, I was asked to luncheon by Lady Cunard. I had met this outstanding hostess several times, but still did not know her well enough to call her Emerald. It was a large party consisting of people much older than myself, the usual mixture of politicians and men of letters, all of them intelligent and interesting. I particularly remember that Eddie Marsh was there, whom I knew from Stanway days. I was seated at the far end of the table, a long way from my hostess. Suddenly, towards the end of the meal, she remarked: 'I think it is time we heard something from little Laura Charteris.' I was slightly taken aback but acquitted myself with an adequately funny story about my grandfather Wemyss and his current mistress, Lady Angela Forbes. Fortunately the silent gathering at the table greeted the story with laughter.

I was now seventeen, but still no one had explained anything to me about sex; nor did they till the day I was married just after my eighteenth birthday. But through watching animals I think I knew more about it than my elder sister Ann. One day when she was about sixteen she went out with a young man who was being 'crammed' for Oxford by our local vicar at Stanway, known as 'The Priest'. Apparently he kissed her good-night on the cheek and she came screaming into our bedroom, saying 'I'm going to have a baby!' In October 1932 she married Shane (Lord) O'Neill, still knowing nothing. When she returned from her honeymoon to their new house in Montagu Square, I rushed round from Oxford Square to ask what it had been like. She just said 'Nothing happened. We got too sunburned and couldn't touch each other!' It was a great anticlimax for me.

It was at my sister's wedding party that I met my first husband,

David Long (Viscount Long). He annoyed me by saying that I must have 'an inferiority complex, having such a pretty sister'. At the time I was really quite in love with a close friend of his, David Spence-Colby. He and David Long were both amateur steeplechasers, and David Long was actually with me watching him ride on the terrible day when he was thrown from his horse and killed at a point-to-point. This ghastly accident drew us together. We met from time to time and he fell in love with me. I was not happy because I thought I loved one of my uncles and also the groom named Bert. I didn't think about marriage very seriously in those days, but I wanted to get away from Oxford Square and have a home of my own. However, David and I were told that we must not see each other for six months, and he went to Germany with his regiment. Nothing was more certain to make us marry than this idea of keeping us apart. But then there was another problem; as a regular officer in the Coldstream Guards and under twenty-one he was forbidden to get married. So he resigned in order to marry me and go to New Zealand as ADC to Lord Bledisloe, or 'Lord Bloody-Slow' as I called him.

Shortly before the wedding David and I motored to Scotland to stay with various relations, travelling in his large, sporting Bugatti. David was very proud of this car in spite of its unreliability. Just short of Harrogate we broke down. Somehow we staggered to a garage where it became clear the car could not be repaired until the following day. David was worried about us staying alone in a hotel, but he remembered that his cousin, Harcourt Johnstone, known as 'Crinks' and a very lovable man, was doing one of his much-needed cures in Harrogate, in those days a fashionable spa. We located Crinks in the Grand Hotel, where he was most welcoming. He helped us book two rooms for the night. Presently we met for drinks and Crinks declared it was a good excuse for him to come off his spa regime. After dinner we were all exhausted, including Crinks, due, he said, to the hardships of his cure.

David and I were given the keys to our rooms, which turned out to be adjoining – perhaps the hotel thought it was a thoughtful thing to do. I said good-night to David and went to my room to have a bath. Afterwards, very properly clad in nightgown and dressing-gown, I suddenly remembered I had something to ask David, so, not unnaturally and in all innocence, I opened the communicating door to his bedroom where I found him reading in bed. To my astonishment he became furious, commanding me to return to my room at once, saying that we were not married and that I was behaving in a provocative and 'cheap' way! I was astounded by his reaction and hastily returned to my room, where I contemplated this uncalled-for outburst. I cannot imagine such a scene happening in the world of today.

The night before my marriage was spent at Oxford Square. I was just eighteen and my wedding dress was all ready for walking up the aisle at St Margaret's, Westminster, for one of those grand social weddings. It was then that I decided I could not go through with it. I went downstairs and found my father in his room on the ground floor. As usual he was looking at his egg collection and I remember his face reflected in the glass. I told him my decision, but he simply looked at me and said, 'If you must marry a man with a mouth like a carp, I'm not surprised, but it's too late now. Everything is arranged.' I went back to bed, cried a good deal, but went through with the marriage. In those days huge crowds gathered to watch brides arrive at St Margaret's. They gazed at me in envy, little realizing how miserable I was. David was only twenty; I had never even crossed the Channel. After we were married, it was one night in London at a friend's house (that was a bit of a flop) and then the programme was all arranged – Paris, the Ritz Hotel, then straight on board a boat to New Zealand, of all God-forsaken countries.

Shortly before my marriage I had been sent to Mr Lane-Roberts, my sister's gynaecologist, to be told how to fit something called a 'Dutch cap', the idea being that David and I were too young to have children. I was a completely innocent virgin at the time. I was embarrassed by the whole thing and marched out of his premises in Harley Street with this small nasty-looking rubber object. Halfway down the street I couldn't even remember what he had said. God alone knows where I put it when the time came; it couldn't have been the right place, because my only daughter, Sara, was born nine months from the night at the Ritz, which was slightly more successful for David than it was for me. I remember taking an apple upstairs at the Ritz that night and eating it in bed, just hoping for the best, though I had no idea what that was supposed to be!

The awful part for me was that we were meant to spend three

years in New Zealand, taking with us maid and valet, linen and china. I was lonely and homesick, and very soon another kind of sickness set in. The captain asked us to his table but David declined; we were on our honeymoon. I looked aghast and said to David, 'We can't sit at a table *alone* for five weeks to Australia.' But we did, for most of the time. I made friends with three much older people I had known as a child – Victor Cazalet (who died in that much-discussed air crash with the Polish General Sikorski), the diplomat, Sir Horace Rumbold, and the well-known hostess, Lady Mendl. They were travelling as far as India. I much enjoyed their company, but David, even then, preferred young people. It was the usual story really; girls grow up to enjoy the company of intelligent and mature people quicker than boys. In my case this was even more true, as I had lived among the brightest and most amusing of the land at Stanway.

In Egypt we made some trips all together, and very enjoyable they were; I felt very grown up, married and travelling. However, I was beginning to feel very sick, and couldn't think why. In our large double cabin life was a shambles. I didn't dare go and lie down for fear that David might get troublesome about our sex life – which at that moment filled me with horror. It must have been awful for David. Years later he told me he did not know what to do for the best, though in fact he couldn't do anything because I was always feeling, and later being, sick. I would go to my maid Susan's cabin. She was sweet but very young. She suggested the ship's doctor, but I wouldn't go to him because I knew he was always drunk. He seldom appeared but one could see the bottles mounting outside his quarters and he reeked of alcohol. The sea was flat calm, so I knew it couldn't be seasickness. I never dreamt I was having a baby – but, of course, that was the simple answer. When we reached Ceylon I was in a poor way, losing weight and not eating, and I had never felt heat like it. I now love the tropics, but in 1933 on my first trip abroad it hit me hard. I was always hanging my head out of my porthole; there was no air-conditioning in those days, just fans. At the hotel in Ceylon they had huge fans on the ceiling which was a great relief. We went up into the hills behind Colombo where it was all very beautiful and strangely thrilling, except that I continued to be sick and all my new trousseau dresses were getting too loose. David made me see a doctor in Colombo, a nice, gentle sort of milk chocolate-coloured man. He asked me many questions and finally did say, when I told him a few personal things, that he thought I might be 'with child', as he put it. I told him that was impossible because of my so-called precautions! In the end he said, 'When you go back on the ship, take plenty of exercise on deck.' I do not know what that was supposed to do for me, but I took his advice.

The next stop was Perth, Australia. Here I really felt I was in the Antipodes. We stayed two days and I witnessed a horrible kangaroo or wallaby shoot. These delightful little animals, some of them with their babies in their pouches, were driven and shot down – a sickening sight to my eyes, but in Australia they were a pest to farming, like rabbits here before myxomatosis. David took part in this slaughter, for which, I fear, I never forgave him. We visited Melbourne and continued to Government House in Canberra, then back to the boat and on to Sydney, which I really enjoyed. We met a mixed bunch of people and went to many different houses round the Bay. We had lovely blazing sunshine and clear skies, but not a bit like the heat I had suffered in Ceylon and on board the ship. One day, a horrible thing happened. We had luncheon with some people who had their bay wired off against sharks, but nonetheless a little boy, who was really no more than paddling on the beach, was seized by a shark which had got inside the barricades. Suddenly there was pandemonium and horror – the fearsome predator had bitten the little boy's legs off. It was a horrible business with blood, screams and ambulances; not surprisingly, I felt even sicker than usual. I couldn't bear blood in those days. I heard later that the little boy died.

We left Sydney for New Zealand on a different ship. Not being very well versed in geography, I had some idea that New Zealand was to Australia as the Isle of Wight is to England. I soon learned how wrong I was. The ship wasn't a very nice one and the sea became horribly rough. The journey was far from fun as it took nearly a week to reach Wellington. We went straight to the Governor-General's house, which I found very unimpressive – large but with a temporary tin roof, because they had had a fire. Lady Bledisloe was his lordship's second wife, a strange woman who wore red wigs; I later discovered she had no hair. They appeared to be very much in love. At church the first Sunday I saw Lord Bledisloe put his top hat on the pew between them, and they then proceeded to hold hands under it. I thought this very droll.

I was still in poor health. Lady Bledisloe sent me to her doctor, who pronounced that I was definitely having a baby. On hearing this she was horrified, saying, 'No child has been born in Government House.' 'But we are getting a house of our own,' I replied. Then there was further trouble. Her lady-in-waiting suddenly had to depart for England. Lady B. asked me to take on this post. Sickly and reluctant, I said I would, having no idea what it entailed. And all this happened in the first forty-eight hours!

David, with his Sandhurst and Coldstream training, soon got into the swing of life with the other attachés. Their room for work and amusement was quite gay. But every time I went there, Lady B. summoned me back to keep her company and to play futile games like 'Peggoty Board' – games I had left far behind me, thanks to my grandfather's tuition in bridge, six-pack bezique and sophisticated games. She even liked to play 'snakes and ladders'. On days with no important engagements for the Bledisloes we went on picnics, which, as I have already said, I hate. Lord B. had a passion for picnics, and in Wellington these were hell as the place is well known for its winds. In fact there was a saying there that you could always tell when a man came from Wellington because he would hold his hat even on a calm sunny day. Lord B. also had a passion for digging up little worm-like things called 'toaroas' on the beach. It was quite an art. You had to be very quick or they disappeared down into the sand like lightning, leaving just a bubble. They made delicious soup. I developed a passion for this soup, as expectant mothers often do for some particular food. The picnic part was just awful – sand blowing into everything you wanted to eat, chairs that constantly collapsed, demented and hopeless servants running round in circles. But I did enjoy that soup.

At the first big dinner party we attended – it was pompous and dull – I sat on the floor after dinner. Next morning I was summoned by Lady B. She was in bed, wearing what I learned to call her 'tousled' wig. She said, 'I must tell you, little Laura,' as she called me, 'you must stop painting your nails red and never sit on the floor.' I was then told my duties for the day, all official stuff. We had to visit a museum in the morning. I was feeling dreadfully sick but at the museum I fortunately noticed an early type of canoe and rushed up to it, pretending interest, and was gratefully able to throw up and continue our tour. By this time I was insisting to David that we must get a house of our own, and he agreed. Servants were hard to come by; one result was that, except at Government House, people had dinner at 5.30 p.m. (5 p.m. on Sundays) even in the hotels. However, we did have my maid Susan and David's batman-valet, and I could cook reasonably well thanks to Katie, the stillroom maid back home.

Meanwhile I was writing frantic letters, mostly to my grandfather Wemyss, imploring him to come out and take me home from this sheep-ridden country, saying that I was having a baby and if I stayed in New Zealand it would be born a Maori or dead. Alas, all those letters took weeks to reach England, but my grandfather did come in the end.

David started to learn to fly aeroplanes; in fact, he always seemed to be in the air. His job as ADC was not at all arduous. Then the Bledisloes said they had to go on their yacht to visit places like Rotorua, Maori land, where there are hot sulphur springs and huge rivers full of salmon and trout, pretty well protected from poachers. No wonder, for you could catch a huge salmon trout simply by tying a knot in a handkerchief. The salmon took hold and you just yanked it out. Here I met one of the fishing warden's wives. I was amazed to see the only books she appeared to have in the house were written by Michael Arlen. At that time I had read his books but had never met him. Later in life I knew that clever little Armenian only too well. When I asked why she enjoyed such reading she replied, 'If you lived in this bloody place, so would you. It is the only sex I get.' As sex was not my favourite subject at that time, I quickly made some banal remark about the scenery. When we returned to Wellington I found, to my great joy, a letter from my grandfather saying he was on his way to see me, accompanied by Lady Angela Forbes. I was thrilled and started counting the days until he might arrive.

Meanwhile at Government House a most unexpected and delightful gentleman arrived for dinner one night – no less than the great Bernard Shaw himself. He was untidy and a bit gruff to start with, though not to *me*. I sat next to him at dinner, and suddenly things seemed more civilized. I poured out many things to him like a long-lost friend. I told him my grandfather, whom he knew, was about to arrive. We made thrilling plans about all going home together, via Panama this time. I never said a word to David about all this. I thought it wiser to await my grandfather's arrival. My baby was due in August and I was determined to be home by then, with or without my husband. Bernard Shaw told me he had seen enough of New Zealand and I heartily agreed. I somehow knew my grandfather would take me home. I told Susan all this; she was delighted as she had a policeman boy friend in England, and she also said that she loved children and had once been a nursery maid. She would learn more and be my baby's first nanny, which indeed she was.

At last time started to pass fast. I had heard that a boat called the *Rangitata* was leaving for England quite soon. Then my grandfather and Lady Angela arrived and came to Government House, and I could explain to him that I was no more use to Lady B. and that she didn't like babies. How my grandfather arranged it all I do not know, but we did sail for England on the *Rangitata* sometime in June. Bernard Shaw sailed with us. David came too and we took everything we had brought out from England. But I had to leave behind a tame raccoon that I had adopted called Tartar, poor little fellow.

It was a long voyage, taking something like six weeks, and I used to walk around the deck every morning with Bernard Shaw. I learnt much on those walks. He was always eating apples and spitting most of them into the sea. He used to say to me things like: 'To be healthy you must have loose boots and an empty bowel.' Then he would continue his conversation on a more elevated note. His wife seemed nice, but very quiet. At meals I used to watch them. He usually had a book propped up in front of him. Naturally, on that long voyage with one break at Panama, we all used to eat together sometimes. I re-started playing games of chance with my grandfather; in fact it all seemed as though I had never been married, except for my now big tummy. I didn't feel well again till Sara was born, but I was much happier.

4

Life Rolls Along

My daughter was born on 9 August 1934 in a little house in Spanish Place, off Manchester Square, which my mother-in-law had rented for us as a temporary base. She was a wonderfully understanding person, always known as Lady Glyn (David's father had been killed in the First World War), and she herself lived in a large house in Manchester Square.

On the day of the birth I fell over my dog, which precipitated things. My monthly nurse (midwife) had not even arrived, but she was on her way. I thought I would help, so before she got there I unpacked the sterilized paraphernalia for a birth at home, called in those days a 'drum'. She was horrified, but realized I knew nothing of such things and sent round to the chemist for a replacement. There was plenty of time. I took something like twenty-four hours to produce a child that weighed nine pounds. Mr Lane-Roberts, the gynaecologist, passed out with exhaustion, and so did my husband. It was not much fun but once it was over the relief was immense. I counted the child's fingers and toes and decided all was well. I sat up in bed and had my first good meal without feeling sick for nine long travel-worn months.

I was now a young mother, still in my 'teens', and for the first time had a very pretty 'doll' in the shape of my daughter, Sara. As a child I had never had dolls; my toys for cuddling in bed consisted mostly of monkeys and well-worn teddy-bears. David was proud of his daughter and loved me. Sara was a lovely baby, with lots of hair and large brown eyes, all her limbs fine and well formed. I took a lot of pleasure in her clothes, right from the time she was born until she married; she had many delicious white baby clothes all full of ribbons and bows. I spent many happy hours in the nursery with my daughter, and Susan, her nanny. We had by now moved to a permanent London house of our own in Gloucester Place, north of Hyde Park and quite near Regent's Park for walking. On Susan's day out I used to love to take my dog and Sara in her pram and just push this very pretty baby along. I had become thin now, and for the first time quite pleased with my appearance; men found me attractive.

Soon I bought a real live monkey at Harrods – he was a charmer but not the ideal nursery pet. My white Pekinese bitch, René, hated the monkey because in the park he was large enough to pick René up and run off with her. He also did this to other people's dogs, which was not popular. But he was clean and loving. When I dressed for dinner he used to copy me, powdering his nose, varnishing his nails, putting on scent, and crying real tears when I went out. At meals with us alone or with visitors he drank too much and became silly. When bored, he had a game of running upstairs to the nursery bathroom which had an old-fashioned lavatory chain which he would pull endlessly, grinning with amusement. Another more dangerous trick was lighting matches and throwing them in the air – his own private fireworks – so all matches had to be hidden away. He suffered a lot from the cold, but he had many smart coats and pullovers in different colours.

For about six months, I was kept busy doing up Gloucester Place to my liking and running a house properly, plus a good deal of social life. David had gone into the City. Accompanied by Lady Glyn, I was again presented at Court, this time as a married woman. I wore a white Molyneux dress for the occasion and some rather uncomfortable shoes. On our way to the Palace I kicked them off under the rug and for an agonizing moment thought they were lost. As the car door was opened, I confided my plight to Lady Glyn. She said simply, 'Find them and put them on.' I also started hunting again and kept one horse and rode others with my Strickland aunt, Lady Mary Lyon as she now is, who still lives at Apperley, near Stanway. David seldom came with me. He rode well; in fact, he still did a certain amount of steeplechasing, keeping horses at Fairlawne (the Cazalet home) with Anthony Mildmay, who nearly won the Grand National twice but for bitter bad luck – once his rein broke after he was well clear of the last fence. (The horse ran out and had to be disqualified.) But David and I were never really settled together. I called Gloucester Place 'the Club' because he had two great friends, one the very rich and charming Bobby Roberts, who died in an air crash. I often flew with him in his own plane. The other, who practically lived with us, was Teddy Phillips. In those days he worked for Cartier, the jeweller. Much later he married a very great friend of mine, Tanis Guinness, who at one time lived in America with her then husband, Howard Dietz, the well-known lyric writer of so many lovely song hits before and after the war. After she married Teddy they lived in Biarritz and in some of the most troubled moments of my life I have gone to her there. In that first year of married life, I began to 'feel my wings' a bit. I hated being caught in the world of young married people, since from Stanway days I had been accustomed to mix with all ages. I was now constantly out at parties or having them at home – all this with people much older than myself.

One day David and I had a silly quarrel, to which, as so often happened, I reacted rather hastily. I had many beaux and decided I would leave home, a terrible thing to do in those days. I picked up a few belongings, nanny, my daughter and animals, then sped down to my sister Ann at Sandwich, where she was spending the summer with her children. I left a note for David, saying, 'Gone away with Sara, we will talk later.' I even left my bath running, which, it transpired, flooded the house. David told me that this annoyed him more than anything as he thought my leaving was just a mood which would change.

In fact, we never lived together again as man and wife, though we did make one brief effort at a reconciliation. David wasn't very well so I went with him to Vichy where he was to do the 'cure'. Vichy in those days was a fashionable but serious spa for various maladies. I imagined the water at the springs, where the band played each morning, would be just like the Vichy water one drank from bottles in England. One day I drank a great glass of this local sulphur-like liquid and was quite ill for a week. Some old friends, Diana and Duff Cooper, were doing a touring trip in France and we met them there. Duff took rather a fancy to me. After that David and I went to Monte Carlo. He seemed better. Here again were many people I knew, and I spent my time gambling, swimming and flirting with all types of people.

On returning from this expedition I fully made up my mind that our marriage was over. I went to my father's house in Oxford Square and took over the top floor for nurseries for Sara and nanny – a new nanny as Susan had finally gone off and married her policeman. My new nanny had previously been with my great friend Didy Asquith and I had known her as a child. Didy 'lent' her to me, but in fact she remained with us until Sara acquired her first French nursery governess. Later, she had a wonderful woman whom we called 'La Vieille Grenouille'. The next move in my personal situation was to go to Stanway to discuss matters with my grandfather, who never let me down. He talked on the telephone to Lady Glyn, my mother-in-law, and one very cold day it was arranged that my grandfather and I should drive to Stow-in-the-Wold, at the top of the Cotswold hills, and Lady Glyn would be driven from Ardington, her home in Berkshire, to an arranged meeting place. It all worked well. I left my grandfather's car and, more than slightly nervous, slid into Lady Glyn's car. To my delight and relief, she remained her true upright but loving self. She just said, 'Don't worry about you and David. I always thought you both too young.' She was sweet and more understanding than my own family. Thus we remained devoted until her death, a long time after the war. It was Lady Glyn who suggested a sort of official separation. David and I went to a lawyer and we both signed our names, saying that we agreed to separate, which as I understood it (quite wrongly) was supposed to mean that in three years we would automatically get a divorce. It never worked out like that. It seems the solicitor was at fault, as so often happens.

For about six months I was treated rather like a leper. I had disgraced myself and my family by giving up a nice, if somewhat dull, married life. Most of this time I spent away from London. In the summer I went to my aunt Kakoo Rutland at Haddon in Derbyshire. The rest of those months were spent between my grandmother Tennant and my other grandparents. My Tennant grandmother gave me so many terrible lectures about my behaviour that I became quite accustomed to it. No doubt it was done with love and one must remember that standards of behaviour were very different in those days. But at least I was free to lead my own life and David his. When I returned to Oxford Square we met almost every day in the thirties when he used to come to see Sara. Then we would go off to our separate dates and parties.

At this time I had a strange ladies' maid called Miss Biddlecombe. She was always saying things like, 'Your life is like a pantomime,' whatever she meant by that. Nanny was wonderful, but she gave me many lectures about having too many boy-friends (nearly always when I was having a bath or getting dressed to go out). What she said was true, but at that moment nothing serious was going on. One very loving friend of mine who was desperately jealous by nature, Frankie More O'Ferrall, did love me for many years, and he used to call all my other men friends the 'performing seals'. I later married two of the 'seals' – Eric Dudley and Bert Marlborough. My father disliked both intensely, and when their Rolls-Royces came to collect me he would ask the chauffeurs to move further down the square away from the house. His dislike may have stemmed from rivalry over shooting as all three were outstandingly good shots.

I was really flirting with life in general. But there were other things in my life which broadened my outlook and education. From 1933 (when I had my first alarming experience at her table) until the war, Emerald Cunard's luncheon and dinner parties played a great part in my London life. I loved to go to her house in Grosvenor Square where she held a salon in the true meaning of the word. Her love for Sir Thomas Beecham and the support she gave him in the world of music is well known. Many people had boxes at the opera and Covent Garden was a glittering sight. In her house in Grosvenor Square, Lady Cunard entertained lavishly, mostly people of musical, political or literary attainments. Into these parties she liked to mix some attractive young women. I fell into this category and I enjoyed it very much. Sibyl Colefax (or 'Coalbox' as she was known) was another major London hostess. I knew her well from Stanway days and enjoyed being invited to her house, but did not find her parties nearly as enjoyable as Emerald's.

I had no money, and with a child and two people's wages to meet, and my only security being my father's roof over my head, it was obvious that I must find work. I was making ends meet precariously by my gambling activities over the weekends; I was lucky but I could not count on my luck running on for ever. So I went to work for a dressmaker in Queen Street, Mayfair. This had the added advantage that, by being in the world of 'couture', I got my clothes for nothing, an important matter at a time when I was out every evening and luncheon too. I had a small car and a bicycle which I used in London, a quick and convenient means of transport. There was a basket in front in which my Pekinese travelled, and a chain and lock to stop it being pinched. One day after luncheon at Quaglino's someone gave me a lift back to work. I left my bike chained to the railings at Quaglino's, which was run by the two Quaglino brothers (one fat and small, the other somewhat taller) and was one of the most fashionable eating and dancing places. That evening at home at Oxford Square with Sara, I was just wondering about my bike when the fat Quaglino brother came pedalling down the square to return it to me. There isn't service like that nowadays! Life rolled along and I never thought what would happen next. London was very gay. Ciro's restaurant was another favourite night haunt, and the Embassy Club in Bond Street with Ambrose's wonderful band. It was here that I first saw the Prince of Wales (Duke of Windsor by the time I grew to know him and his Duchess very intimately after the war). I was devoted to him; he had great qualities and charm. Since he gave up his kingdom which he loved so deeply, no one will ever know how good a king he would have made.

Some time in 1936 I met Eric Dudley (Earl of Dudley) staying at Belvoir Castle with my aunt Kakoo. Strangely enough, before that I remember standing with him out shooting at Stanway as a child. He was well over twenty years older than I was, very good looking, powerful in every sense. I found him, on sight, fantastically attractive. He was all-powerful in the world of industry and he had also been a politician. He was used to his own way over nearly everything. He had reconstructed his father's coal mines and steel furnaces which had fallen into almost as bad a state of productivity as they are now under nationalization. But Eric rebuilt his empire. He worked hard and he also played hard. Deep down he was a sad and, in some ways, even a sentimental man. He had a devilish temper but was soon sorry for his outbursts and, strangely enough for a man of this character, his tears were quick to flow. Many years before I met him he had married an enchanting woman called Lady Rosemary Leveson-Gower (the sister of the Duke of Sutherland). She and several others of her generation were killed in an air crash returning from Le Touquet. Eric had taken an earlier flight for business reasons, so he survived. Her death was a bitter and terrible blow. They had three sons, but the middle one was killed in a horrifying accident, being run down by a van on Chelsea Bridge. After these tragedies at the end of the twenties, he turned his energy even more feverishly to business – and many love affairs. When I met him that weekend at Belvoir Castle I fell in love with him almost at once. I remember after dinner there was bridge and other games. Eric asked me if I could play six-pack bezique. Luckily I could, and was flattered and excited to be asked. We played for many hours and all the time I remember thinking: 'This is what falling in love is all about.'

He left for London on the Monday, telling me to make good use of some very large hunters he had stabled nearby, as he had not the time to ride to hounds. Later, I discovered that at one time he had enjoyed hunting, but by then it seemed to me that he had no further enthusiasm for the chase, preferring shooting, although he continued to do both. Before we said goodbye he said, 'By the way, will you dine with me in London next week?' I gulped out 'Yes'. I was so thrilled at the prospect that I could scarcely speak. We dined at the Embassy Club and went on to the Four Hundred nightclub. I remember that night so well. Many eyes seemed to look at us and there was obviously much gossip, for he was greatly sought after by women in the London social round. I cared nothing about that; all I was certain of was that I was for the first time deeply in love with a man many years older than myself. This was the beginning of a long, romantic, tumultuous love affair which, in the end, led to marriage.

I was not free of David. The three years 'separation' would soon be over, but anyway at this moment there was no talk of marriage. I'm sure that Eric still had many other entanglements of heart and body. So, indeed, did I, but nothing that meant anything after I met him. Indeed I think it was better this way, for Eric only liked a challenge –provided he thought he could win in the end. Eric was a contemporary of King Edward VIII, and one of his closest friends. They had travelled round the world together when the King was Prince of Wales. Yet another link in the chain leading up to that agonizing event, the Abdication, was that Eric had a romance with an American, Foxy Gwynne (now the Countess of Sefton). Foxy and Mrs Wallis Simpson were close friends. Eric took little part in the matter of the Abdication; indeed some people thought too little, in view of his long friendship with the King. But I know that by then Eric and Foxy had more or less parted. (I have been accused of causing the break but this simply isn't true.)

I started to go and stay at Himley Hall, Eric's family seat near Birmingham. I also went to stay at many other places during this run-up to the war, and many men were in love with me. I enjoyed it all. I probably behaved fairly outrageously on occasions but, looking back, I am pretty sure Eric would not have wanted me for his own if I had behaved differently. Also, it was my nature.

I was still living with my father at Oxford Square. Sara does not realize how spoilt she was. She was given fantastic presents like huge rocking horses and every other kind of toy by my beaux. The time between tea and dinner in the nursery (because I didn't drink and hated the cocktail round) was a party in itself. Nanny held court, keeping a beady eye on all who came and went. This was often when flowers arrived for me and toys for Sara; at that moment in my life the most frequent and regular flowers came from Frankie More O'Ferrall, Bert Marlborough and Dickie Mountbatten. Others did send me what Frankie called 'dreadful floral tributes as for the dead', although his were among them! Bert – although fond of Frankie – called him 'the More Awful'.

I made my life in the thirties a mixture of working in my Queen Street couture shop, going out for luncheon with various men friends, rushing back to Oxford Square to my child, and a short rest, usually interrupted by the telephone ringing and Miss Biddlecombe asking what dress I was going to wear that night. I read little. The gramophone was almost constantly thumping out the popular hit records of the period. A rather fruitless and pointless way of life, one might say, but I was young, gay and thoughtless, and felt I had already had enough of the harsh realities of life. Little did I know!

Weekend parties played a great part in my life. I went to stay at many houses, including Blenheim. Although even that long ago Bert Marlborough said he loved me, it was nearly forty years later that I married him, and I still bear his name after going through another, and perhaps the worst, of all the tragedies in my life.

One weekend I stayed at Belvoir with my Rutland aunt and uncle at a house party in honour of the Duke and Duchess of York (later King George VI and Queen Elizabeth). The Yorks had to attend an evening public function in Leicester, and for fear of fog a special Pullman train was laid on to take us all there from Grantham. We boarded the train in evening dress at Grantham, where a considerable crowd had gathered. The Duke was very shy and rushed along the carriage, pulling down the blinds. I was very impressed by the way that the Duchess snapped them up again immediately, saying to her husband, 'Bertie, you must wave.'

Barbie Agar, as she now is, was then Mrs Euan Wallace, with a lovely, happy family and houses in Scotland, Sussex and London. In her house I was always happy and at peace. She has always been like a mother to me and remains to this day one of the few people I talk to many times a week. Her life has been full of tragedy with the loss of all her sons, but she rises above the blows of life even though they have been many and cruel. After one visit to the Wallaces at Kildonan I had to go south to London. Barbie booked me an overnight sleeper on the train. Duff Cooper and Paul Munster were also travelling south and my sleeper was sandwiched between Duff's on the one side and Paul's on the other. Before retiring we three talked for a while in the corridor, then I went inside my sleeper and locked the door which communicated with Duff's compartment. Alas, any hopes that I may have had for a peaceful night's sleep were in vain, for Duff kept knocking on the inside door while Paul banged repeatedly on the corridor door. Both were disappointed but it was one of the noisiest and funniest journeys I have ever experienced, and it made my bread and butter letter to Barbie both easy and amusing. Knowing the habits of both these charming men, there was nothing extraordinary about the journey and I was not nearly as surprised as the good-mannered brown-uniformed sleeping car attendant who witnessed their frustrated efforts with considerable amusement.

Travelling on those wonderful, beautifully clean old sleepers puts me in mind of a story Eric once related about Lord Hugh Cecil. Lord Hugh was nothing if not absent-minded. One evening he boarded his sleeper at King's Cross and prepared for bed. He could find no convenient place on which to hang his umbrella, until he noticed a tempting-looking chain. He hooked his umbrella on it with the result, of course, that the train ground to a halt and one of those splendid brown-uniformed attendants arrived to enquire what the trouble was. Lord Hugh was bewildered and protested that he was very comfortable. His actions were then explained to him and he settled the matter most apologetically with a flutter of £5 notes. As the train started up Lord Hugh again began to prepare for bed and once more spied the miscreant umbrella. Without further thought he hooked it on the emergency chain a second time with identical results, more trouble and more £5 notes. After this the attendant placed his umbrella firmly behind the door and the train proceeded unhindered to its destination. This was the same sort of Cecil absent-mindedness that caused Lord Hugh's nephew, David Cecil, to kiss all his relations after his wedding when he was on the point of leaving for his honeymoon, and then to kiss his bride, close the car door without joining her and stand with them waving her goodbye!

Besides weekend parties there were many balls and evening parties in the years before the war, and they seemed to be on a grander scale than ever. At Blenheim there was a ball for the coming out of Sarah Spencer-Churchill. The state rooms were filled with flowers and popping bottles of champagne and the Long Library was filled with ladies in lovely ball gowns and magnificent tiaras. I was feeling well and gay and had a carefree time apart from losing an ugly fur wrap which was returned to me at a later date. Laura Corrigan, a rich American, used to rent the Marlboroughs' house in 'Millionaire's Row' (Kensington Palace Gardens). Her wigs were the subject of much joking. Once she lost one in the indoor swimming pool at Himley but, being amazingly acrobatic for her age, disappeared under water and retrieved it with very few people aware of her change in appearance. At a very grand ball she gave, all the lights went out at about one in the morning and the dancing couples drew to a halt. My partner was Dickie Mountbatten. In this sudden blackout he clicked his heels together and informed me, 'I am now going to do to you something I have longed to do for some time' – whereupon he gave me a peck of a kiss on the top of my head. I understood Dickie better after this curious episode!

For the following Ascot, I stayed with Laura Corrigan in a

house she rented close by the racecourse. It was the first time I slept in heavily monogrammed *crêpe de chine* sheets. I kept slipping out of bed. Among the other parties just before the war was an original and attractive ball given by Nancy Lancaster at Dytchley. All the guests had to be dressed in red or white and this colour combination even extended to the marquees and flowers. I had great fun, but inspired jealous scenes between Eric and Bert. Then the Ilchesters gave a grand party at Holland House in London. The party continued to be rather formal until the early hours of the morning when some of the older people departed. Then it became really 'swinging'. I danced incessantly with the eldest son, Harry Stavordale, who, though married, was one of my beaux.

Naturally there was much talk of what was going on in Germany, but with no television the 'media' then had nothing like the effect it has today, when every grim and disastrous bit of news is flashed into the home, very often doing damage by influencing people who might otherwise think for themselves. I was still very young and, looking back, I know that right up to Munich and the 'Umbrella Man' Chamberlain's hopeless and ridiculous peace talks and pacts with Hitler, I never really believed there would be a war. I suppose all those parties were 'one last fling' before the coming of war. Throughout history this has often happened.

5

A 'Pancake' Landing

In the summer of 1938, I was staying with Eric in a house he had rented in the South of France. There was a large house party and there seemed to be a weird kind of fever in the air as larger and grander parties were given. That August, on my birthday as it happened, there was a ball which I went to in a dress made mostly of those sweet-scented tuberoses which grow in profusion in the South of France. It was a hot, romantic evening and I danced with Bill Paley (head of CBS in America). He was young, good-looking and, I suppose, enormously rich. Beyond enjoying myself, there was nothing going on between me and this powerful chieftain of US broadcasting. Shortly after dancing with Bill I went to the loo where I met a very attractive girl called Lady Mary Dunn, whom I knew, but not well in those days. She came up to me and, with fire in her eyes, suddenly said: 'Lay off Bill!' Years later, strangely enough on a cruise ship called *Blenheim*, I reminded Mary of this incident. She recalled it well, and furthermore had recently met him again. He is now a widower and she a widow, and it appears that old flames were re-kindled!

The following summer I again spent time with Eric in a house he had near Cannes. By now many people were against my liaison with Eric. Among these were his older guests, Commander and Mrs Colin Buist. Gladdie and Colin Buist had been wonderfully kind and hospitable to me during my early hunting days in the shires. During the winter months I practically lived at their hunting box, as those houses were called, in the Quorn country. I think it was Gladdie who thought Eric too old a man for me, because the Buists were of an age and much greater friends with

Eric than almost anyone except his particular women friends of the past, like Freda Casa Maury. The Buists and Arthur Forbes (later Lord Granard) were going off on a trip round Europe in Arthur's own plane – just themselves and his radio operator – and they asked me to join them. I knew Arthur, but just thought him rather young, fat and funny, reminding me of my childhood pony, Arbuckle. I was keen to go as I had seen little of Europe and now I knew we were on the brink of war. Eric was not pleased about my plan to leave him in Cannes and go off on this air jaunt but at the same time did not want to get involved in my divorce situation – which irritated him – and up to a point he was still leading his own life.

It was all very gay and carefree. Arthur didn't really love me; it was just a piece of match-making on the part of the Buists. They collected me at Nice airport to which I promised Eric I would return, and we flew to Venice. I was in good form and thrilled, as who wouldn't be, to see Venice for the first time. We stayed at the Gritti, on the Grand Canal, but only for one night. What can one see of Venice in so short a visit? A picture-postcard glance maybe, but enough to make me very excited over the sight of so much beauty, all criss-crossed with water to make it a unique gem of a city, like nowhere else on earth. There were real gondolas then, not the *vaporetti* of today; it was almost too romantic. I longed for Eric.

Far too soon we were preparing to leave. Then we ran into a little trouble, or at least anxiety, for a short time which seemed much longer. Apparently the heat had thinned out the oil in Arthur's plane engine and he had so little power that it was only with great difficulty, and alarmingly slowly, that he was able to get us airborne. It seemed to me that we only just grazed over the tops of some of the loveliest churches in the world, whereas our route should have been straight out to sea. However, things eventually became normal and we headed for Budapest. The aeroplane was comfortable, an eight-seater biplane, or fore-runner of today's 'executive jet'. We were five in all, Arthur, the Buists, myself and the wireless man. There was plenty of room, delicious food and lots of jokes once we were on our way again. Alas, more trouble lay ahead. There was a miscalculation on how long it would take to get to Budapest. Arthur, having never landed there before, wished to land in daylight. It began to get dusky, then black night descended. We came down pretty low and there was a lot of talking between the radio man and the control tower at Budapest. Beneath me I saw the blue Danube, looking anything but blue, and horribly near. Any second, I thought, we would plunge into this vast river winding its way through the two towns. Apparently Budapest airport had in those days a difficult runway – narrow and short. We just made it.

We rushed to the best hotel and from there to a most delectable restaurant, where we ate like wolves – I think sheer relief must have given us a very much greater appetite for life and food than before. We spent a few days of enjoyment here as the plane had to have some kind of service, not very well done as it transpired. After Budapest, we decided to fly further east, heading for Rumania and Bucharest. This was achieved with skill, and we had fun. In Bucharest, like everywhere in Europe in August 1939, there was a feeling of fear and tension. I confess I noticed little of this; I had for the moment forgotten Hitler and all the death and disaster that threatened us.

The holiday continued. Arthur wanted to have a look at Constanta and also wished to refuel. Not far from the Black Sea the trouble began. I was up front with Arthur in the co-pilot's seat and we were coming in to land when, to my horror, Arthur said, 'The undercarriage and wheels have jammed. Go back to the tail of the aeroplane and strap yourself to the seat.' I rushed to obey his command. I was so frightened because he said he would have to do what he called a 'pancake' landing that I tied my seat belt in knots. All was heat, haze and dust. We landed, or rather slid along the ground without wheels. Arthur became a true captain giving orders. 'Get out quick. She's on fire!' Of course, this was not true, or we would have been killed. Thick blinding dust surrounded us. I could not undo my belt; the knots I had tied were knots indeed. Colin managed to open the exit door and – as I have many times since reminded him – rushed hundreds of yards from the aeroplane.

It was some time before the rest of us disembarked, but there was no fire. Colin was teased for his 'gallantry' in leaving us to burn while he galloped across what looked like a dusty dirt compound – no grass or green of any kind, just sunbaked earth, a small desert with no signs of habitation. When the dust had settled, Arthur surveyed his beloved aeroplane, a sad, distorted sight, the luggage compartment and tail all twisted and immovable. This dusty quiet did not last long. From a distance we heard the sound of vehicles and soon a small army of police and soldiers arrived. They were rough and pretty rude in a language of which I understood only the reiterated word 'passport'. But even our hand luggage was apparently jammed in the twisted part of the aeroplane. Gladdie and I tried to clean up, she with her permanent white gloves – a long-standing joke as they seldom left her hands for fear of some infection, especially in foreign countries. Eventually we were ordered to board the frightening-looking police trucks. There followed a bumpy drive over dried-up marshland. Before we arrived at the police headquarters in Constanta Colin brought out a camera and took many photographs, but soon afterwards cameras and most small personal possessions were confiscated.

At police headquarters we were locked in a small, stiflingly hot room. Some hours later, when we wanted at least some water and refreshment, a uniformed official arrived and told us that our luggage, passports, etc., had been removed by force from the crumpled aeroplane and he went on to ask what we were doing in this part of the world. Luckily, he spoke some English. It was clear that he suspected us of being spies but we explained we were simply on a holiday. Time passed very slowly, but at long last we were driven to a seaside hotel and given back some of our documents and bags. We gratefully tried to thank our custodians, then rushed to bath and generally clean up. Oh, the relief of being in a really quite pleasant hotel on the edge of the Black Sea, shaken and bewildered as we were by the whole extraordinary episode! Dinner was a real delight; clean, and with no thought of the next day, we sat filling ourselves with caviar which, of course, was in no way an expensive luxury at Constanta, the Black Sea being, I imagine, one of the happy hunting (or breeding) grounds for sturgeon. Arthur decided to remain with his beloved aeroplane and somehow get it repaired. The Buists were hell-bent on returning to England. Somehow, I had to get back to Cannes. We all tried to make plans but it was very complicated. I decided to take the first available flight to Rome, from where I could get to Cannes. The hotel kept saying that a plane from Alitalia, the Italian airline, would arrive shortly and transport us to Rome, but at least five days went by with no sign of any aeroplane. All the news we got by then made it clear that war was imminent.

Some days I walked to the railway station, well guarded, for horrible and diabolical things were taking place. Trains like cattle trucks came through jammed full of anxious Jewish people, old men, children and women. They were allowed out for a short time with buckets to empty out their excrement, then tearfully pushed back on to the train. I really must have been very stupid and ignorant for, upset as I was at seeing these horrifying sights, I simply did not realize what was going on. Now the whole world knows this was the beginning of the hounding of the Jews out of Germany.

Eventually to my great relief the long-awaited Italian plane arrived. August was nearing its end and I feared that Eric might have left Cannes. On arrival in Rome, all seemed in a turmoil. I went to the Grand Hotel where I immediately landed in new trouble and frustrations; my luggage was lost and I had no money. I should have gone to the British Embassy for help but it never even occurred to me. I met a young Englishman who was frantic to get home. He was kind and understanding of my plight. I explained I had to go home via the South of France, so he lent me money for my fare and gave me his name and address, but I lost both so I remain in debt to him. I took the first train to Cannes. Eric was there, but not in the best of moods, though he was at least pleased to see me safely back. There was little time for talk. His car was already loaded. Although we knew the roads going north would be jammed with traffic, Eric thought we could not risk the train. I scrambled into the car, exhausted and bewildered; I had seen no newspapers but, judging by the general panic and Eric's attitude, I thought the war had started.

As it turned out, we had plenty of time to talk. He had his chauffeur driving and we only crawled along, as the traffic was so dense and many petrol stations had run dry. Poor darling Eric, he was in such a frenzy to get home. I spent the long drive to Calais sleeping and eating when we could; watching and, for the first time, seriously wondering what part I would play in a war that was now a certainty. I thought about my daughter and was glad that she was for once not with me but safe at home with nanny, staying with her grandmother, either at Wraxall or at Ardington in Berkshire. I also thought of David, knowing that, as an ex-officer of the Guards, he would be back in uniform on declaration of war. I swiftly decided to train as a nurse, near wherever Eric was to be. I could not bear the sight of blood but realized that the quickest way to get over this childish phobia was to plunge into the very heart of things.

On arrival in London after a hectic journey, Eric delivered me back to my father at Oxford Square and we arranged to meet for dinner at the Savoy Grill the following night. My father was collecting his belongings to leave for the country. By the following night, Eric was calmer and had done much work. He had been appointed Regional Commissioner for the industrial belt of the Midlands near Himley – a very important and responsible duty for which, of course, he was the ideal man. Britain was divided into various regions such as his. The Midlands was just about the most important for it was here, later, that some of the worst bombing attacks took place, such as that on Coventry. All the large motor car and other factories were quickly turned over to the war effort, making munitions. My father joined the Home Guard, which was perfect for him and which he enjoyed very much. He looked like so many of the characters in 'Dad's Army' – and I'm happy to say he lived to watch that original and evocative television series.

Eric asked me to pack up and come to Himley with his youngest sister, Patsy. At that moment she was not particularly friendly with me, but soon we became devoted to each other and remained that way until her sad death. I took few of my belongings and I have never seen the rest of them, or Oxford Square again. Nanny and Sara went to Didy Asquith in the depths of the Cotswold country for safety's sake. I went on one last shopping spree to Jaeger to buy a very warm type of boiler-suit, thinking it to be a useful garment for a war. Miss Biddle-combe went home. I stepped into my small Hillman Minx, with my dog and a little luggage, to drive to Himley as Eric had suggested, and as I naturally wished to do. My last recollections of that September 1939 are of those huge and monstrous-looking barrage balloons floating over London.

I stopped one night at Blenheim with Bert Marlborough and his wife Mary. Mary was always very kind to me; in fact, before the war she actually used to ask me to go out with her husband. She said it 'kept him happy', and as he often walked up and down the street where I was working we had luncheon together many a time. I was nursing from 3 September 1939, but must have had a night off because I well remember coming to London to have dinner with an old friend, Dickie Mountbatten, on his ship, the destroyer *Kelly*, which shortly afterwards was nearly sunk but for the determination and skill with which he managed to bring her limping back to harbour. I remember the drive through blacked-out London to wherever the *Kelly* was anchored. Dickie was determined not to ask the way, so, with a torch, he studied every little back street of a map of London while his driver continued our seemingly hopeless task of finding his beloved *Kelly*. We did eventually find her and had a delicious dinner, just the two of us. When I heard she had been nearly sunk I was very sad for Dickie as he so dearly loved his ship.

The final tragedy of his life was infinitely worse than anything one could have anticipated.

6

Nursing Times

A new life began as I headed for Himley. Perhaps for the first time in my life my thoughts were wholly serious. Today Himley would be considered a very large country house, though it never struck me in that way. It was beautifully proportioned, as most true Georgian buildings are, consisting of a middle block with two large wings that formed the house into three sides of a square. The fourth side was open, leaving plenty of room for the drive to sweep up to the front door. The wings, one of which was mostly occupied by an indoor swimming pool and squash court, were covered in magnolia trees, trained round the windows so as not to obscure the light. The southern side was terraced with stone and balustraded. From there great stretches of lawn extended to a large lake which in summer had many lovely groups of water-lilies. There was a kitchen garden, a stable yard with a clock tower and many loose boxes, all of this situated in a large park with fine trees. The only thing that made one realize it was in the 'Black Country' was the dust and dirt that lay on trees and shrubs. Also one's hands soon became grubby. The inside of the house was full of light and sunshine and the rooms were wonderfully proportioned. To me it always seemed a happy house.

I was acquainted with the staff. The older ones would stay on, but obviously, as time went on, many of the others of both sexes would be called up to go into the forces or other war service. Miss Pinner – or 'Pinny' as she was called – was a kind of 'Mrs Danvers' to me (the fearsome housekeeper of Daphne du Maurier's novel, *Rebecca*). The Ward family adored her. She had loved Eric's first wife, Rosemary, for every possible reason, hence her very real resentment of me. She was all-powerful at Himley. Fortunately, her attitude towards me changed gradually and she became less unpleasant.

I went to Birmingham for an interview at a municipal hospital called the Dudley Road Hospital. It was situated in the poor district of Ladywood and consisted of some eight hundred beds in a sort of compound which included the prison and, in those days, a vast building called 'the Workhouse' which was intended for the old, penniless, and sometimes insane, but alas there were also some young people among them. It was a really horrifying institution. Herbert Morrison, Home Secretary in the wartime Coalition Government, always told me that such places would be done away with after the war when a Labour government would be in office, as he was certain would be the case. He was correct in that presumption, but his promise was not carried out.

Dudley Road Hospital was run by a matron called Miss Snowden, a relation of the Labour politician Philip Snowden, with political views akin to his. My first interview with this most formidable lady did not give me much encouragement to enter the profession of nursing. Nevertheless I started my nursing career, the arrangement being that I would sleep at Himley and drive to the hospital each morning at some God-forsaken hour, returning home in the late evening. Eric was well pleased with these arrangements, although at that time I scarcely saw him. As Regional Commissioner his headquarters were in Birmingham with what was called the 'War Room' underground. The War Room was really the most vitally important place. It was supposed to be safe from bombing raids. On enormous maps with pins stuck in them at the vital places the movements of our forces and the enemy's were plotted. This room was under full security, but Eric took me there many times. He spent most of his time there and slept, in the early days, at the railway hotel, the Great Western, as he was a director of the Great Western Railways before nationalization.

I had now become a very humble nurse at the Dudley Road Hospital, with the full intention of going through my whole training. The hospital uniforms seemed badly made, so I had mine greatly improved at a real dressmaker's; very becoming it was, greyish-blue with starched aprons (I used at least three a day), and a wide starched belt. The cap was a problem. The uniform

one for a first-year nurse was small with one stripe. It was hard
to keep on my head, however many kirby grips and pins I used,
and I was teased for my cap being always awry. The outdoor
uniform I loved – air force blue with a scarlet lining and hood
to match, much needed in the severe winter of 1939–40.

The matron was a woman of many qualities but she was very
severe with me when I went to work. I was to be called Nurse
Long as she did not wish the hospital staff to realize that I was a
Viscountess. In 1980 this would have little consequence, but it
happened that one of the nurses discovered my full name from
some photographs in the *Tatler*. This was a pity for me, as the
other nurses did not then treat me like one of them for quite some
time. The training in hospitals in those wartime days was entirely
different from the present. My first experiences were in Casualty.
Inevitably I saw many dreadful sights. On one occasion I passed
out and another time I was violently sick. But at least I was soon
broken in (for want of a better word) to blood and mangled
bodies. For example, I had no idea that paupers' funerals still
existed as an archaic survival from another century. Some
frightened girl had had the misfortune to become pregnant and
in desperation had sought help from a lugubrious woman in the
slums of Birmingham, who, for a fee of ten shillings, had performed a hit-or-miss abortion with the aid of steel knitting
needles. As so often happened, the girl had developed septicaemia.
It was then the nurse's duty to lay her out with her arms along-
side her body and not, as is more normally done, folded over
her chest. The coffin was thus able to be narrower and she could
be buried anonymously, without further complicated enquiries
being made. I learned more of these sad goings-on when I visited
the women's prison. There these abortionists explained to me:
'Well, it might be you, dearie, coming to me in trouble. It would
be a hard-hearted woman who didn't try and help you out – for
a small fee.'

During this period of the war the hospitals were evacuating
all the patients they could to various 'uncertified' asylums,
institutions for people not actually 'certified' but not well enough
to be at home, nor indeed wanted there. The reason for this was
to have as many beds available in case of the expected air-raids.
These institutions, in turn, sent their inmates home. Once I was
sent in the ambulance to transport a man from one institution to

another. By this time everyone had been issued with gas masks; those in the services had a better and a more sophisticated mask than the general public. In the ambulance sitting behind the driver, alone with this by no means sane individual, things became both frightening and funny. He strapped on his gas mask and then proceeded to make obscene and quite extraordinary talk-noises, the gas mask obviously exaggerating the unutterable things he was saying. He was a large and powerful man. I must admit to feeling a certain fear, yet at the same time I had to control the laughter within me as the situation was funny in a grotesque way.

After my time in Casualty I was sent to work in a surgical ward of some forty patients. The sister in charge was a domineering and in many ways sadistic woman, and by no means young. Here, my duties were distinctly menial. I smelt constantly of disinfectants, one of my many jobs being to wash down bedsteads with Jeyes fluid, or some such thing. Also, most new patients were full of lice, so we junior nurses had to delouse them on admission to the ward. These minute but prolific insects were to be found mostly in the hair. We used special steel-tooth combs and very nasty liquids, and each patient had to be treated several times owing to the great proliferation of the lice and their eggs. Naturally, through carelessness, I got them myself. Worse still, on my day off I passed them on to my daughter, much to nanny's rage. By then there had been no air-raids, so Sara and nanny had moved from the Cotswolds to live at Himley, so that I could at least be with her sometimes. Among other distasteful but necessary jobs as a junior nurse was testing urine from the patients as they entered hospital. Then there was a constant flow of bedpans to be emptied. This first ward was for women, so there was nothing so simple as a 'bottle', as such receptacles for men are called. But even at this early date in the war I had nearly got over all my repulsions; furthermore I enjoyed my work and started to read medical books, apart from our lectures from the Sister Tutor, as Dudley Road was still a teaching hospital. One thing was always with me – a small pocket medical dictionary. The other things visible on my uniform were a pin-on watch, scissors and pen sticking out from a small pocket on my left breast.

But I had really started to love my work, even the basic things like the evening round of bedmaking that go with a young nurse's duties; I found a surgical ward comparatively cheerful. Our patients seemed to recover pretty quickly or die. Of course, there were the cancer patients, but even they seemed remarkably gay and friendly. They were all so unspoilt and grateful for every small thing one did, or when one had time to chat with them. I grew to love them all. I became rather left-wing or socialist, seeing really for the first time the other side of life from the one in which I grew up, and even then was returning to every night – the very rich set-up at Himley. I still had a personal maid, French and elderly, someone from Eric's family. She must have had precious little to do, although when I was on day-duty there were many dinner parties and, arising out of Eric's job, much entertaining of important people from all over the world. We were still not married, but I acted as hostess for several years before our eventual marriage in 1943. The reason for the no-marriage situation was my inability to get a divorce. The three years of the arranged separation were past. The fact that David and I had signed our names to a lawyer's document agreeing to separate had no standing in the eyes of the law. In fact, our case came up in the House of Lords. Two judges said we should be allowed a divorce without any third party being involved, but the third judge would not agree. So we returned to square one in the whole business.

During the thirties David had many entanglements with women. In one instance he was desperate to get out of marriage to a certain American lady. He asked me to lunch at the Ritz in London and then begged me to go upstairs to this lady's room and tell her that I was sorry, but on no account would I divorce my husband. I carried out this request, because we remained great friends. I met him for lunch or dinner on many occasions. Eventually I did divorce David on some rather cooked-up evidence that Eric arranged with him. Eric always said that in his position he could not be cited. He met David many times to discuss these matters during 1941 and 1942. I had to go to court for the divorce as it was I who was bringing the action. My sister Ann came with me. The judge took so long summing up the case in the form of a lecture to me that I thought he was not going to give me the decree nisi, but in the end he smiled and said, 'There is no merit in this case but on account of your age I will give you a decree.' I felt like going up and kissing his rather dirty-looking wig.

One night in 1944 I had dinner with David near the coast, little realizing that it was to be our last meeting. A mere three days later he was dead, killed by a sniper's bullet as he led his men in Normandy. I received the news in a strange and painful way. The trains carrying our wounded from the coast to various hospitals throughout the country were so organized as to try to send the men to the areas nearest their homes. One of Eric's many duties as Regional Commissioner was to meet these trains, which nearly always arrived at small stations or 'halts', usually in the dead of night when there would be the minimum number of people about.

One day Eric was exhausted from many engagements, so he asked me to meet the hospital train instead of him. It was to arrive at a small station near Wolverhampton around two o'clock in the morning. By this time (as Himley was now a Red Cross Hospital and I was in charge) I was in full Red Cross Commandant uniform. When I arrived at this 'halt' there was a long, winding snake-like line of ambulances waiting; their lights were dimmed and all was deathly still and silent. I had by now seen much of life and death, but I was not prepared for the tragic and pitiable sights about to confront me. The train came puffing to a standstill. The arrangement was always that any German wounded prisoners of war were taken off first, then the officers, and lastly our soldiers. The train had doctors and nurses on board, but not enough to cope with a full complement of stretcher-cases of burnt and mutilated men. In fact, one of the doctors on this train actually said to me that he wished penicillin had never been invented; in other words, he thought as I did that many of these men would be better dead. In France they had received some attention at front-line hospitals, even amputations. Others had mounds of cotton wool covering their burnt and disfigured faces. It was a dreadful sight.

On this first of many trains I met, there was one German, very young but hardly wounded, with nothing more than a scratch, but he was terrified. I think he feared he would be put to death. The idea was for me to go aboard the train and talk to as many as possible and take messages to send to family and loved ones. There were only three officers, none of them too badly wounded. One of these I vaguely remembered from David's steeplechasing days. I thought he would know me but when I asked him if there was anything I could do for him he both shocked and surprised me, as he clearly did *not* remember me. He said, 'No thank you, I'll be all right, but I am very sad. A friend and brother officer of mine was killed today. His name was David Long.' I felt quite sick and shaky, but pulled myself together in a way I doubt I could do now.

The rest of the train's wounded men were either too near death for communication, or very brave and covered with blood-stained bandages. Some talked and laughed and asked for cigarettes. In many cases I held the cigarettes for them, as they either could not use their hands, or their faces were so swathed in cotton wool that any form of flame from a lighter or match would have been dangerous. On future occasions I took paper cigarette-holders. The whole night was heart-rending but by dawn the train was cleared and the ambulances had moved off. Now I was faced with the knowledge that I must return to Himley and break the dreadful news of David's death to Sara. She was much the same age as I had been when my mother died. She adored her father, though, in some ways perhaps fortunately, she had not seen so much of him since the war began. I told her all I knew, which was little beyond the hard and final fact that her father had been killed in action and in France. She cried a great deal, which I knew from my own experience was better than bottling up one's emotions till one felt like breaking into pieces.

Nanny was loving and a great help. The harsh and inescapable fact was that we were in the middle of a ghastly war, yet life had to go on. Now, as I look back, I feel that although I spent as much time with Sara as possible I do not think I talked to her about her father nearly enough. I had the hospital at Himley to run and many other things on my mind, and in saying this I make no excuses if I was inadequate for my daughter's needs.

Life continued at the hospital at Dudley Road. Within six months of my entering as a nurse the matron had somewhat softened towards me. I often worked longer hours than was my duty. This she realized and, in return, moved me to different wards to gather all possible experience. She told me that however hard I worked and whatever examinations I passed I could never become a State Registered Nurse. At the time this was a bitter blow, especially as she gave reasons which seemed to me quite ridiculous. They were, first, that I did not live in at the nurses' hostel; second, that I could not produce what was then called a 'School Certificate'. This latter and most important reason was quite futile to argue about as I had never been to a real school and never even heard of a School Certificate. But she said that when I left hospital she would give me letters stating how hard I had worked and the responsibilities I was trained to take and was capable of. These letters I have to this day; they meant a great deal to me at the time of leaving the Dudley Road Hospital and even more later, and of course they helped me to become Commandant at Himley Red Cross Hospital. I give one of her letters here, written on 16 July 1942:

Nurse Lady Long has worked as a Nurse in the medical and surgical wards at this hospital since September 4th, 1939.

She has attended lectures in medicine, surgery, and theory and practice of nursing, and is quite capable of taking considerable responsibility in the nursing and care of patients.

She has carried out full-time duty on the nursing staff of this hospital.

(Miss) O. M. Snowden
Matron

During my time at Dudley Road two friends of mine came to work there for a short period. One was Mary Dunn, the other a very great friend, Virginia Gilliat (who married Sir Richard Sykes shortly after the war). Virginia, who was my own age, died some years ago and I miss her very much, as do many others. Both Mary and Virginia were gay and amusing. Mary seemed to spend most of her time talking and laughing or standing on hospital beds shouting out political speeches. Virginia, or 'Bird Brain' as I affectionately called her, was indeed loved by everyone. I remember her carrying on a conversation over the top of some screens where *she* thought she was giving a patient a pre-operative enema. In fact, no such thing was taking place. She had all the right equipment, rubber tubes, etc., but to my great amusement there was a river of soapy water coming from her position by the bed and running down the middle of the ward. It seemed to me that the ward was getting a 'wash down' and her patient was getting no enema. But, as usual with Virginia, she managed to laugh it off.

All the nurses were much attached to Virginia and each would try to keep a place for her near them in the dining-room, or at least at the next table. The mood in the room in which we ate those filthy meals was always lighthearted, no doubt a reaction from our 'on duty' hours. The more macabre the day, the more flippant and silly the jokes. I remember hearing the news of Pearl Harbour in our dining-room. To my amazement, this news seemed to mean nothing to all those nurses. They appeared not to grasp the significance of that horrible attack. I remember that day for a different reason too: I was nearly killed by a man throwing his heavy and full china bedpan over the top of the screens surrounding his bed. The bedpan incident was so disgusting I can hardly bear to write about it. My head was cut and had to have some stitches, and I was slightly concussed. Even more frightening, it was discovered that this patient had GPI (general paralysis of the insane) – almost the last stage of syphilis.

One of my patients was an elderly Jewish woman. She was very ill and rightly believed that she would soon die. She took a great interest in me and, as time went by, she became convinced that I was Jewish. She liked me to attend to all her needs, whether they were the indignities of illness or simple things like combing her hair and arranging her flowers. One evening, shortly before I went off duty, she died. When the doctor had left, the sister and staff-nurse being absent, I asked another nurse to help me 'lay her out'. Our task was completed by 8 p.m. and I was on the point of going home when the day sister appeared unexpectedly and called me to her side. 'You surely haven't done the necessary to that woman?' she asked. She was furious, explaining that as she was a devout Jewess she would not have wanted to be touched by someone of another faith after her death. She even obliged me to remain until the Chief Rabbi in Birmingham arrived, so that I could explain to him that I had acted without her instructions.

I also did work in the operating theatre. Here I was, in the early days, what was then called a 'dirty nurse'; in other words, I was not all 'scrubbed up' and sterilized. My first experience of theatre work was the amputation of a leg. It was very hot in the theatre; the temperature had to be kept at this level. As I stood back from the operating table, I could see all that took place, and with interest. It was quite unlike a bomb or motor-car

accident. It was impersonal and no one was in pain. The doctors
and surgeons did talk, I heard some 'sick' jokes coming from
their masked faces and skull-capped heads. They also sweated
from their brows, which were always wiped for fear of any drips.
It was when they came to the amputation on their list of more
minor operations that I came more into the picture. The patient
was wheeled in on the usual type of trolley. He was an elderly
man suffering from a rapidly spreading gangrene. The surgeons
cut the leg and then used a small surgical saw for the bone.
The work continued, but I was told to take the leg away and
deposit it outside the theatre. I must admit I really was sickened
as I carried away this limb. I have to write of these experiences
as they all had a great effect on me.

Another experience, almost Grand Guignol in its horror, befell
me at that time. The bodies, or parts of a body, had to be put
together (for identification by us nurses) on the beds and sometimes on stretchers in the passage, where a notice hung saying,
'No running in these passages with the exception of fire or
haemorrhage.' (In the general holocaust of air-raids these notices
were obviously ignored.) One very horrible and hectic night the
sister of the ward in which I was working had labelled a corpse
wrongly, but the body had already gone down to the mortuary,
so she asked me to go there and remedy her mistake. The
mortuary had an attendant who I think was quite mad. He
admitted me to the mortuary, which looked like a vast re-
frigerator, and, having never seen anything like this before, I
stared around at the marble-like slabs with bodies on them
covered by a sheet with a label on top. I was just about to try
and explain my mission to this ghoulish man in charge when
he slammed the heavy door behind me saying, 'Now I've got
you' – and it was not a joke, for he chased me round the
mortuary and I was truly terrified. By the grace of God, he suddenly changed his mood and I was able to escape. When I sped
back to the ward and told sister what had happened she was
most understanding and gave me some kind of sedative.

In certain cases leeches were used (they still are in France)
and I was sent to fetch these slug-like creatures from the laboratory as the sister wished to use them on a patient. I brought
back two glass receptacles, one empty and the other containing
the leeches. When they had done their work and were fat with

blood, I put the fat blood-suckers back with their friends without thinking and returned them to the laboratory where they lived. When I got there I was horrified to see that the leeches which had been used had seemed very succulent to their friends and had been set upon and nearly eaten alive; no question in this case of 'dog don't eat dog'. I was reprimanded and accused of ignorance but how could I have known any better, having no real knowledge of leeches and their habits!

It was while I was nursing at the Dudley Road Hospital that the historic and terrible German air-raid on Coventry took place in 1941. Birmingham is the nearest big city to Coventry, which was surrounded by factories engaged on making armaments, especially aircraft, and so was an obvious target. Some of us nurses were drafted from Birmingham, and the worst of the raid was over when we got there near dawn. But it was still a horrifying sight, with the centre of the city and the famous cathedral almost obliterated; and there were still German fighters overhead, using their machine guns on everything at random. Many of the buildings were still burning (I believe the cathedral, on high ground overlooking the city, burned for twenty-four hours). The anti-aircraft defence had long since run out of ammunition and the water supply had been cut off, and guns and fire engines lay abandoned, with the men who had manned them lying dead or dying at their posts. In what was left of the streets I saw elderly people and women and children wandering, too stunned by what they had seen to be able to speak. The number of casualties was unbelievable and I think I am correct in saying it was the only time during the war that England had a mass burial.

We nurses remained there for about forty-eight hours. All that really remains clear in my mind is that when night fell all was silent except for the ambulances, with their bells ringing, winding their way among the ruins. It was indeed a massacre.

The Germans did some damage to the factories, but Billy Rootes, Eric Dudley as Regional Commissioner and the mayor (a very remarkable woman) were soon organizing the recovery process with great energy and determination. Billy Rootes's factories, which before the war made motor cars, had to be got back into full production urgently and they all worked night and day. He and his wife Nora played an important part in producing the necessities of life for his work-force – tarpaulins to cover the roofs of their houses, food and cooking utensils – and he never waited for government grants, he just went ahead and did things himself. One of the few lucky things was that many men who might have been killed or wounded had they been at home were working at the factories on night shifts. I remember Eric telling me that the Rootes factories were back to eighty per cent production in under a week.

Some time after leaving Dudley Road I was invited to witness a brain operation by a skilled surgeon from America. He came to the Queen Elizabeth Hospital in Birmingham to operate on a particularly sad case. There was a twelve-year-old girl who had suffered since early childhood from epileptic fits. Recently these had become so severe that her parents decided to risk surgery, fully realizing that the alternatives were complete recovery or death. I was allowed to witness the seven-hour operation from within the theatre, whereas many students, mostly male, stood in a type of glass-enclosed dress circle. The operation was carried out under local anaesthetic so that the patient and surgeon could communicate. I stood transfixed watching the grey matter of the brain exposed to view, the head open like an oval door three-quarters ajar and still attached by a hinge. The interior looked like uncooked sweetbreads interspersed with blood vessels. It was too much for the watching students in the gallery, who fell like swatted flies. The surgeon whispered to the child, asking her to tell him the moment she had the sensation of a fit coming on. Meanwhile he delicately touched pieces of her brain the size of a pin. When she told him what he wanted to hear, he swiftly removed a minute amount of grey matter and then closed her skull. After the operation the surgeon asked his brave patient to grip his hand with her right hand. This she did, proving all was well. But the story has a sad ending, for five days later (without having any more fits) the child unexpectedly died.

I am now going to say farewell to Dudley Road and all the sad and funny things that took place there between 1939 and 1943. The matron actually kissed me goodbye when I left. I saw her once again when I was Lady Dudley. She asked me to present some prizes which I did with much enjoyment, and talked to many old friends, even some of the doctors that I have not mentioned who spent their time when I was on night duty making my life quite difficult with their advances.

7

Himley

I left the hospital for reasons connected with my divorce. I had to spend some months away from Eric and Himley while waiting for my decree to become absolute or we might have run into trouble. As I was divorcing David I couldn't be near Eric or there would have been a chance of the mysterious man called the 'King's Proctor' finding out about us, and his intervention would have meant that I would fail to get my divorce.

I wanted to do something, and indeed had to, as I was already 'called up' for war work. I decided on London. Eric took a small room at the Dorchester Hotel for me and when in London he stayed at Claridge's. My letters of recommendation from matron helped me find some private nursing to do, and as nurses were in short supply they did not mind my not having my SRN. The few cases I looked after were quite routine except for one at the Strand Palace Hotel. A couple had returned to England from somewhere in the East – I think the man was in the diplomatic service. The husband was my patient and although he was quite ill he continually made passes at me, and when I gave him a bed-bath he was delighted to get a huge erection. This had happened to me before in hospital so I threw a glass of water over him. After I had been there about a week he seemed to get much worse and his wife and I became very worried. The doctor seemed to come rarely, no matter how many telephone calls we made. Eventually he did come and said that tests showed the patient to be a case of paratyphoid fever and that he and his wife must be isolated in a hospital for tropical diseases. Fortunately for me I escaped infection, as I was always particularly careful when dealing with this patient and scrubbed my hands constantly because I had had a suspicion of what his illness might be.

After this I decided that until I could return to Himley I would take my name off the books of the nurses' agency and find some other job. My next idea came from a great friend of mine, Rosie Fiske (formerly Countess of Warwick and later Rose Bassett). Rosie suggested that I join her at a large American canteen in the Washington Hotel in Curzon Street, where Americans from all the forces, men and officers, could eat and sleep or just be merry. The Washington stayed open twenty-four hours a day and Rosie and I worked long shifts, though not necessarily at the same time. We were really no more than barmaids, constantly wiping down tables, and I rapidly learnt how to carry at least eight empty bottles of Coca-Cola or beer by putting my fingers in the bottle necks. It was all rather fun and I knew it was just filling in time till Eric and I could be married.

I continued with my bedroom at the Dorchester while Rosie lived at Grosvenor House in a much grander way. Both hotels were only a short walk from the Washington, but it was always difficult getting home at night or in the early hours for the 'Yanks' were a saucy, sexy crowd and they pursued us from the doors of the Washington with wolf whistles and remarks which were still ringing in my ears as I hurried to the refuge of the Dorchester. During this period London was really very gay, so when I was not at work I went out with many different people, although I had no love affairs. Nevertheless I enjoyed myself and it was certainly a change from hospital life, though even when I was nursing I would come to London on days off and stay with Patsy Ward, Eric's sister. It was from her flat that on one occasion I joined a party of six friends, and because of a strange feeling I had that night I probably saved the lives of several people, including myself.

This little dinner-and-dance party on 8 March 1941 was to take place at the Café de Paris. We met and had drinks at my old friend Frankie More O'Ferrall's flat. To this day I do not know what came over me, but I suddenly said to Frankie, 'I don't want to dine at the Café de Paris.' He was very surprised because he knew I liked the place, and particularly the band. Anyhow, I got my way and we went to the Mayfair Club. We were not more than halfway through our dinner when the sirens went off indicating an air-raid. None of us paid much heed until the head waiter came over to our table looking very grim. He wanted to tell us that the Café de Paris had suffered a direct hit. All he knew was that there were many dead and injured. We were all shocked and wondered how many of our friends might be there, as indeed we ourselves should have been.

After a time we decided to go to the most obvious nightclub in London, the Four Hundred, but to get there we had to pass the Café de Paris, and since the road was blocked with ambulances we got out to walk the short distance from Piccadilly Circus to the Four Hundred in Leicester Square. The sights outside the Café de Paris were indeed horrible, men and women in full evening dress lying on the pavement or being taken to a small hotel on the other side of the road. There appeared to be too few nurses and doctors; and I was shocked to see for the first time some dreadful looting going on. Diamond bracelets, brooches and even silk stockings were being stripped off the badly injured (if not dead) women. The Café de Paris appeared to be no more than a smoky hole in the street. Many people had been killed by blast alone. The band-leader, 'Snake Hips' Johnson, was killed outright with, I think, most of his band. At this time in the war people had an idea that as you went downstairs to the restaurant and dance floor it was safer than most places. In fact, the Café de Paris had a large glass dome covering it and into this the bomb had dropped. It was a miracle that anyone dining there that night survived at all. One officer on leave was there with his girl-friend when the bomb fell. She was sitting at a table with him, but died from blast without so much as a mark on her. A waiter tried to remove her jewellery and the officer, quite rightly, hit him. The man fell back on the stairway, hitting his head, and died. I am glad to say that the officer got away without a court-martial, but it was a near thing.

Having seen the horrors at the Café de Paris my party still went on to the Four Hundred. It sounds very callous and unfeeling, but that was the way the war went when one was not actually at work. I never even thought to tell Patsy, so on my return to her flat she was frantic with worry, thinking I was dead. She had also telephoned Eric, making matters far worse. I had told my great friend Didy Asquith where I was dining and she actually spent hours looking for me among the dead and wounded. I am far from proud of my behaviour that night; it was thoughtless, to say the least.

I recall one curious little episode from that period when I was staying at the Dorchester: Lord Beaverbrook invited me down to spend the night at his house, Cherkley, near Leatherhead. I was surprised, as he was a very busy man in his Ministerial capacity and being very close to Winston Churchill was called upon to meet him most days. Also I knew he was not well. Yet he kept me up virtually all night, using all his powers of speech – which were considerable – to stop me from marrying Eric. So far as I could make out, it all stemmed from some long-past feud he had had with my future husband.

I returned to Birmingham and went straight back to work. At this time, and even long before, there were of course many types of air-raid shelters. In London the Underground stations were often packed with whole families who spent their nights in such places, not even waiting for the sirens to give their three-blast warning. The 'all clear', always a welcome sound, was just one long blast. In the country towns and the Midlands, with which I was more familiar, there were many more small shelters. There was the early 'Anderson', named after Sir John Anderson (later Lord Waverley). Then there was the 'Morrison', called after the then Home Secretary. This was a hopeless and dangerous bit of construction, just a large concrete slab above ground held up by bricks. I used to tell Herbert Morrison, whom I knew well and liked despite our different views on politics, that his shelters should be called 'the mouse trap'. I know he agreed with me and few of these shelters were built. I demolished one myself by driving into it during a raid on Birmingham. I was on my way to the hospital when the sirens sounded and with dimmed lights on my car, late for night duty, I pressed on but remember little except running into this 'Morrison mouse trap'. The people inside fled, thinking a bomb had struck the shelter. The front of my small Hillman Minx was damaged but I could still drive it, though not for long. A basket of incendiary bombs landed on the back of the poor thing. That was enough for me! I quickly skipped out, leaving the car to burn, and walked on to the hospital, shaken but quite unharmed. I was lucky.

I knew Herbert Morrison well because as Home Secretary he was Eric's direct overlord or boss. Herbert, despite his attempted socialistic ideas, loved the good things of life. He also loved women. Ellen Wilkinson was his real steady girl-friend; she became Minister of Education in the first post-war government. Myself, I preferred his wife. She was a very mouse-like woman who, I now know, wished they had remained among their friends of humble origin. When they stayed at Himley I always felt she was far from being at ease. Her husband, on the other hand, was ambitious and enjoyed life. When he stayed with us he never stopped smoking Churchill-type cigars and drinking a great deal of champagne. He also had a passion for dancing, which he did with little accomplishment but great fervour. I remember one day after dinner he asked for music. He was accompanied by neither his wife nor Ellen Wilkinson, so I realized I was in for some pretty violent *palais de danse* exercise. He was well dined and wined and there were not many people staying with us. He grasped me to him. Eric was never jealous of Herbert and I can well understand why! At his best, he was amusing, a true London cockney with a great sense of humour; in appearance he was rather small and squinty-eyed. I couldn't imagine he had any attraction for women but he was a great one for trying and did not mind the rebukes he must have suffered. His passion for dancing after dinner became a great bore. One night he bit my ear, removing an earring, which I told him he was welcome to provided he either choked or spat it out. Herbert also suffered from another unfortunate habit, so much so that during a large semi-official dinner I felt obliged to rebuke him: 'Please stop scratching your head with your fork.' Perhaps I should have admonished him privately but either way it would have made no difference.

Miss Wilkinson, I can only imagine, was in love with him. Fortunately, during the course of his many visits to Himley she only came two or three times. She was certainly a clever woman, red-headed, and she smelt like a fox. I used to tease Herbert about her strong, overpowering smell, saying that her bedroom took days to be aired on her departure, and that it was fortunate there was little fox-hunting in the Black Country or she would be in grave danger if hounds got wind of her presence. He never replied to these remarks, but perhaps this 'foxy' smell was the great attraction for him.

Such nonsensical frolics with Morrison after dinner affected our two permanent guests, Francis Queensberry and Michael Arlen. They were both working for Eric in Birmingham, Arlen in some journalistic capacity and Francis doing something in Eric's War Room. Both these men I liked, but that was all. On the other hand they imagined they were in love with me. Francis used to say to me when I returned from the hospital, 'You make me long to get ill, provided you would care for me in that uniform.' One weekend a woman called Mimi Gore Chunn came to stay. She was madly in love with Francis. She did not play bridge and so sat on the sofa while we played, asking futile questions. Francis dropped his h's like an eighteenth-century buck. Suddenly he left the bridge table, seized the largest volume he could find and threw it at her, shouting: "Ere, heducate yourself!' With that he returned to his game. I grew very fond of Francis and after the war, when he lay dying at the Dorchester Hotel, I went regularly to see him. By then he had married Mimi, a woman who spent all her time trying to convert him to be a Roman Catholic. I believe she succeeded, but literally on his deathbed.

I remember little more of Michael Arlen after the war. He was wildly self-conscious about being an Armenian Jew, which was ridiculous in England at that time. He had had, after all, considerable success as a moderate novelist; in fact his book, *The Green Hat*, was very successful in its time and was later made into a film with Greta Garbo. He had a wife in America to whom he could return at any time. Indeed he did eventually, and died there.

People came and went at wartime Himley. The Russian Prince Dmitri rather surprisingly sent his first wife and child to Himley during the early days of the war. A woman of little interest, she had a hat shop in London and when she and her child returned there to stay with her mother, it was to my great relief. Major 'Fruity' Metcalfe was another man without war work until Eric took him on. I think he mostly posted letters or did any small chore that had to be done. But there were other visitors of much greater interest.

Besides official guests, many friends came to visit us at Himley, including Sir John and Lady Anderson. I did not know Sir John well. He was a dour Scotsman (then in the Coalition Government), but I had often met Ava either at parties or at her interesting little salon in Lord North Street. She was an ultra-feminine, petite, whispering blonde, but under this fluffy exterior she was clever and had a cruel tongue. She seemed to know about everything from politics to trivial gossip. Her first marriage to a diplomat had ended in tragedy and their one son would have been better dead. More or less insane, he lived at Ava's cottage in Sussex, surviving well into his twenties. It was there that I once caught a sad glimpse of him and later heard some awful howls. In many ways Ava and John were an unlikely pair to have married. Nevertheless in October 1941 they did, and, unable to leave these shores, they came to Himley for their honeymoon. Ava's room was close to mine and John's dressing-room was only a yard or two away. I was constantly hearing poor John pattering down the passage and tapping timidly on his wife's door. Nearly always he was told to go away. I saw him once, standing there in a long old-fashioned Jaeger dressing-gown which was too large even for the big-framed man that he was, and I felt sorry for him. He looked more like a reprimanded schoolboy than a formidable political figure.

HRH the Duke of Kent, better known and remembered by me as Prince George, came to stay with us in April 1942. I shall always remember his visit with love and gratitude for his charm, tact and gentleness towards me, as I was acting hostess for Eric but still not married to him. One night when Walter Monckton was in Birmingham as a judge on circuit, he and his very large entourage came to Himley for dinner. I made a pretty good mess of 'placing' the table by having Prince George on my right and Walter on my left. Eric seemed somewhat perturbed. I was oblivious of my error until after dinner when Eric told me in no uncertain terms that I should have known that a judge on circuit represented the King and therefore should have been on my right with the Duke of Kent on my left. It was of little consequence and I am quite sure nobody minded even if they noticed. Quite early after dinner those who were not actually staying at Himley returned to Birmingham. The Duke of Kent did not appear to have any wish to retire to his room. He was perfectly relaxed, knitting a long, grey scarf or muffler. He and I stayed up chatting into the early hours of the morning. He told me many fascinating things, but apart from talking about his adorable wife and children he talked almost entirely of the past – of his brothers and sister, his early upbringing and his mother and father. He asked me when Eric and I would be married, and all about the divorce hold-up. He was understanding and sympathetic about these personal matters and as we sat talking his muffler grew to an immense length, spreading right across the room and curling its way out of sight, like some long grey-coloured river.

When we eventually ended this memorable and enjoyable evening, I was totally unprepared for the tragedy that was to follow. The next morning the Duke went off in his aeroplane to visit various military and civil headquarters and not long afterwards he was killed in an air crash while on such duties. Sometimes I wonder if he didn't have some kind of premonition about his death. He only spoke about the present when referring to his own family; otherwise, it was always the past. Nor did he seem to want to talk about the situation of 1942 nor indeed about the war at all, our possible futures or the very likely dark and grim days ahead.

On another of Herbert Morrison's visits to Himley – he only signed the visitors' book when in the company of his wife – we went to a prison near the hospital I had worked in at Birmingham. We were conducted round by the governor and it so happened that the first few prisoners we talked with were all COs – 'conscientious objectors'. I could not resist saying to one of these quite harmless inmates, 'Cheer up, you will probably be Home Secretary if we ever have another war.' I said this because I happened to know that Herbert Morrison had himself been a CO in the First World War. Herbert, not being certain that only he and myself were sharing the point to my joke, did not think it funny. On leaving the prison he did laugh, but all the same he told Eric that he had objected to my behaviour. Herbert and I remained great friends even after the war. I remember visiting him at the Freemasons' Hospital when he was ill, taking with me the usual fruit and flowers. I must say for Herbert that he never changed much and certainly he was still scratching away with the fork. We laughed about many wartime stories, but he continued to say that there were many things I should never have said. I presume he was referring to Miss Wilkinson, the prison, and various other experiences we had shared. I really do not know whether his political views changed with his second marriage, but they may well have done as his father was a policeman with strong Tory inclinations.

8

Randolph

Something that was of great importance to my life all through the war was the constant flow of letters from Randolph Churchill. We did not meet, except at the odd party, until 1937 or 1938, but from then on I know it to be true that he loved me deeply. His marriage to Pamela Digby was of short duration; they had a son, the present Winston Churchill, who is proving to be very courageous, and all through the years leading up to the war Randolph had many girl-friends. But from the time we met till the day he died I was always devoted to him. When Randolph met me I was in love with Eric Dudley, but he had that very strong Churchill quality of determination, so whatever I said or did made not the slightest difference to his attitude and determination to marry me. When he was out of England, which he was for the greater part of the war, he kept me well in touch with the goings-on wherever he might be, through an enjoyable and fascinating correspondence. His letters, which were many, used to reach me via the 'bag', in other words uncensored. They went first to his wonderful and devoted secretary, Miss Buck, who gave them to me in person if possible.

I have re-read many of his letters. There is much of interest about the war – his time in Yugoslavia with Evelyn Waugh and Fitzroy Maclean, and many letters from Cairo and Turkey. They are to a great extent love letters, and continue in this way before and after I married Eric. There is one scribble he must have persuaded Virginia Cowles to write, begging me to think again before marrying 'the Earl' as she called Eric, and how much more exciting my life would be if I reconsidered and married Randolph. His own letters do not change much towards me, except when he accuses me of writing insufficiently. He says things like, 'Tie a knot in Beany's tail to remind you to write more often.' (Beany was my dog at that time.) His letters reached me quickly, not always through the 'bag' but sometimes through friends of his or mine returning from North Africa. One letter, written in February 1943 soon after I married Eric, recalls what he knew to be one of my favourite films. He writes: 'The night you saw *Casablanca* I just left for Marrakesh, en route again for Cairo, which will mean more presents I can send you.' Sometimes his letters sent direct to me just had a date with no real address, for example 'February 20th 1944, Advance HQ Force 133, CMF', but this was rare because Miss Buck used to give me further details. One very depressed letter was written when his relationship with 'W', as he referred to his father, was at a low ebb. This was a recurring theme right through Randolph's life. He explained from Cairo: 'It's the same old trouble in the back of his mind, reinforced by his belief (so true in political affairs) that he can get his way by obstinacy and bullying. Matters have now really reached a crisis and I can't bear to stay with him any longer. He has done wonders out here – but I am neither a Chinaman, a Turk or an American!' The only thing that really got him down was any form of argument with his father; in fact, like Eric, Randolph's tears flowed easily about the few things he deeply cared about.

There are many references to Marshal Tito, and to the sumptuous meals he was having with our Russian allies if Tito was present, and another occasion when he met Stalin, or 'Uncle Jo' as he calls him. He talks of quantities of smoked salmon and the best caviar (two sorts, grey and black) and mountains of this delicious stuff – in fact, as he says, the most satisfactory meals he had had 'since arriving in this primitive and hungry land'. He says in another letter from Yugoslavia,

We now have been joined by an American colonel, which gives us a bridge four. Money has no meaning here so we play for one cigarette a hundred. We all over-bid and play many goulashes. My partner is Sir Andrew Maxwell, a cousin of David Stirling's. He is an agreeable addition to our party. The American is a 'flash Alf'. He knows all the answers, but he means well, in spite of his manner which I fear gets on my nerves, having a pronounced Cockney accent, which is particularly jarring in an American!

In 1944 there are several letters from the British Embassy in Algiers saying how lovely it was staying with Duff and Diana Cooper, both of them, as he puts it, 'doing a wonderful job and being at the same time as gay and charming as ever'. I think he was then recovering from a car smash he had with David Stirling. In later letters he says he has done several parachute jumps and his back is giving him further trouble. When he was at what he called 'Advance HQ Force 133, CMF' which was again, I think, Yugoslavia, he says that, 'They are going to give a great party for Uncle T [Tito] and the Russians, a blowout, which cannot hope to be as sumptuous a repast as the Russians gave us, but capitalist countries can hardly hope to vie in a modern world with the luxury that is suitable for the officials of Communist Russia.'

I have many letters of Randolph's but have just quoted a few things from the hundreds I received during the war. Amongst these there are two very unhappy ones. When I tell him in 1943 that I have actually married Eric, his letters continue as though nothing had changed, which is understandable as I had always told him I loved Eric and when I was free I would marry him. A year later he writes: 'Do you ever have time to think of me or are you too busy sitting under apple trees with a lot of other guys infatuating them with your shutters? You always get into trouble when I go away. Last year you got married. What will it be this time?' The other letter has no date beyond Saturday, but it was during the war and it came from Chequers. He says something about *himself* becoming very difficult, but it is really all about not getting on with his father. Fortunately, as in other letters when he talks of 'W', he does go on to say, 'It will pass and next time I see you I shall be as gay as a lark.'

Our correspondence went on till he died at much too early an age in 1968. He was capable of long and lasting love and indestructible friendship. One of his favourite questions was: 'Who would you go tiger hunting with?' 'Randolph,' would always be my reply. When he left this earth it was hard to believe. For so long he had been like a huge bonfire, flames licking out in all directions. When his health was failing, the fire and enthusiasm for life which had always seemed unquenchable were diminished by the almost unbearable burden of constant pain. For years he kept himself alive by sheer determination and for one reason alone, to complete the overwhelming task of writing his father's life story. He completed two volumes before death overcame him. His father was always the most loved, admired and important influence on him since childhood. Randolph loved arguments and revelled in promoting them when possible. But any disagreement with his father made him deeply unhappy. His courage, both moral and physical, was unique, and his dynamic and irrepressible personality inevitably made him enemies as well as friends. In my view he was the most colourful character of his generation; death, like life, held no fear for him, and he lived life to the full.

9

'Queen of the Midlands'

In the early months of 1943 Eric and I finally married. First we went to Caxton Hall for a register office marriage, then, because Eric wanted some kind of blessing in church, we went on to Holy Trinity, Brompton, a pretty church but nearly invisible as it lies behind the large Roman Catholic Brompton Oratory. The Bishop of Lichfield, an old friend and constant visitor to Himley, took the service. When he was staying he often made me laugh by kneeling and saying his pre-breakfast prayers in the garden, 'Come snow or high water!' as he said. He should really have been called the Bishop of *Lech*field, as he was of a lecherous nature, but nevertheless a very dear and kind friend.

After the church service, which was attended mostly by family, we went to Henry ('Chips') Channon's large house in Belgrave Square, sometimes called the 'Chippodrome'. Chips had very generously offered to have a sumptuous sort of wedding break-fast for us. It was beautifully done in every way and many people came. It was very different from the few other parties given during the war, with food of excellent quality and drinks flowing; even the flower arrangements were really lovely. It was rather late to return to Himley so it was arranged that Eric and I would spend the night at Claridge's and return home the following day. It was not a very memorable wedding night for we had been as good as married for a long time.

I was still certainly very much in love with Eric, but his attitude seemed to change. He became tremendously possessive towards me, which I then liked because there had not been enough time for the possessiveness to turn into a form of manic jealousy, which it gradually became. That night at Claridge's we were both very busy, but not, as you might think, in the manner of 'newly-weds'. Eric, obviously, had much to do, arising out of his position as Regional Commissioner. He was dictating to his secretary. I was fully occupied with thinking about and writing a speech I had to make in the Town Hall at Dudley the following evening. I was far from practised in such things but realized that this speech was of considerable importance, as the Mayor of Dudley (a Mr Hillman) was going to introduce me to a large gathering as the new Countess of Dudley. It was my speech in reply to the mayor that I had to compose, so that very night at Claridge's I wrote and memorized the first of my many speeches. I think it must have been quite good for the audience sat still, except when laughing.

The mayor, Mr Hillman, became a useful and devoted friend for a long time, and Eric, whom I most wished to please, shed tears of joyful emotion as we were finally driven back the five miles to Himley. For me the drive was much too short as Eric, between his loving but emotional tears, was very sweet to me, making me realize that I could at last play my part in an important public life. I remained nervous on all such occasions, although I did have a kind of inner confidence. I remember Duff Cooper telling me not to worry, because the first time I made a public speech *without* 'butterflies in my stomach' it would certainly be a bad performance. I always suffered from this 'butterfly' feeling, therefore I know that on the whole I was not too bad, however much I dreaded those speeches, whether they were of great importance or just for some village fête.

That winter and spring of 1943–4 was hectic with every kind of work. I also began to realize I was in a very powerful position. The mayor used to call me alternatively 'Queen of the Midlands' or 'The Hillman Minx' (I now had another car of that make) but he helped me with many things.

My first objective was to get Himley going as a Red Cross Hospital. I had as matron a most charming woman called Lewis. She had been at Lady Carnarvon's luxurious and well-known nursing home in London; she insisted not only on its being well run, with excellent food, but that her nurses should be pretty and the rooms attractive, all of which she said contributed to her patients' recovery. In theory I think she was right, but I also think it quite possible that some male patients hung about this delectable establishment longer than was absolutely necessary! Matron Lewis and myself as Commandant made Himley Hospital as comfortable and carefree as we could. This was all-important to us, especially as our patients were almost exclusively cases with burnt or badly disfigured faces; mostly it was a hospital for patients undergoing much plastic surgery. Usually they had been operated on by that wonderful surgeon, Archibald McIndoe, whose headquarters were at East Grinstead. The patients came to us either when awaiting surgery and skin-grafts, or between the many operations they had to undergo. Naturally, they were often psychologically upset. In the worst cases it was of great urgency to get them out of hospital to face the world, and it was of immense importance that they should gradually realize this, even if they sometimes underwent as many as thirty to forty separate operations for appalling burns to their faces and hands. In fact Mr McIndoe and his team rebuilt faces, giving them new noses, ears and sometimes eyelids. The skin for this purpose was taken from behind their ears as it was fine in texture and therefore suitable for such a terribly difficult type of graft.

Our patients were mostly mobile, but the few exceptions often proved the most difficult to handle. As a hospital for such gravely injured, as well as psychologically damaged men, I thought we had everything well arranged. Eric still had his home farm so I was able to get far more than the usual ration of butter and other milk products for my patients, who often had to rely on this kind of food as they had to take their sustenance through straws. In the park around the lake they spent many hours coarse-fishing for pike, roach and suchlike. In the summer they could lie about in the gardens or park without fear of being seen – this was often their gravest fear. In the evening, if they had reached a point when I could persuade them to have a night out, I would hire a bus and take them to the theatre in Birmingham. One thing I did not like was that they had to be dressed in that startling blue with red ties, the same hospital uniform as in the First World War. For men whom I was doing my best to coax out into the public eye it was not the best of ideas, but it was a very definite rule and one I could not break. I did, however, smarten up my own Red Cross uniform against the regulations, though I think Sir Philip Chetwode secretly liked my small improvements.

Patients well on the way to recovery used to keep photographs of themselves during the various stages of plastic surgery. This was a good and healthy sign, much encouraged by matron and myself. As they progressed, however, they became more difficult and went missing as many had their homes in that very populated area of Wolverhampton and Birmingham. But it was not always to their families they went. Some had girl-friends in the neighbourhood and many girls used to stand about the Lodge gates, which were only closed at nightfall. Most of this form of rehabilitation was a good thing, provided they came back at night which, with very few exceptions, they did. They also spent much time in my office and if I was not there they would come through a large green baize door to the private part of the house. As Eric was in Birmingham most of the time it did not matter. We used to play games and there was a piano that some of them could play while others would sing and joke. Fortunately they were used to me and never appeared self-conscious about the way they looked. Some of them were really quite a frightening sight. My daughter Sara also used to be around, certainly most evenings, and she grew accustomed to these gallant and disfigured men in blue. I remember one outing to the theatre in Birmingham when I took a dozen or so of them. When it was over they scattered to various public houses. That was one of the very few occasions when they led me a pretty dance before I could collect them to go home. Even then, on our return drive to the hospital, they said they had only done it to tease me, which I think was the truth.

They were really very happy at the Himley Hospital and many people famous in the world of entertainment, both British and American, would visit us and go to the hospital, sometimes just to chat, but others, such as Gracie Fields and Frances Day, to sing and entertain them in a wonderfully natural way. Many of these men wrote charming letters to me when the war was over, and, for the most part, said their time in hospital had been enjoyable. Some used the word 'Ritzy'; this was because some bad cases, who needed all the so-called 'spoiling' I could give them, loved to have breakfast in bed and I managed to provide this, even if it was difficult. As I missed real nursing I used to attend to small comforts such as this myself.

During the early stage of my marriage I was involved in work of all kinds, quite apart from the hospital, for I took on a certain amount of my husband's work. I had an excellent secretary and matron was efficient and dedicated in her work, so once it was all running well I didn't have too much to do in the hospital except for the many small but sometimes difficult problems usually brought to me by the patients about their private lives – broken marriages and unsatisfactory love affairs owing, in most cases, to the fact that they had often been away too long on active service. Also, their pathetic disfigurements gave them every kind of complex, and it took many hours of talk and sympathy to try and sort out mental or psychological problems of which I had little experience. All I could really do was to make them feel loved and secure.

My activities in connection with my husband's work took the form of constantly going to his steel plant and down his coal mines; the men I met were wonderfully jolly and friendly. (It seems a far cry from the situation of today.) Petrol being no problem for me I went all over the Birmingham area, usually driving my own car, but at night Eric insisted I took one of his cars with a great flag flying on the front, driven by the old chauffeur Roscoe who was too ancient to be doing war work. There was also a wonderful butler called Bullock who, between terrible rows with Eric, ran the house to perfection. Even the rows were of little consequence, beyond giving them both a great deal of pleasure! Mrs Wakeland, the superb cook, also had her moments of tempestuousness, usually because she couldn't get every single ingredient she wanted for the kitchen where she prepared her unbelievably good food, just the same as before the war. Though Eric worked hard, there were certain things he would not have considered doing for himself. One such thing concerned cleaning his teeth. His toothbrush was put out for him every night by his valet and the toothpaste already squeezed on to it. If the valet forgot, then Eric was furious and demanded an explanation.

One night Eric asked me to cook and run the canteen over the War Room in Birmingham to replace someone who was ill. I had done some 'nights' there before, with great enjoyment. It was a large room where firemen, ambulance drivers and everyone to do with the war effort could come and eat or drink coffee at any time during the night. It was equipped with one of those old-fashioned machines for making tea and coffee that used to be in railway station buffets. They ran on gas and were not exactly easy to work. The food I produced was simple but, I thought, excellent breakfast fare – kedgeree, eggs and bacon, accompanied by home-made bread. Eric and his staff slept underground and, for that matter, worked there too if it was a night with sirens and air-raids.

One night the sirens sounded, shortly to be followed by the familiar drone of German aeroplanes. I always had a horror of air-raid shelters, thinking it better to be killed than huddled up, or even buried alive, with a mass of probably sweaty, frightened people. So this night in the canteen I was almost alone, with only a few other people who seemed unperturbed, continuing to eat and drink their coffee. My machine for hot water, tea and coffee was not working very well, so realizing that once the 'all clear' had sounded the place would be full of people I decided to try to get this 'ancient monument' in proper working order for making my hot beverages. As I was not of a mechanical turn of mind my attempt was a ghastly mistake. The wretched thing blew up, making a noise as loud as any explosion, confined, as it was, in a comparatively small space. I was fortunately only slightly scalded, mostly from steam. But the War Room beneath me was fully staffed, and, hearing the explosion above, Eric, followed by his staff, rushed upstairs, thinking there had been a direct hit. Meanwhile, fortunately for me, a bomb *had* fallen in the street not far away. I shall never forget the look on my darling husband's face when he saw me covered in milk, tea, coffee and water, a bit ashamed and also dazed from my home-made bomb! Having taken in more or less what had occurred, he at once became the Regional Commissioner and, however chaotic the scene before him, he returned to the safety and peace below stairs to start giving orders (the opposite to *Upstairs, Downstairs*), because that night there was a serious blitz and, as I knew, Birmingham was running short of water. Fires were starting up all over the town. In fact, had the German Intelligence been better, one more night like this and Birmingham might well have burnt to the ground. For some unknown reason, they did not raid the following night.

An interesting episode that I well remember took place when I was Commandant of the Himley Hospital. We had a visit from General Wavell. He was accompanied by Chips Channon and Peter Coats as ADCs; they made up a merry and happy party.

General Wavell was particularly carefree – having not long returned from India his wife Queenie did not accompany him; she remained at the Dorchester in London. Peter and Chips were also in good form.

The following day poor Wavell nearly met his death out riding with me. He decided to jump a gate. Neither he nor the horse seemed capable of such a performance and they both came to an appalling crash. I am sure he was suffering from bad concussion, but he insisted on re-mounting, just glancing at his watch and mumbling, 'It is exactly a minute to this day that some years ago I escaped death.' I imagine he thought he had escaped death on this occasion too. He certainly made little sense at luncheon on our return.

We had many interesting and important people to stay at Himley during the war. One to whom I took an immediate liking was the renowned violinist, Yehudi Menuhin. He came to stay with us for two nights and gave a splendid concert for the Free French, as the exiled Gaullists were called. Another talented visitor was Irving Berlin. He spent hours entertaining my disfigured soldier patients and they thought the world of him. Although in the realm of music Yehudi Menuhin and Irving Berlin were poles apart, there were certain similarities. The one with his ragtime and the other with his pure, classical, almost ethereal sounds, achieved an emotional effect in different ways and certainly brought tears to my eyes. General de Gaulle came to stay to visit the many establishments of Free French in the Midlands. Although I speak pretty good French I found him not an easy man to talk with, the very opposite of Yehudi Menuhin who was gentle and full of charm. On the night of his concert, accompanied by his own orchestra, I had real 'butterflies' in my stomach as I had to make a speech in French, introducing him and thanking him for honouring us with his presence. Also present that night was 'Crinks' Johnstone, David Long's cousin, with whom we had dined in Harrogate before our marriage. He was in government as Secretary of the Department of Overseas Trade. He had much charm and a first-class brain. He said to me after my speech that he was very proud of me, a great relief for he was not the type of man to say such a thing insincerely. One characteristic of 'Uncle Crinks', as he liked to be called, was that he really did love food, and he never hesitated to get the 'grub' or even cigars that he wanted from a 'black market' farmer friend of mine. Sometimes he would leave for London after staying with us with a suckling pig squashed into his government despatch box.

His love of food and drink brought 'Crinks' to an early death in March 1945. Towards the end of the war he came to stay and when he arrived I thought he looked very ill. I had taken some trouble over the food and produced one thing he adored – marrow bones, done up in napkins so that the hot marrow gushed out on to toast. Marrow bones cooked this way are a very simple dish but they are also very rich and fatty. 'Crinks' told me he was pretty certain he had jaundice, a most unpleasant illness, as I well knew having already suffered from it once before the war. I naturally told him to go to bed and eat something suitable for his condition. But he would have none of that and came down to dinner (already an ominously yellowish colour) and ate and drank everything, including the marrow bones. He returned to London but I do not think he ever recovered. I visited him and he was gay and fun-loving to the end, but my own theory was that his liver was in a state pretty near to cirrhosis; and so he died, a great loss to all his many friends. My friend and ex-mother-in-law, Lady Glyn, never really recovered from his death. She always adored him and was the real 'mother figure' in his life, apart from being his first cousin. From his point of view, his end was the best way out. He could never have changed his mode of living; there was certainly never anything in the slightest bit jaundiced in his way of looking at life.

In November 1943 we had a strange and interesting guest in the shape of the Amir Abdul Illah, Regent of Iraq. He came to Himley with sad little King Faisal, his nephew. Like the Duke of Gloucester, the Regent's one passion after dinner was to play hide-and-seek. But he always hid in the same place and, when discovered, shrieked with childish laughter! I related this curious tale to Randolph, who was in Cairo with his father. By chance they met the Regent the very next night and Winston said to him, 'I hear your Royal Highness is very fond of playing hide-and-seek in the dark and that you always hide in the same place.' The little man was astounded that the Prime Minister should be so well informed but Winston assured him that he had excellent sources of information. He then asked the Regent why it was that he

always chose the same hiding place. The Regent said it was de-
liberate policy. He didn't think it would occur to anyone that
he would do so unlikely a thing! The story has a sad end, for
in the *coup d'état* in Iraq in 1958, the Regent, the King and other
members of the royal family were assassinated.

Another visitor we had at Himley was General Montgomery.
He stayed only one night, and the following day I accompanied
him on a much-heralded drive through Birmingham. I found him,
as a man, to have little charm and fantastic conceit, but already
he was undoubtedly a great hero and adored by the British people
with good reason. The streets of Birmingham were crowded with
people eager to see and cheer him. His large car, with flag flying,
was driven by a soldier, beside whom sat an ADC. Monty and
I sat alone in the back. Our conversation during the drive was
not memorable – but something else was. At Monty's feet lay
a hat-box. The thronged streets reduced the car to a crawling
pace many times and it was now that Monty showed his theatrical side. He wound down the car windows, waved and grinned
at the massive crowd, and then tossed out the beret he was wearing. The crowd scrambled for it like a football scrum. A little
further on the box at his feet was opened, revealing a heap of
duplicate berets! As we progressed through the excited crowd
Monty, at intervals, threw at least two dozen examples of his
well-known headgear to the eager crowds. On our return journey
I asked him if this was his usual behaviour. He simply said, 'That
is my own secret,' at the same time looking well pleased with
himself. That evening he departed late; socially he was an easy
guest as it was not difficult, or indeed necessary, to keep up a
conversation, for he more or less conducted a monologue on his
own prowess, both in the battlefield and in his knowledge of his
men and their problems at home or in the field.

Now a final guest story of those days at Himley. Sara's young
and pretty nursery governess had replaced nanny and one morning on my return from night duty I was dismayed to find this
young woman in true hysterics, lying on her bed, with a glazed
look in her eyes. She told me she could not move her limbs. It
appeared that Sir Malcolm Sargent, who was staying with us
while he was conducting several concerts in Birmingham, had
assiduously pursued poor Mademoiselle round the house. What
else happened I have no idea for she was far from articulate. I

called our doctor, who sedated her. Then I reprimanded Malcolm but I feel certain this had no effect, for, although a charming man, as regards women he was impossible, having little control over his instincts as I knew from my own experience.

About the spring of 1943 I started thinking, but not more than that, of having an enormous Red Cross fête in the grounds at Himley, with every intention of doing it all on a very grand scale. I discussed this project with my now great friend the mayor, Arthur Hillman. He was very enthusiastic on the subject, which my husband was not. I did realize it would be difficult to arrange as I was quite determined that all the work involved would be done on a completely voluntary basis. My dear friend the mayor agreed and we planned that we would do all the secretarial work in his own factory in Dudley which made leather goods; this was in a way his donation. His office was also the headquarters for the fête which, in the end, took place on the August Bank Holiday in 1944. This was, as things turned out, a very good date for such an enterprise as by then the war was going our way, the invasion of France having been successfully completed. Speaking for my area of Birmingham, Wolverhampton, Dudley and all the smaller towns in that densely populated part of England, the people were all ready for the sort of 'day out' of which my fête became the focus.

It took time to get to know all the heads of industry so that I could inveigle them into taking advertising space either in the programme or in the drive. But in those days I was very young, attractive and full of energy, so it was with little difficulty that I rushed around the inner sanctums of offices and factories and soon left with fat cheques. Meanwhile, I was gathering together attractions like Henry Cotton to give golf lessons, and a most attractive American tennis star, Jack Kramer. I arranged whippet racing (a popular local sport), a horse show and jumping. There was a training camp for paratroops nearby and I persuaded the officer in charge to lay on a practice jump over the park on the day of the fête. There was a bit of trouble over this venture and a question was asked in the House of Commons. What gave rise to this was quite ridiculous. One of the paratroopers landed in the stable yard, breaking a leg. In fact, it most probably saved his life as he was one of a battalion training for that most disastrous venture as far as human life was concerned, the Battle

of Arnhem. When he was in hospital with his smashed leg I visited
him. Arnhem was over by then and he told me he was sure he
would have been killed – so he was not a bit worried about his leg.

I had hoped to get the great Winston Churchill himself to open
the fête and when I first wrote to him he said he would, but as
the time drew near Mrs Churchill communicated with me to say
her husband just could not find the time but that she would open
my fête in his place. On the platform I introduced her to well
over 100,000 people. She was backed up by Sir Philip Chetwode
and all the other local Red Cross dignitaries, and also my husband, who wore a patch over one eye on account of a bad sty
on his eyelid which did not put him in the best of tempers. That
night I went to bed in tears, partly from being over-exhausted
but much more from sorrow because Eric, who usually approved
of this kind of activity, would not admit that the fête had been
a success, although I told him I had raised over £40,000. I did
not tell him there was more to come – and that is a story in itself.

It all began with my 'black market' farmer friend suggesting I
should ride in what is known as a 'Flapping Race'. This is a form
of flat racing on an oblong course and it was a popular sport
in the Midlands and Wales in those days. It is in no way illegal,
provided you do not have horses running under Jockey Club rules
yourself, but by 1944 I had two rather good horses, one called
Pantalette, by Panorama, and the other called Fair Trial. The
farmer made the suggestion that I should ride in the middle of
Birmingham on what he assured me was a good horse that had
once belonged to the Aga Khan. However, he added that he didn't
know what colour the horse would be or its name. But, he said,
this was normal in the world of 'Flapping'; horses changed colour
and name pretty frequently! He knew I could ride, but I had not
been on a horse since 1939 except for the odd day with one of
our house guests. My last riding experience had been an equally
dubious one when Eric had let me ride Journey's End, a mad,
strong horse he had bought with hopes of winning the Grand
National. On the second time I rode him I took a cracking fall
on to a tarmac road, and 'Roley' Cubitt (later Lord Ashcombe)
said to Eric, 'What is Laura doing riding that mad horse? It
should be ridden by a boy of no consequence.' This time, the
arrangement was that the horse-track owners would give a
quarter of the gate money for the Red Cross if I rode, thereby

very much enlarging – to £47,000 – the cheque I finally sent to
the Duke of Gloucester. I had no idea about the Jockey Club
ruling on this matter, so I agreed to ride. I told Eric the day before
the event. He was not over-interested but said he would look in
at the meeting.

Sara, her then very young French governess, the farmer and
I all set off for Birmingham. Though I had hunted out my riding
clothes, there was apparently no need for colours; you just wore
a large number and I was to be provided with a fearsome amount
of dead-weight in a saddle cloth. It was a grilling hot day and
when we arrived at the overcrowded course the first race was
taking place. I had but to glance at the situation to see it was rough,
with pretty dirty goings-on. My race was the third on the card.
Even now I remember that the name of my horse was Firebrand.
Just before my race I saw that someone else's name was up on
the black and white boards as Firebrand's jockey. The farmer
seemed very excited and was surrounded by friends, and a good
deal of talk, inaudible to me, was going on. At this moment my
horse was clear favourite at ten to one on! Then came the
announcement over the deafening loudspeakers that there was
a change of jockey for Firebrand, the horse I had not even clapped
an eye on yet. The brief but noisy announcement just said, 'The
Countess of Dudley will be riding Firebrand instead of the jockey
down on the race card.' The effect of this announcement was
electrifying and pretty insulting to me, but it was exactly what
the farmer and his buddies had wanted. The bookmakers, and
there appeared to be hundreds of them, wasted no time on their
boards changing the odds on Firebrand from ten to one on to
ten to one against! The farmer and many others rushed to make
their bets. He then returned to me, escorted me to the weighing-
in room and then, carrying the saddle and all the dead-weight,
we went to find the famous Firebrand. I wonder how many names
that horse had had and how many times he had changed colour!
Today he was a rather drab chestnut and, I suspect, slightly
doped. He couldn't keep still and was already sweating profusely.
The farmer said to me, 'We will hold up one of his legs so that
you can mount, but once the race starts get out in front and stay
there or one of the other jockeys may try and put their knee under
yours to pitch you off!'

From then on, everything happened very fast. The heat was

terrible and the reins were already slippery from my crazy Fire-brand's sweat. I was hoisted up and went straight to the start, which was a man with a flag. I have learnt since that the betting at 'Flapping' meetings is substantial, hence the excitement of the farmer and his friends. All I could do was think how funny it was to be on a horse again and under these conditions, when down came the flag.

Firebrand was well-named that day. He went off like a shot from a gun, nearly leaving me behind. It was a hazy and dusty track, not grass, just dirt or peat (like Rotten Row) which flew all over one at the start. I had no alternative but to follow my instructions. I cannot possibly remember now how many times round I had to go to win, but the howls and cheers from the crowd, and particularly from some of my patients who had come to watch, left me in no doubt as to when I had won. But the problem for me was how I would ever stop. Each time we passed the winning-post Firebrand's ears went back, but his pace didn't seem to slacken. By now the reins were useless and, worse still, the saddle cloth and weights were getting loose. Then I heard the honking of a car and was just able to see Eric arriving with his huge Regional Commissioner's flag flying. He got out and, purple with fright and fury, started to yell, 'Somebody stop that horse before my wife is killed!' By this time Firebrand and I were both exhausted; finally we came to a halt. I think it was the farmer who led me back to weigh out. All was well; somehow the weights were still in place. So I had won the race, not once but I should think ten times over.

Eric calmed down, they gave me something in the region of £7,000 for the Red Cross, and I imagine the men at the back of it all, the farmer and his friends, made a killing at ten to one. Sara made some money and so did the soldiers from my hospital. I was glad to reach home and have a bath, but it was an experi-ence that in retrospect I would not have liked to miss.

Naturally the adventurous ride, my one and only experience of 'Flapping', did not end there. The all-powerful Jockey Club telephoned to ask if it was true that I had taken part in a 'Flapping Meeting'. There was nothing to do except tell the truth – I didn't know the rules of such matters, and, anyway, I had only done it for charity. Nevertheless, I was summoned to Newmarket to explain further in person to some members of the Jockey Club,

QUEEN OF THE MIDLANDS'

most of whom I knew. They were all understanding and rather kind about this escapade, saying they would overlook my little 'Flapping' enterprise as it was done for charity and as I was ignorant of racing rules. This made it possible for a short while to continue with my flat racing; my trainer, Victor Smythe, was much relieved as my horses were doing well. In fact, Pantalette won a race at Ascot under wartime conditions the following week. Eric and I drove to Ascot to watch her run. On the way I opened a new canteen in my husband's steel-works and performed some other public function in Dudley, and on both these occasions many of the men, who liked a weekly flutter on the horses, asked me what my chances were. I rather stupidly said she had a chance, although not completely fit for this race. They must have misunderstood me, for I learned afterwards that so much money was put on Pantalette that the best-known bookmaker in Dudley went bust. My mare won with the greatest ease at long odds so she and I became heroines overnight. I should add that I hadn't a penny on her myself.

My career as a racehorse owner had begun in rather an odd way. Some weeks after Eric and I were married he remembered that he had given me no wedding present, so he decided that, if I wished, he would give me £3,000, of which £2,000 was to buy racehorses and the other £1,000 for their keep and training. Frankie More O'Ferrall was not only one of my greatest friends, but the senior partner of the Anglo-Irish Bloodstock Agency and therefore an expert in this field. I discussed this project with him and he certainly did me proud in buying me two horses, Fair Trial and the filly Pantalette, by Panorama, who had been a well-known sprint horse, in other words fast over a short distance. The amount of money involved sounds unbelievably small in 1980 and would be ridiculously inadequate as capital for entering the sport of kings today, but in 1943 the venture was not only possible but in my case very successful.

Frankie thought Victor Smythe a good trainer, so my horses went to his stables at Epsom. He was not the grandest trainer, but a charming man and less expensive than some. I won many races in a short time and from prize-money and betting I was able to extend my racing activities by purchasing a Gold Bridge mare in foal and another yearling or two. The mare and foals were kept at Frankie's brother's stud Kildagon, near Dublin. Eric thought it all seemed too easy, so he asked Frankie to buy him two really well-bred racehorses and he naturally wanted them trained by the best-known trainer of the day, who was Fred Darling. His establishment in Wiltshire, with its wonderful gallops and stabling, now belongs to Jeremy Tree, who has continued in Fred Darling's successful steps. One of Eric's horses was called Clippie, and he was a complete 'dog', never to be counted on. The other, whose name I forget, was bought by my husband for one of the highest prices ever paid at that date. It was a beautiful horse to look at, and Fred Darling did everything in his power to persuade this incalculable animal even to set foot on a racecourse; the nearest he ever got was the paddock! Eric was not pleased.

We had moved from Himley to Ednam Lodge, Sunningdale, in the early days of 1945, much to my displeasure. I never liked this house, and also I felt deprived of my hospital and all the other work in which I was deeply involved in the Midlands. Some horses that at Himley had been turned out to grass, and also my beloved little grey mare, Doodlebug, came south. I acquired a key for the gates into some parts of Windsor Home Park, which then became an ideal place for riding and jumping, being beautiful and deserted. Sometimes instead of using my key I jumped the gates. Sara and I spent many hours of pleasure exercising ourselves and the horses.

The débâcle of my racing came soon after the end of the war. One of my horses was running at Windsor. Wartime conditions still prevailed so Eric and I set off with a large, rather elaborate picnic luncheon. In what had once been the restaurant there were tables and chairs and a long bar at the end of the room behind which stood a barmaid. It was early so there were few people around. We settled down and I opened up the picnic baskets and arranged glasses for the drinks. There was too much of everything by the standards of those days of rationing and it must have been a surprising sight! Before long a few friends joined us in our rather sumptuous meal. I was absent when the trouble started, having gone to the stables to see my horse and Victor Smythe, my trainer. Then I went into the paddock – and suddenly I cocked my ears not unlike my horses. From the loudspeakers, clear above the noise of crowd and horses, I heard, 'Would Lord Dudley go immediately to the Stewards' room.' I was horrified to hear this announcement, and to make matters worse Kenneth

Wagg, who was with me in the paddock, said he thought it must be something pretty serious or they wouldn't have summoned Eric in this way.

I made my way back to the luncheon room. Most of the people had scattered to watch the race from the stands and I noticed that the barmaid was absent. I shall never know exactly what had taken place, but the information I gleaned was as follows: Eric had apparently gone to the sink behind the bar to wash out some glasses for late arrivals who wanted a drink. The barmaid considered this her territory and forbade him to use the sink. Eric paid no heed and pushed her aside. She then reported him to the powers that be, saying he had called her 'a bloody bitch'. The result was that Eric and the barmaid had to tell their different stories in front of the Stewards, and unfortunately for Eric they believed the woman and not my husband's version of this unpleasant affair, which ended in a nominal fine. But far worse was to follow. The incident was reported on the front page of the next edition of the *Racing Calendar*.

After Eric had gone (as he put it) 'like a schoolboy, cap in hand, to the headmaster', he put out a message on the loudspeakers for me to go at once to our car. This I did, to find him trembling with rage, at the same time looking like a deflated red balloon. Whatever the truth may have been the incident was badly handled, especially as Eric knew the Stewards. As we were driven back to Ednam Lodge, Eric was too furious to do more than mumble about the whole ridiculous episode. I was utterly confused by the different stories. On reaching home Eric took to his bed for something like ten days, sending me to London now and again to hear what was being said about him or what had happened at the Windsor meeting. He then announced to me that all the horses, his and mine, had to be sold and that I was never to set foot on a racecourse again. For the sake of peace I gave way to him over my horses – which was extremely foolish. They were all sold under the hammer at Newmarket, at the wrong time of year. One foal of mine which I had named Delirium went for £300. I had carried this delicious little animal across a field soon after it was born. Within two years of the Newmarket sale he was sold at Deauville for £40,000! I realize how stupid I was in giving in to Eric's wilfulness; perhaps the most sensible thing I did in my short racing career was to christen my favourite foal Delirium.

Glimmering Manhattan

The first Christmas after the war, Esmond Rothermere rented Lord Moyne's fantastic house on the south coast near Margate and invited a house party. The house was dark from too few mullioned windows and created the atmosphere of a Shakespearian play. There were dried flowers for decoration, weird cutlery with two-pronged forks (difficult to manipulate), and plenty of mob-capped maids.

Esmond had married my sister Ann the previous June. (Her first husband Shane O'Neill had been killed in action in Italy. They had two children, Raymond (the present Lord O'Neill) and Fion.) Besides Eric and myself, the other guests were my daughter, Sara, Cecil Beaton, Ed Stanley (Lord Stanley of Adlerley), Loelia (Duchess of Westminster), Helen and Evelyn Fitzgerald, and the O'Neill children.

On Christmas night Ann decided on a fancy-dress evening. There was not much material to dress up in and a fair amount of imagination was needed. Cecil of course appeared in some splendid get-up, while my sister and I resorted to stockings and suspenders and not much more than a skimpy scarf. When Eric saw my lack of clothing his mood changed to one of silent disapproval. He hardly entered into the spirit of the evening at all. Matters deteriorated when a pre-dinner round of bridge turned into a form of strip poker, played by Loelia, Eric, Esmond and Ed Stanley. It was arranged that the loser's penalty was to find Cecil Beaton and kiss him! Unfortunately Eric lost the first rubber and was forced to plant a kiss on Cecil much to everyone's amusement including Cecil's. Eric carried out his penalty in a cloud of fury. From then on all hell broke loose. Eric was in a rage, insisting we should leave at once. It was only with considerable difficulty that I persuaded him to wait until Boxing Day morning before we drove away after some hurried farewells. I should add that Eric was always fond of Cecil, but clearly not to the point of a public embrace.

There was another occasion when Eric made a precipitous departure from a Rothermere entertainment, this time at Warwick House. He was very touchy about 'place à table'. So when we went to dine with my sister, he assessed the fellow guests and concluded that he should be seated on my sister's right; instead he found himself seated below the salt. In disgust he literally turned his plate face downwards then, since he insisted that I join him, we swept out of the dining-room. Ann always said she disliked Eric.

I have said little of my relationship with Eric. We had been as good as married for nearly eight years, but from the time we actually married in 1943 I found a change in him. I loved him just as much as ever, but *he* had become more in love with me; already some kind of frantic jealousy had crept into our relationship. He was proud of me but at the same time he began to show a side I had never seen in him before. His possessiveness was really pathological. He seldom took his eyes off me and it seemed to me he was less dynamic in his work. I began to fear for the future of Himley when the war should end. I wondered if he might be slightly 'burnt out' through all the exceptionally hard work he had done, in particular building up his steel-works, coal-mining and the other industrial projects which he revived and developed after his father's death. He talked of leaving the Midlands when the war ended, leaving his real roots for a more light-hearted social life in 'Café Society'. We already went more often to London, staying at Claridge's, as his own very pretty and conveniently placed house in Brook Street, Mayfair, had been quite badly damaged by bombs that fell nearby and would have to have extensive work carried out down to its very foundations.

One Christmas at Ednam Lodge I experienced great difficulty in finding Eric a present. A man such as my husband had everything imaginable that money could buy. Nonetheless he was fascinated by shillings and sixpences. So I bought him a full-sized 'One-Armed Bandit' from a games shop in Tottenham Court Road. I cannot describe the pleasure it gave him. He fixed it in such a way that no one but himself could win the jackpot. The many visitors to Ednam Lodge, both adults and children, would pass their time pulling the machine's handle, while Eric ensured there was always a ready supply of small change at hand. Very rarely did a row of three lemons or cherries appear at the little window. Eric's greatest delight was to empty the amassed silver when his lucrative toy was bursting full.

Eric's two sons were safe; my favourite, Peter Ward, had been taken away from Eton at an early age and sent for safety and schooling to a relation called Dudley Ward in Calgary, Canada, but he returned to England towards the end of 1944 to join the Fleet Air Arm. He amused me when he returned home with a strong Canadian accent. He was longing to meet people of all ages, and I helped him to do this. We spent much time together, for it seemed ages since the day I took him to the Adelphi Hotel, Liverpool, to see him off on the ship for America, whence he went to Calgary. We had corresponded and I remember very funny letters from him about his love for a girl in a hat shop. My husband adored both his boys but after their mother was killed they had no real home life. In the holidays they travelled much, either on Eric's yacht, the *Anna Marie*, or to shooting parties and such amusements, but it seemed to me that Peter craved for love and for a more normal upbringing at home, which I tried to give him. One thing he did not like was horses and hunting. One night when he was still very much a child I went to say good-night to him and found him deep in prayer, kneeling by his bed. I asked him what he was doing, as he was not inclined towards religion; his reply was tearful as well as truthful. He said, 'I'm praying it'll snow and freeze tonight so that we can't go hunting in the morning.' His first marriage was to Claire Baring, a most beautiful girl, and they had two daughters and a son. The girls are now real beauties. That marriage broke up and Peter remarried, while Claire went to live in Italy with ever shorter visits to her London house.

Eric wanted me to send Sara to the USA, like Peter, but I took a less grim attitude to the war than he did. He had his reasons though, having been through one World War and losing so many of his contemporaries in the massacres of 1914–18. During the last months of 1944 I went to the Cotswolds to see my old friend Didy Asquith (or Holland-Martin, as she is now) and I also visited my father, who lived nearby. He came occasionally to Himley, but he did not have much in common with my husband. He attended my Red Cross fête and I remember his joy at winning a bottle of tomato ketchup at a coconut shy!

My brother had left Eton in 1941 to join the Scots Guards and, after a very short training, was sent out to Italy where he fought in the Battle of Cassino. He was wounded and was awarded the MC for bravery, although his story is that his sergeant had been killed and he was really running away and should never have been given a medal. But I know this to be quite untrue. After the war Hugo went to the Far East where he stayed for some time.

My cousin Martin had a strange wartime experience. He was paralysed by some ailment and had to be returned to England from the Middle East as a stretcher case. During the journey his ship was torpedoed and he found himself on a raft with several others, including a clergyman. To his amazement he suddenly found he could move again. Meanwhile everyone was engaged in tea-at-the-vicarage type of talk when all at once the vicar said, 'Do you mind if I pee into the sea?' Martin wrote a brilliant short story about this whole episode.

Many horrible things happened in the last six months of the war, such as the flying bombs and rocket attacks on London. They were accurate and most dangerous in a densely populated city like London. Everyone was told that if they heard a flying bomb – or 'doodlebug' as they were called – they should lie down at once to escape flying glass. I only came near one once in Regent Street. The dangerous time was when the engine cut out as they struck a few moments later. I remember watching a queue at a bus stop collapsing like a pack of cards. I also got down on the ground, but more slowly. I was amazed to see such quick reactions, but it was very necessary when surrounded by shop windows which smashed and threw glass most alarmingly in all directions.

In the early spring of 1945 we knew that the war in Europe would be won and that victory for the Allies was in sight. It came on 8 May – VE Day. Eric's work as Regional Commissioner ended and my work at the hospital was left to matron, much against my wishes. We followed Eric's plan to leave Himley for Ednam Lodge, Sunningdale, and Claridge's in London. Sara and her new older French governess (known as 'La Vieille

Grenouille') and my dogs and horses all moved to Sunningdale.
VE night was tremendous fun; people who had not met for years
seemed to congregate in London. There was a good deal of drinking (not on my part; I simply did not like it and my own spirits
were quite high enough without alcohol). It was a mad kind of
night with street parties of every sort, and when people wanted
to go to bed the hotels and houses seemed to be overflowing.
Eric got very angry when we met at Claridge's in the early hours
of the morning to find the Duke of Northumberland asleep in the
sitting-room of our suite. I knew Hughie Northumberland more
as an acquaintance than a friend; however, he had persuaded
the wonderful head porter, Mr Gibbs, that I had said he could
share our rooms that night. I had gone up to bed first, and finding
Hughie fast asleep and fully dressed, I left him and went to bed
next door. When Eric came up he was furious, accusing me of
all kinds of things that had no word of truth in them. But, as
I have said, his jealousy was becoming pathological. It seemed
particularly silly that night.

In this post-victory period of 1945 we were invited to a reception
one evening at the temporary French Embassy in Cavendish
Square by the ambassador, M. Massigli, and his wife, as I was
being awarded a minor French medal for no good reason that
I can think of but just, I imagine, as a token reward for the work
I had done in the Midlands with the Free French. Anyhow I felt
very honoured and wore it when show-jumping in France. It was
called *La Reconnaissance Française*. There was a big gathering
at the embassy, which must have had a good shaking up from
bombs as there was damage all around. The Massiglis took up
their position in a room on the second floor and all of us who
had come (with friends and relations) to receive medals duly lined
up for the presentations. When it came to my turn I walked up
to the platform where the ambassador and his wife were seated
behind a long trestle table and Eric followed me closely. I was
in the midst of a short talk with them when suddenly there was
a terrible cracking noise behind me. Eric was not particularly
heavy but he was the proverbial last straw on this occasion; the
floor had given way as there were too many people for its war-
weakened condition. To my horror I saw that it had collapsed
taking Eric and quite a number of other people with it. He was
lucky because he landed on top of other people who broke his fall,

but some were hurt though fortunately none seriously. The dust and pandemonium were awful. The Massiglis and I remained marooned but safe. Eric, as may be imagined, was not at all pleased, even though he had been lucky not to be injured.

After the war, for the only time in my life I attended a state opening of Parliament. I sat for what seemed like hours amongst the other peeresses, most of whom were ill-clad for a morning ceremony, with too much flesh showing, their dresses too *décolleté*, and their jewels plastered on them in a clutter with no thought for the type of dress they had chosen. I wore a classic long-sleeved dress and a sprinkling, but not *all*, of the Dudley jewels. Much of the coming and going of the various dignitaries was dull, until the King and Queen arrived. From then on my attention did not wander. I was glad to have been but have no wish to repeat the experience.

There were two things I was looking forward to tremendously – a trip to Paris to buy some clothes (badly needed after years in uniform) and to help choose the trousseau for 'Baby' Carcano, the very pretty eldest daughter of the Argentinian Ambassador to whom Eric's eldest son, Billy Ednam, had become engaged; and the second prospect to which I looked forward was my first visit to the United States early in January 1946. Paris had made a rapid recovery and was already very chic once more. For my clothes I went to Pierre Balmain and there met for the first time Ginette Spanier, who ran his *maison de couture*. In later years she and her husband became great friends of mine and we had much fun in their flat in Paris. In 1945 Pierre Balmain himself came to London to arrange for the making of 'Baby' Carcano's wedding dress and all her trousseau. He brought such wonderful silks and satins that it seemed hard to believe that Paris had been under German occupation for so many years. I managed to obtain some very pretty dresses from Balmain, particularly important for my forthcoming trip to America, where Eric had a great deal of business to do. We sailed on the *Queen Elizabeth*, which was still a troopship, with a few civilian passengers classified as VIPs who included Eric and myself and Lord Kemsley, the newspaper baron, and his wife. There were thousands of American soldiers on board and it was a round-the-clock task for the kitchen staff to keep pace with feeding them. The VIPs had sandwiches twice a day and a cup of tea in the morning – if they were lucky! Our cabin was very small, so I found a certain amount of fun in learning to play 'craps' with the soldiers, throwing the dice against the corridor walls or doors. The noise was deafening.

The Atlantic was still considered quite dangerous from un-swept mines and we were ordered to have a life-jacket on or at hand continually. I was many times reprimanded for not stick-ing to this sensible but irksome rule. On the whole I enjoyed the voyage and it was a thrill to pass by the Statue of Liberty, that welcoming green lady, for the first time and then to dock almost in the heart of Manhattan, a wonderful sight after the black-outs we had been through in London. It seemed like an enormous star-lit city. Eddie Ward, Eric's brother, who was also in America on business, was meant to meet us but something held him up. When he finally arrived all hell broke loose between the brothers. Then our luggage got mislaid, delaying us from going out to dinner. Finally Eric had a row with some newspaper reporters; they were only doing their job, but Eric kicked their cameras into the sea. However, nothing seemed to matter to me; it was all too exciting.

We stayed at the Waldorf Towers and I enjoyed meeting masses of people Eric knew, apart from the entertaining he had to do with such people as the heads of Bethlehem Steel and many other firms. The fantastic cold, dry air that is always so wonder-fully invigorating in New York went to my head. I loved my new clothes from Paris and was delighted when some American women Eric knew asked if they could borrow various dresses to have them copied, since New York had been starved of Paris fashions during the war. For the first few days I was on the crest of a wave, then I was suddenly struck down by a virulent attack of pneumonia. Eric called in a Mr 'Piggy' Weeks, who was really a surgeon not an ordinary doctor. He was a man of considerable charm, attractive and understanding, and very much in the social life of New York. I told him he must get me well enough to fly to Palm Beach in three or four days as we were going to stay with Madame Balsan, a woman of exquisite looks and charm, born Consuelo Vanderbilt, who married the ninth Duke of Marl-borough. She had two sons, one of whom was the late Duke and my last husband. I was very anxious to stay with Madame Balsan in this lovely climate and I also had been told that Mr and Mrs Winston Churchill would be staying, he having a well-earned rest after carrying Britain through the war, working all hours of the day and night, and then being (most ungratefully in my opinion) thrown out by the British public in the general election of 1945. Piggy Weeks understood my feelings, and also it helped that I found him most attractive and he felt the same way about me. He dosed me full of every antibiotic and the fever passed, leaving me not well but able to travel.

On arrival at Palm Beach, all was sun and gaiety. Sarah Russell (*née* Churchill), Madame Balsan's eldest and favourite grandchild, was there. The Winston Churchills were well settled in. For the first few days I was thrilled and fascinated by all I saw and heard. Eric was happy and in the best of humours. All looked as sunny as the weather. In the mornings I used to watch Winston Churchill painting. He stood out in that boiling sun, an easel in front of him and his valet nearby, replenishing his brandy glass as required. I felt I knew him better than I did from the endless discussions I had had with Randolph. In fact I found him extremely moody, but this may have been due to his recent defeat at the polls. When seated next to him at meals I never knew whether he would be easy and most flattering or whether he would be dour and difficult, making me feel less than adequate company for him. I realized then how difficult it must have been for Randolph, whose devotion was constant, to cope with these continually changing moods. One thing was certain, though – however hot the climate he tucked in with relish to such things as roast beef and yorkshire pudding; his appetite never failed him.

Madame Balsan's house was lavishly comfortable and luncheon and dinner were served at a conventional hour. But at the large dinner parties I attended, the guests arrived at eight o'clock and we were lucky to sit down for dinner before ten or ten-thirty. By this time the heads of the men, which to begin with were not very interesting, were so befuddled with spirits as to make sensible conversation impossible. These parties continued for some days, while I found myself in a state of nausea. I saw the local doctor who thought it was just the aftermath of pneumonia. This condition continued for several days and I went on dining and playing golf on the superb courses which are such a part of Palm Beach life. It was almost with relief one morning that I awoke completely yellow and knew I had contracted that most unpleasant of diseases, jaundice, or in my case, infective hepatitis. I was quite seriously ill and Eric took me to what was considered one of the best nursing homes in that part of the world – a convent hospital run by nuns. I sank into bed feeling simply dreadful and was fed on what seemed to be mostly baked potatoes without butter, and boiled sweets. I was also given injections of some kind of therapeutic serum.

For the first week I felt so ill I was really conscious of little except the disappointment that my lovely holiday should end this way. I had many visitors and flowers and everyone was most sympathetic and kind. The present Countess of Bessborough, who is American, was doing part-time work in the hospital and she was particularly kind to me. One day an old boy-friend from England turned up. In the war Colonel Stichfield had been a medical officer with the American troops in Britain. (Now he is one of the leading orthopaedic surgeons in the USA.) He was very attractive and there was a time in the war when, in spite of my relationship with Eric, 'Stich', as I called him, was a very serious part of my life. About twelve years ago we had luncheon together at the Astor Hotel which reminded me of the old song ('Meet Me at the Astor'). He told me then that he would never have been the success he is as a surgeon had our love for each other gone any further, because he would not have been dedicated to medicine in the same way. Maybe he is right; it is long ago and so many things have happened it is hard to remember how I really felt, and I am sure the same goes for him.

I also received visits from Madame Balsan's husband, Jacques. Although Sarah and Caroline had warned me how he had pursued them round their grandmother's house from an early age, I had not realized quite what a maniac he was about women. He used to arrive looking as innocent as Little Red Riding Hood, with a basket of fruit over one arm and a bunch of flowers in his hand. Having deposited his gifts he became a public menace, for in spite of his seventy-six years he was strong and agile. I was lying in bed and not feeling well so I was all too vulnerable a target. His first visit ended in a ridiculous situation with me pinned to the floor, my hand firmly on the bell, hoping that a nurse would come. Subsequently I insisted on being informed of his arrival and openly asked a nurse to stay in my room. I was in hospital in Palm Beach for about five weeks. Eric had to leave me and return to his work in England, where plans for the nationalization of coal and steel were taking shape under our new Labour Government. On leaving hospital I spent a few rather shaky nights with friends of Eric's before returning to New York. Here Tanis Dietz (*née* Guinness) and her wonderful maid, Selina, were very hospitable to me in her house in Greenwich Village.

I stayed once more at the Waldorf Towers, but led quite a different life. I made great friends with Cole Porter. Though he was now crippled, he frequently played the piano for me and sang his songs for as long as I asked. I saw another side of life from the New York I had seen with Eric. Much of my time was spent at that vast and gruesome hospital, Bellevue, with my doctor friends, watching operations and all the things I was so vitally interested in. Howard Dietz took me to dance halls in Harlem – unthinkable today. He also took me round the Bowery district of New York where a mixture of great entertainment talent was to be seen in the various night haunts. There was also dreadful drug addiction. The police seemed to pick up these dangerous maniacs in search of a 'fix' and put them in cages like the monkey house in our zoo. In a special ward at Bellevue Hospital they screamed all night like wild animals, and when morning came they were released without any further treatment. At the time, it seemed to me a diabolical way of handling these addicts. I know it was a very difficult situation, and it did at least reduce crime during the hours of night when these pathetic creatures would have done anything to obtain money to give the pedlars of heroin and other hard drugs. I had been in contact with many dreadful sights during the war, but the impact of seeing these 'animals' – they scarcely looked like human beings with the terror in their eyes, their clutching hands and twitching limbs – was a haunting and despairing sight I shall never forget.

By this time everything in my life looked different. I was still very fond of Eric, but by the early spring of 1946 I had not left New York. I had constant telephone calls – even more than letters – from Eric asking what I was doing as he had heard I had attended few of his American friends' parties, and saying I must return home, which somehow I had a dread of doing, beyond wanting to see my daughter Sara. I had heard that Himley was to be taken over as the headquarters of the Coal Board. I fully realized that life in England for me would be Sunningdale and

Claridge's, neither of which had much appeal. Eric had more or less promised that he would put up the money for me to have my own nursing home in London. Before leaving for America I had seen Aneurin Bevan, who had started setting up his health service. He had said that he would give me all the help possible, as he intended to have a mixed health service – unlike the recent Labour Government which wanted to do away with all private practice. When I did return to England in the spring of 1946 the idea of the nursing home was very much uppermost in my thoughts.

The Duchess's Jewels

I travelled by ship on the *Queen Mary*, sleeping a good deal to recover from my most enjoyable time in New York. There were on board plenty of interesting people including Isaiah Berlin, who never stopped talking in his brilliant way. Arrival in England was obviously a slight anticlimax. Eric seemed even more changed. He was so often in a rage against someone, either friends or people in a subordinate position to himself. It was difficult as, apart from petty jealousy, he continued to be very loving towards me. I admit to being changed myself and much more grown-up, which, of course, I was by now, and no doubt very tiresome to Eric in many ways. Almost immediately Eric said the nursing-home idea was off. One reason he gave was that he couldn't afford it, which was not true; the second, probably true, was that he said I would always be at the nursing home and not with him. So that was the end of that plan.

I was pretty busy with Elizabeth Leveson-Gower's wedding preparations. She was a niece of Eric's first wife, who was the daughter of the Duke of Sutherland. Elizabeth had neither a mother nor father and had been brought up by her Sutherland uncle and aunt. Eric adored her and she spent some of her time with us at Himley. I was devoted to her and we had great fun making the preparations for her wedding to Charles Janson. Later in life she became a great friend of my brother and sister-in-law. My brother was working in Paris and Charles was also working in some journalistic capacity in the same city. Elizabeth is now the Countess of Sutherland in her own right, which her husband found a droll situation since he remained Mr Janson!

Things between Eric and myself were not going well, so it was decided in an amicable way that we should have a few weeks apart. Eric arranged that my great friend Didy Asquith (whose life was also in trouble) and I should take a trip to Sweden, of all places. So in May 1946 we went by ship to Götenburg, then by train to Stockholm. At this time I was having a mild affair with Philip Dunn, but never thought he would follow me to Sweden. However he did, bringing as a companion our mutual friend Toby Milbanke. The boat trip was rather odd, neither Didy nor myself speaking a word of Swedish. We seemed to spend a lot of time eating, which is unlike me, but I soon realized that the Swedes are a very greedy people. On ship every meal began with *smörgasbord*, their version of hors-d'œuvre, but in vast quantities and varieties, including a great deal of raw fish, mostly salmon. One helping of *smörgasbord* was a large meal to the average person, but not to the Swedes. It was just the start of a vast 'blow-out', lasting for hours. At first it was a novelty to us and we picked about amongst the wooden boards on which the various items of food were laid out, but by the time we reached Stockholm I was sickened by Swedish eating habits.

Sweden itself was an enjoyable novelty. We lived at a modest small hotel, everything spotlessly clean; one almost longed to see a house that was not newly painted, or even a child normally, if slightly, untidy, but that was not the way of Sweden. There were many gossip comments in the main newspaper, called *Spungust*, about our arrival, and we had plenty of invitations to dinners and parties. Eric rang up Didy every evening to find out what was going on. We spent a lot of time in Nordiska Kompaniet, a large Swedish store. We bought bicycles to get around on. We also wore rather becoming caps, which we had no right to as they had written on them 'Uppsala', which is their celebrated fifteenth-century university near Stockholm. Philip and Toby Milbanke stayed at some much grander hotel and gave vast and rather dull parties. In Sweden Philip and I had many disagreements, so in a way it was a good thing that he pushed off, although we always remained great friends.

About this time, Didy and I met Thorsten Kreuger, a brother of the 'match king' who killed himself before he could be jailed. This Kreuger, I knew, was probably a pretty dreadful man. He certainly had plenty of wives, in various houses surrounding the one in which he lived with his latest bride. This sounds strange, but in Sweden at that date you could get a divorce (at least a man could) by going to the post office and giving any trumped-up reason. When we met Mr Kreuger he appeared to have masses of money and a very large yacht, in spite of a socialist government and a general effort to give the impression of equality, which was far from the truth. On the yacht we took a most interesting voyage among all the little islands in the fjords around Sweden. Kreuger had one rather pathetic daughter, plain and uncertain of herself, who came to stay with me later in England. Not Kreuger, but most of the men I met in Sweden were almost sex maniacs, particularly towards midsummer. There was a saying in Sweden that most children were conceived on Midsummer Night. They also had a ridiculous form of entertainment called 'bathing on your honour'. This meant that nobody was supposed to don a bathing dress and the men all promised not to look in the women's direction – a likely tale!

I had a great admirer who was no less than the owner of Bloomingdale's, the large and well-known store in New York. He was a small and rather insignificant man, completely overpowered by his mother, a very domineering American lady, but he was rather kind and nice compared with many men I had luncheon or dinner with. Very often these men were quite impossible. One night I dined with such a type. Before we had so much as ordered our food he had the nerve to ask me if I would go to bed with him that night. When I said, 'Certainly not', he left the table without a word, leaving me to find my rather hungry way home! One night we attended a large and very grand ball which provides a picture of the strange way things happened in Sweden in 1946. This ball started in the usual rather conventional way, with Swedish royalty present. By midnight I was dancing merrily away when I suddenly noticed that the ballroom was empty. 'Is it all finishing at such an early hour?' I asked my partner. 'Oh no,' he replied. 'Most of the couples have gone upstairs to make love.' As you may imagine I was astounded by his answer. He went on to explain that the party would soon recommence, which indeed happened. The much-bejewelled guests returned in dribs and drabs; there was an excellent band and, as always in Sweden, a mountain of food was served and we danced the night out. I had never attended a party like this before, nor have I ever again.

It was now approaching the end of July. The messages from Eric continued. Didy left for Denmark, so Eric suggested I should meet him at Cannes and there we would try out our marriage again. I complied with his wish. I would go further than that, because I was not only becoming bored with Sweden but I rather longed to see Eric and my daughter Sara, whom he said he would bring with him. I also looked forward to the luxury of being joined by my Swiss ladies' maid Mlle Dupuis, who remained with me for many years. She was a woman of understanding and intelligence, much needed in the years that followed. My reunion with Eric was emotional but happy on both sides. He had always longed for a child by me and even before the first parting – my Swedish expedition – we had undergone many tests. From the medical angle all seemed well so there was always hope, although I had undergone an operation after the war for what is known as a prolapsed uterus from too much standing during my nursing career. That time in Cannes was at least successful from this point of view. I did start a child, though, of course, I did not know it until our return to England.

In Cannes I met for the first time the Duke and Duchess of Windsor. They were then living at La Croe on the Cap d'Antibes with gardens and lawns running down to the sea. The Duke had not seen Eric since the Abdication, but they remained long-standing friends and one night they invited us to dinner. It was a very hot night and Eric and I put on ordinary thin evening clothes. When we arrived, the Duke was dressed in full Scottish regalia down to the smallest detail, all worn with his usual elegance, and though I could not but think that he must feel somewhat hot, he did not show it. He greeted me with his usual impeccable manners and I at once found him easy to talk to and full of charm. Soon the Duchess appeared in some lovely but simple creation of a dress, which was typical of her incredible chic. She, too, was gay, happy and full of jokes that night at dinner and all through the evening. The Duke, as I got used to later in my life, never took his eyes off the Duchess. We had dinner by the sea and all went very well; many plans were made for future meetings, including that the Windsors would stay with us in England whenever they so pleased. We were still living mainly at Sunningdale which, being adjacent to Windsor, suited the Duke very well as he told me he had many private papers to go over which were still lodged at Windsor.

The Duke was without doubt one of the most charming men I have ever had the pleasure of knowing, always easy-going and un-moody. He was perfectly natural and had a great understanding of almost everything. He loved England, but having given that up took great solace in his garden, especially later on at his *moulin* near Paris. He had a passion for outdoor life, particularly golf. There were some moments when he looked desperately sad but nonetheless he had no regrets over surrendering his inheritance for the woman about whom he was so besotted. However, he was deeply hurt that the Duchess was not granted the title of Royal Highness. He felt it was an insult to her and it worried him till the day he died. I was fond of her too. She was gay and friendly and dressed beautifully. Always quick to see the funny side of life, she was also a perfectionist, a superb *maîtresse de maison*. Some said this was due to an abundance of money, but many houses are ill-run where money is no problem. She had style. Only once did I see an unpleasant and to me unexpected side of her character and that was at the time of the robbery of her jewels at Ednam Lodge. Another strange thing was that nobody except the Duchess, not even their closest con-temporaries, called the Duke David. This puzzled me particularly in the case of Eric, who had been a childhood friend and was once even beaten with a leather belt by King George v for some misdemeanour in the royal presence.

When Eric, Sara and I returned to London towards the end of August Eric wanted me to see my own gynaecologist, Mr Lane-Roberts, who pronounced me pregnant. As the weeks went on, I suffered increasing pain. I was at Claridge's with a nurse. My health deteriorated and after three months I was put into a charming small nursing home in Bentinck Street. Lane-Roberts did not seem very interested, while Eric was half out of his mind – longing for a child yet hating to see me in such pain. It was beginning to be clear to me and my nurse that I was in an ad-vanced state of ectopic pregnancy, in other words the baby was in one of my fallopian tubes and not in my womb, hence the pain because it had already ruptured. I was lucky to live. Even then, the doctors delayed cutting me open in order to save my life until they had done a curettage. Eric was at his most sympathetic and sweet, scarcely leaving my bedside. I remained very ill for some weeks. Then I was put into a most luxurious Daimler ambulance and, with my favourite nurse, driven down to Ednam Lodge.

Eric's mood changed at about Easter, and the cause was a petty one. My nurse, to whom I was by now devoted, accidentally burned a hole in the carpet outside my bedroom door. It was no more than a round patch where she had placed an electric kettle. Eric simply blew up, little thinking of the effect it would have on her and me. He simply chucked her out, leaving me in tears, as I was still far from well and loved my nurse. Furthermore I knew she only had a small flat of her own to go to and it being Easter Saturday, all the shops were closed. He said to me that he would engage another nurse, which was of no comfort. It was this kind of thing that made living with him so hard to take, and eventually made my eyes wander more in other directions even if he suffered from remorse afterwards.

The Duke of Windsor wrote to me once: 'In spite of all the disparaging things you say about your "surburban villa" personally I have no complaints whatsoever over Ednam Lodge and always find it most enjoyable and luxurious.' But I liked neither it nor our way of life, though Angie and Bob Laycock, Dot (Lady Dorothy Head) and her husband Anthony, all lived in this part of the country, which made life much more bearable. Also Pat Laycock (first known to me as Lady Jersey), was often staying with her mother, Lady Kent, literally next door. Kenneth Wagg and his then wife were in the same vicinity. We played golf and tennis and we had a swimming pool, and there was much bridge and poker with rather too high stakes in the evenings.

I started riding in Windsor Home Park, which I much enjoyed, except on one occasion when Paddy Leigh Fermor, the novelist and explorer, turned up to stay after his mammoth walk from Crete. He said he would like a ride, and knowing all his many capabilities I took it for granted that he was an adequate horseman. I mounted him on my favourite horse called Doodlebug. He suggested it would be more fun to ride around the many golf courses of Sunningdale. His choice was Wentworth, where it was perfectly all right to ride on the rough grass. I don't know what happened, whether Doodlebug got out of hand or Paddy was just having a lark, but either way it was a disaster. They went off at full gallop, crossing at least six greens; the precious turf that had been carefully tended even during the war was cut to pieces and the greens looked more like ploughed fields than their normal green baize. Paddy roared with his most endearing laughter. On our return, however, things did not seem so funny. Eric had already been informed and told that *he* would have to replace this priceless turf! I need hardly say how he took this news; he almost asked Paddy to leave, as he had done to other characters of a less ebullient type. Once Alastair Forbes was told to quit after a joke about Billy Ednam, inspired by a comment in the *Sunday Express*. Sometimes, if there had been a row at bridge or canasta and I had gone up to change for dinner, I would hear a tap on my door and even some of Eric's oldest friends would say, 'I have been asked to depart this house at once.' I always said the same thing: 'Don't be absurd. Eric's mood will change by dinner.' This was by no means always true, but he usually calmed down or at least this was my constant hope. And it is true that if I could get him to listen to me when he came upstairs, he took a more sane and rational view of whatever the ridiculous hullabaloo was all about.

It was not long since I had taught him one salient lesson by leaving him and going to Sweden, but there had to be more 'bolting' (as Randolph Churchill called my departures), and of longer duration on my part, till I left for good in about 1953. Meanwhile there were many times when we were still happy, as his uncontrolled temper was never directed towards me except in jealousy, and over this he did at times have cause to be angered.

A couple I was always pleased to see arriving for a weekend were Bobby and Freda Casa Maury. She was a fascinating woman whom the Duke of Windsor had worshipped for many years before Mrs Simpson came along, and after that affair came to an untimely end Eric had loved her for many years and wanted to marry her. It appears that she gave it some thought, but then met Bobby (Marqués de Casa Maury). He was good-looking, of Cuban origin, and although I thought him limited in many fields of conversation I fully admit to finding him attractive. As weekend guests they were perfect. Eric always loved Freda, not in the same way as he loved me, but at least for old times' sake, and never as far as I can remember made stupid scenes when she was present. He also behaved equally well when the Duke of Windsor was about. One time when I left Eric the Duke wrote to me imploring me to return home. I had to write back explaining:

Dear Sir,
I do not think you appreciate the complex character of your friend and my husband. If you, dear Sir, were always with us, my life would be both happy and easy for he would never show the temper and insanity that becomes more tedious and difficult for me as the years go by. At this moment I have little else to say, beyond thanking you for your kind offer and sending you and the Duchess
Much love,
Laura.

I must now tell the story of the fantastic robbery of nearly all the Duchess of Windsor's jewels from Ednam Lodge on 17 October 1946. We had lent the Sunningdale house to the Windsors, complete with our staff, but could always go down there at any time. Sara and 'La Vieille Grenouille' remained, and my dogs and horses. On the day of the robbery another arrangement had been made. My personal maid, Mademoiselle Dupuis, was going to look after the Duchess as her maid was going home to Scotland for a holiday. Fortunately the change-over had not taken place. When the Windsors arrived, our butler had suggested to the Duchess that her jewels should be put in his strong-room, which was a large room made like a safe in which the silver and other things of value were kept. But the Duchess's jewel case was no ordinary affair. It was a trunk in which she had many of HRH's fantastic collection of Fabergé boxes and a great many uncut emeralds which I believe had belonged to Queen Alexandra. The Duchess liked jewels very much, though this is rather an understatement as she was continually having them re-set, mostly in Paris. One of these priceless baubles had only just reached her, a vast sapphire which she had had converted into a bird of paradise by Van Cleef and Arpels. But the butler's prudent suggestion that this trunkful of things scarcely to be found in an Aladdin's cave should be put in the strong-room was rejected by the Duchess. Her jewel case, she said, would remain, as it always did, under her maid's bed! On the afternoon of this disastrous day her maid, in preparation for her holiday, asked that this trunk of valuables should be put in the Duchess's bedroom temporarily, later to be put in the strong-room at the request of my maid, who did not fancy having such a treasure under her bed. In those days a very loud bell was rung at 6 p.m. for the servants' high tea. There was a detective hanging around the gate at the entrance to the house (or, possibly, having a doze in the sun or a stroll on the golf course). The robbery must have taken place around 6.30 or 7 p.m. My dogs were around, but they were not ferocious types. It was still quite light.

Eric and I were in London and so were the Duke and Duchess. They went back to the country that evening, whereas we remained in London. What the highly organized thieves must have done, according to Mr Capstick, the CID man in charge of the case, was to have swung a white rope up to Sara's windowsill in the front of the house, then crossed the passage to the Duchess's room to find the whole treasure trove sitting in front of the fireplace, where it had been put while the servants were eating their meal. The thieves left the white rope with the hook on it hanging from the sill while they proceeded to get at the loot. Much of this they left, including the collection of heavy Fabergé gold boxes, on a tray on another windowsill where I found them. Either they had forgotten them or this was not what they had come to get. Some of the Duchess's jewels which they took were not even mounted. The detectives found something like eighteen odd earrings scattered over the Sunningdale golf course but, much to her fury, not one pair.

Our butler rang Eric at Claridge's. I was in the room and was much amused to hear Eric say, 'Are you sure they haven't touched my guns or fishing rods?' Eric and I then joined the Windsors at Ednam Lodge. The Duchess was in a bad way. She wanted all the servants put through a kind of third degree, but I would have none of this, all of them except for one kitchen maid being old and devoted staff of long standing. By the following night the Duke was both demented with worry and near to tears. The Duchess started the next day with a grim face and wearing on her dress about the only jewel that remained to her. Just before we all went out for a little stroll she said, 'David, put this brooch in a safe place.' On our return he could not remember where he had put it! He thought the most likely place was the room he was using for sorting the papers he had fetched from Windsor. There ensued a frantic search, but to no avail.

When it was time for bed the Duchess and Eric went upstairs;

it had been a grim day. The Duke said he was going to continue the search although he looked grey with worry and exhaustion. I was desperately sorry for him, and anyhow I would have stayed to help him in his search, hoping at least to find this one remaining jewel to which the Duchess appeared so attached. We stayed up most of the night; he obviously feared to go up to bed empty-handed. I made endless cups of black coffee while the Duke went through his papers, which he seemed convinced was the likeliest place. At about 5 a.m. by some miracle we found it, under a china ornament. Never have I seen a man so relieved. He was still ashen in the face, but he rushed upstairs.

For days the house seemed filled with CID men. Eric and I returned to London. Soon afterwards I was walking down Bond Street with one of the Dudley jewels, which happened to be a diamond brooch, on my dress. It was small but its shape was that of the Prince of Wales's three feathers, no doubt a gift to Eric or his family. I was suddenly tapped on the shoulder by a plain-clothes detective, who wished to know about this brooch. The incident was really rather foolish and funny for, the moment I told him my name, the detective was naturally embarrassed. It was all over in a matter of seconds but it did bring to my mind how fortunate I – or rather Eric – had been that none of the Dudley family jewels had been touched in the robbery. Inspector Capstick's investigations went on for years, but as far as I know nothing has ever been discovered to this day. The Duke must have spent a fortune on giving the Duchess a fantastic new collection of jewels which she still wore until recently.

12

I Bolt

In about 1947 Eric took me to Rome and we went to watch the International Horse Show. This was really the turning point in the field of international show-jumping largely brought about by Colonel Harry Llewellyn and Colonel Mike Ansell. Not that Britain figured prominently at this show; the Italians had their own way, and rightly so. But it was from that date that Britain entered the international field, led by Harry Llewellyn and his famous horse Foxhunter. Mike Ansell, partially blind from injury in the war, had an incredible talent for building jumps and for the arrangement of the show-jumping arenas in England, which he continued to design even when his sight deteriorated further. At the same time Harry Llewellyn did marvellous work, gathering a British team that before long was hard to beat.

I did not start to compete seriously until 1948. There were many reasons for this, the dominant one being that, although Eric and I were having many troubles of a personal kind, he had at least said I could find another house and we would be able to leave Sunningdale. I was therefore fully occupied in finding a house that would please both of us, thereby, I hoped, giving our marriage a better chance of survival. Late that summer Sara (now nearly grown up) and I found a very pretty small Queen Anne house near Kings Langley with a certain amount of land, but there was much to be done to it. It had lovely stables, which was very important as we had both taken up show-jumping and started hunting again in the winter. I was thrilled with the new house and Eric grew to like it, but things did not start well as my great friend Patsy Ward, Eric's sister, remarked to Eric more or less as a joke that she thought it 'Too small and not a house for a gentleman!' This was soon put right by Eric building on two large rooms downstairs, a dining-room and a library, more domestic quarters and another bedroom and bathroom. With his usual luck, he was also able to purchase something like a further 2,000 acres of land remarkably cheaply for such pretty country, a mere twenty miles from London. He also built a large walled kitchen garden with old bricks I managed to find. The house was called Westwood, but that name was soon upgraded by Eric who re-named it Great Westwood.

During the autumn I set about the interior. The furniture we had was not particularly attractive, the wrong period and too big. I bought some really lovely antique furniture from the most expensive shops in London, such as Blairman and Partridge. When Eric returned from shooting grouse in Scotland he liked what he saw but, like a fool, he returned the greater part of the furniture, which was cheap compared with its price a very few years later. This was rather unlike him as usually he had a nose for sniffing out where money was to be made, and God knows what these exquisite, small but perfect antiques would be worth today. This was one of the very few mistakes he made in favour of quick profit. In those days 'doing up' and structurally extending a house went at a great speed, unlike nowadays, and for less than a quarter of the price that it would cost in the 1980s. During this transitional period from Sunningdale to Westwood I was very occupied. Sara and her governess, 'La Vieille Grenouille', moved from one house to the other. It was not an easy time, but I enjoyed it and I was well pleased with Westwood. My horses and Sara's ponies spent their time mostly with a man called Phil Oliver, a real rough diamond with a great knowledge of horses. His son, Alan, was a well-known rider, and Alan's second wife had much to do with Princess Anne's successful Three Day Event career.

All was well after our move to Westwood, but Eric didn't have enough to occupy him. He was on many company boards as a director and still had certain industrial interests in the Midlands, which took him there at least once a week; my night off! We also moved back to the house in Brook Street and spent the middle of most weeks in London, where we entertained. It was a lovely house and garden. Peter, Eric's youngest son, was living at home so most weekends there were parties at Great Westwood. Sometimes Eric invited old friends, like the Casa Maurys. But his jealousy was getting worse by the day. Among the people I knew was a kind and gentle person called Gerry Koch de Gooreynd. He had been a prisoner of war, captured very early, but repatriated about 1943 because of ill-health. I had known him a little before the war, but only at the odd party or playing golf. In those days he was married to a lovely girl called Elizabeth, but she fell in love with a young man called Wallace, and left him just before the war. (Later they married.) I was always fond of Gerry but I had no idea how he felt about me until the night of a scintillating ball which Diana and Duff Cooper gave in Paris when Duff was our ambassador to France. It was a fantastic occasion, just before Christmas, and many people went to Paris specially for the night. This is what Eric and I did, taking a pretty ball dress of mine, made in Paris – a mass of pale tulle, no shoulder straps, just a broad band of real leopard skin making a bodice finishing under my arms. I also took the Dudley tiara, which Cartier's had almost remade to suit me as in its original form it was much too heavy and cumbersome. The jewels and the dress (plus the things I travelled in) were the only clothes I took to Paris, knowing we had to return to England the next morning for a business engagement of Eric's; besides I had further arrangements to make for a Christmas house party which was now close upon us.

I know I looked attractive at the dinner and the ball, the first really grand and beautifully arranged party since the war. I was also in very high spirits, as I had been looking forward to this occasion for some time. To my despair, nothing went well from the very start. Eric, for some unknown reason, looked thunderous. I was quite used to him never taking his eyes off me, but something worse was happening to him that night. He was not even particularly nice to me yet every time I spoke or danced with any other man the thunderclouds within him seemed to go out of all control; he either interrupted my conversation or broke in on a dance (an American habit), making some feeble excuse. Whatever I did or said was ruined by his even more than usually psychopathic behaviour. It was not long before, in a most disappointed and half-tearful way, I said to him, 'Your behaviour is quite impossible. I think we'd better go back to the Ritz and go to bed.' Eric claimed to be delighted with the idea but his face was still as furious as ever. When we returned to the Ritz I saw

no point in discussing the evening and did not mention it. I hurriedly removed my dress with the intention of going to bed. Eric
had other ideas; he provoked every kind of argument, interspersed with totally untrue accusations. This unpleasant and unfair state of disagreement continued till nearly daybreak, at which
point I told him he had better take the early flight as arranged,
as I was too exhausted and upset to go with him; I would return
later in the day. He was not pleased but, as was his way, realized
that he had been both selfish and absurd and finally agreed with
much reluctance to this arrangement. When he departed I looked
ashen grey.

I tried to sleep but I was far too unhappy even to close my
eyes. I organized an afternoon flight home. Then around midday
I decided to have a bite of food on the rue Cambon side of the
hotel. I went down in the lift to the principal entrance on the
Place Vendôme and here I sat, a huddled bundle of misery, before
walking down the long passage filled with show cases to the Cambon side. I must have looked a pitiable sight, and my mind was
a complete blank. Suddenly I heard a voice that seemed somehow
far away saying, 'What is the matter?' I slowly raised my head
to find Gerry Koch de Gooreynd standing by me. He asked a
few questions; on hearing my immediate plans, he said he was
thinking of returning to London in the afternoon and suggested
taking me out to luncheon where we could talk. I cannot describe
my feelings. I seemed to be in a very weary distraught dream.
We went to Maxim's. Gerry had apparently observed Eric's behaviour at the embassy ball and been infuriated. I knew he disliked
him. We talked endlessly about my impossible marriage and, to
my surprise, he appeared to know a lot about me from hearsay
or observation at various parties and at the board meetings of
the Chest Hospital in Brompton Road, of which Eric and I were
directors, Eric being chairman.

I was tearful and poured out all my misery in a flood of self-
pity. He listened with understanding and something more than
sorrow for my undisguised and unhappy plight. Time passed and
before I realized it was far too late to return to London. Suddenly
Gerry became very serious, taking all matters into his own hands.
To my complete and utter amazement, he said, 'You do accept
the fact that I love you and have done so for some time.' I blurted
out the truth that I had no such knowledge. He went on to say

that I must leave Eric, and, once free, he hoped I would marry him. I had no time to take all this in before he continued with more immediate plans. He said, 'You must telephone Eric and tell him you are never going to return to him.' I did what he told me, and the result was a dreadful and stormy telephone conversation. Gerry then telephoned the British Embassy and spoke to either Diana or Duff, who said I could take sanctuary with them. Gerry took me and my one and only dress to the embassy. I remember so well how funny Duff and Diana were, and it was certainly time for some light relief! Diana was the most practical, saying the staff had scarcely recovered from the ball and that they were going out to dinner and needed an extra man, so Gerry had better go with them, while Venetia Montagu, who was staying at the embassy, would have dinner on a tray with me. This arrangement was perfect. I was nearly dropping on my feet and was fond of Venetia, who was not only a contemporary of Eric's but had had a love affair with him years before which had resulted in a child, Judy Montagu (later Mrs Milton Gendel), who was a great friend of mine. I thought it would be a chance to talk to Venetia, a woman of the world and of high intelligence.

That evening once again seemed to pass in a hazy fashion. I was both mentally and physically exhausted. Venetia was far from well (she was in fact dying of cancer but was wonderfully brave). She was most understanding and able to look at all I said with a dispassionate eye. The next morning everything was again discussed in Diana Cooper's lovely Borghese bedroom, which she turned into her own private salon. Diana, as always, was most entertaining and begged Duff not to venture outside the courtyard of the embassy for fear Eric would mistake him for Gerry and shoot him on sight!

I telephoned my sister Ann asking if I could go to Warwick House, the Rothermeres' huge house overlooking the Green Park. She was sympathetic and agreed. I then went out to buy a few necessities, having arrived equipped only for the ball. Christmas being upon us, Gerry and I remained only a few days in Paris, and there was no further talk of love or marriage. I had explained to him that I still loved Eric and although I had left him before I still had hopes for the survival of our marriage. To all of this he made no comment. Duff Cooper amused me by saying, 'I quite understand you leaving Eric, but I don't understand the "Gerry" side of it.' This was no surprise to me, but I was lost in my own unhappiness and Gerry appeared the person who most understood my predicament.

I went back to London and stayed at Warwick House. Eric, by now out of his mind with fury, went ahead with his Christmas party. We had many further dreadful conversations on the telephone. I returned all his diamonds and pearls, but he would not release my maid, my dogs or any of my personal belongings. Fortunately, Sara was spending Christmas with her grandmother, Lady Glyn. It was at least ten days before Eric's lawyers told him that he must let my maid, dogs and clothing be sent to Warwick House. Here I spent the rest of the winter, making my home on the top floor of Esmond Rothermere's house, and very charming he was to me. My sister Ann soon went off to Jamaica to be with her later husband, Ian Fleming, at Goldeneye. During my stay at Warwick House I saw a great deal of Gerry, who lived in Buckingham Street, but I remained very unhappy. Eric went to America, crying on everyone's shoulder and making them write to me, as he did, begging me to return and promising to be different in the future. All this I told Gerry, which made him unhappy too.

By the time spring came I knew Eric would be back in England. He telephoned from Brook Street. I agreed to a meeting with him, but made no promises; in my heart I already knew I would return to him, although this was complicated by my also knowing I was having Gerry's child. Eric and I had been apart nearly five months so when we met at Brook Street it was all very tearful on both sides and in many ways slightly theatrical, making me feel, 'I've been here at least once before'. We talked about the future and whether I really would return to him. He rang for the butler and, to my amazement, told him to go to his son Lord Ednam's house and collect my jewellery, as he called the Dudley jewels. I knew and liked 'Baby' Ednam, Billy's first wife, and I was astounded when Eric gave the butler this instruction. Naturally 'Baby' had assumed the jewels to be hers and had had some pieces altered to her taste; it can never have occurred to her that Eric regarded them as, so to speak, 'on loan'. Anyhow it seemed rather ridiculous of Eric to send the butler off on this mission when we had not yet talked about things of much greater importance – our future life for a start!

I had plenty to say and indeed I had already written, in large letters and in red ink, quite a long list of things Eric must promise not to do should I return to him. I showed him my list of 'Don'ts'. He immediately said he would adhere to everything I had written; he went even further and said he would keep the list by his bed at Westwood and have a copy made for London! He asked me to move from Warwick House to his house in Brook Street that very night. I said it would have to be the next day, knowing I must first tell Gerry that I was leaving Warwick House to resume my marriage to Eric, a task I deeply dreaded. I then bravely informed my husband that, though it was early days as yet, I was definitely having a baby. He was neither surprised nor shocked, obviously guessing it was Gerry's child, as there had been much talk about me and Gerry. If anything he seemed pleased, although he repeated that he would never give me a divorce at any time, so if I had the child and did not return to him the child would be a bastard, as he so charmingly put it! I said I would pay one of my extraordinary visits to Mr Lane-Roberts, my gynaecologist, but he was opposed to this.

I had my painful talk with Gerry, and though he had an angelic personality he was so upset that he completely broke down and I feared for his health. I knew he had Hodgkin's disease and had undergone lengthy and unpleasant treatment, which had lately much improved his health. I had talked to his doctor, also a great friend and surgeon, Sir Archibald McIndoe, whom I had known in the war when I cared for many of his patients at my Himley Hospital in between surgery done by the hand of Sir Archibald. I therefore felt instinctively that he would tell me the truth about Gerry's disease. He said there was no reason why Gerry shouldn't live his full life span, but he also said that, as Hodgkin's disease is a form of cancer, one could not be certain – though more was being discovered every day and in the case of Gerry, who was strong in general health, he felt very hopeful. I understood this easily because of my nursing experience. Nevertheless, that day in May 1946 was an agonizing one. Gerry, as usual, was not thinking of himself; he seemed certain that Eric would never change his ways and this made him unhappy for me as much as for himself. So he wrote me endless letters during the years that followed and we also met sometimes.

When I settled back home again I visited Lane-Roberts, who

advised me not to have the baby. He kept me in a nursing home for one night, but I will never know exactly what he did. All I do know is that on my return home I felt quite extraordinarily ill. Lane-Roberts, who I think must have gone mad, assured me it would be quite all right to accompany Eric to the South of France as planned. It was early June and the luxurious Eden Roc Hotel was empty. As soon as we arrived in the hotel I felt even worse. I rushed to the bathroom and collapsed. Thereafter it was all a nightmare which I was fortunate to survive. In the pain of what happened I remember Eric's voice calling me and his look of horror and terror. Presently I found myself in bed with two nurses preparing me for the first of three blood transfusions. Eric summoned the best gynaecologist he could find from Paris and he telephoned Lane-Roberts. This crazy doctor merely stated that he had 'promoted a miscarriage'. As I regained my strength over the next few months, Eric remained at his most charming. As I got better I was able to bathe in the warm, clear sea-water. Eric was so sweet and understanding to me and I was happy. I was full of hope for the future and soon longed to go home. I had made up my mind to take up show-jumping and return to the hunting field the following winter. Eric agreed to all my plans.

During the late 1940s Eric, Sara and I had some very entertaining times in the South of France. Eric longed to have another yacht, not a large vessel like he had before but a small yacht that we could sleep in and bathe from as we wanted, and which would provide an easy means to travel along that already congested coast from St Tropez to Monte Carlo. He soon made his dream boat come true by ordering a small yacht to be built in England, and he named her *Saralong* after my daughter. She was to have a one-man crew so that Eric could wear a captain's cap and fly his beloved 'white duster', or white ensign. My stepson Peter was to take her south through the lovely canals that trace their way to the sea, meandering along the artificial watercourses of France. I wish I had gone on this trip. Billy Wallace accompanied him, taking bicycles to enable them to seek out delectable bistros en route in which they had delicious simple meals. When the *Saralong* reached Cannes she was not in the best of conditions, being somewhat bumped and scratched, but she was soon restored though Eric was not best pleased with Peter over the cost of re-conditioning his new toy! I in no way blamed Peter, as in the

Midlands of England I had ridden along the towpaths of our wasted canal system and realized how difficult the locks are to navigate.

For several years we spent a few weeks each summer on the *Saralong*. I remember one year there was an unfortunate incident in Cannes. At that time no one was allowed to take more than a small amount of money out of this country, but Eric would go completely mad in the casino on occasions, playing *chemin de fer*. One night in the Summer Casino Eric was playing in a crazy fashion, losing vast sums of money – and, even more alarmingly, drinking heavily, which was unlike him. I made several attempts to stop his spectacularly foolish behaviour. By the early hours of the morning many people had gathered round the table where he was playing. He had brandy by his side and he looked furious – and was apparently unaffected by the stir he was causing. In despair, and worried about the repercussions that would follow, I decided to go back to our hotel where Sara and my maid were asleep. I went to bed but with little chance of rest till Eric returned.

He came to my room around 4 a.m., still in a fury – mostly with himself – and informed me he was going to take an overdose of sleeping pills. I had no fear of him carrying out this threat. He explained how serious the matter was for him, being a director of the Westminster Bank and countless other businesses, as I was quite well aware. He then calmed down, for he remembered that Loel Guinness's yacht was anchored between the two islands off Cannes. I said Loel was not aboard, but Eric replied that a Mr Auniac, then the manager of Loel's many lucrative enterprises, was there, and the plan was that I should go to him and ask for help (in other words for him to pay off the many thousands of pounds Eric had lost) and Eric would repay Loel in some other way. I agreed to this and Eric fell asleep, thinking his problem solved. Later that morning Sara and I boarded our boat and anchored some distance from Loel's. It was a glorious hot day. I thought it would be a good idea to swim the rest of the way and ask to speak to this Mr Auniac, whom I had never met. When we reached Loel's yacht I shouted to a member of the crew, gave my name and said I wished to have a few private words with Mr Auniac. We scrambled up the ladder and met Loel's key man who was most understanding, and after a brief talk said all would be arranged provided I would go with him to the casino when it opened. He said there was no difficulty and he would have all dangerous cheques destroyed. He then offered us coffee and a change of clothing – I had forgotten my wet bathing dress and dripping hair! I thanked him and said it would be better if my daughter and I returned to our yacht now, meeting him in the afternoon at the Carlton Hotel and from there completing our mission at the casino. All went according to plan as Loel was not only a friend of Eric's but enormously rich, and as an expatriate it was easy for him to do as we asked.

I was hopeful that Eric would have forgotten his folly of the previous night, but when I returned to the hotel it seemed to me he was most ungrateful and began to moan about the money he had lost, which was in no way serious for a man as rich as he. Nevertheless that evening he said we must eat in some cheap bistro (that being all he could afford!) and then return to England.

Another year at Monte Carlo we slept aboard the *Saralong*. One evening, at that lovely moment of dusk after a perfect day of sunshine, all was still except for the familiar sound of boats being washed down and the murmur of voices as people sat over drinks on various decks. We were to dine on shore and as I was changed and ready before Eric I was passing the time wandering about on the *Saralong*, when a pleasant (as I thought) working man, as scruffy as my father (whom Eric used to call 'the scruffy old bastard') came up the gangplank. I was rather off-hand, asking him what his business was on our boat. He just laughed and went on his way again. A few nights later I sat next to this gentleman at a dinner party and then recognized him, much to my embarrassment, for he was Prince Rainier of Monaco.

Another incident on the Côte d'Azur was not so funny and made me very angry with Eric. We were not far off Cannes harbour about dusk and Eric, at the helm, cut right through the local French fishermen's nets, completely ruining their catch and tackle. The fishermen quite rightly screamed at us but my husband paid no heed and, much as I begged him, he would not even stop and apologize or offer them compensation. Thus he did one of the many things he had promised me would never be repeated.

13

Hugo, Ann and Ian

When my brother Hugo came back from the Far East, Esmond Rothermere gave him a job in Paris as a contributor to the *Daily Mail*. Later he turned to writing novels. I thought he had real talent and had he lived he might have become a great novelist. Soon after he returned to England he met and fell in love with Virginia Forbes Adam. They were married in 1948. Virginia had nursed throughout the war, and her father Colin Forbes Adam (who is still alive) was recovering from an operation to his throat for cancer. She nursed him back to life. My brother's first and probably best book, *A Share of the World*, was published at this time. It was partly about the war, the rest revealing how consumed with jealousy he was about his future wife's adoration of her father. To make matters worse, Virginia's mother, Irene, typed a great deal of this book, which contained some very harsh comments about herself and her family; so much so that when I was trying to defend the book to my mother-in-law, Lady Glyn, who was a great friend of the Forbes Adams, she said: 'She may have typed it but with tears pouring down her face.' In the publicity for one of his books, *Pictures on the Wall*, it states: 'As in all Mr Charteris's work, comic or serious, the scenes and characters belong unmistakably to our own day.' If anything this was un understatement for Hugo's characters were often all too easily identifiable. Sometimes this got him into trouble.

I have referred briefly to the occasion in the war when Eric sent his son Peter to a relation in Canada for safety. In contravention of all the laws relating to taking money out of the country, Eric ensured that Peter would be financially independent by an old-fashioned method of smuggling. 'Pinny', the housekeeper at Himley, was sent out to buy an old coat into which many thousands of pounds' worth of precious stones were sewn. The coat became heavy from the little shammy leather pockets and their contents, Peter's future in the event of our losing the war. Peter was then given this coat and told to guard it with his life. I accompanied him to Liverpool to see him safely on to the boat and we stayed at the Adelphi Hotel. More than once I found he had left the valuable old coat in as dangerous a place as the billiard room, where many unsavoury characters gathered, but in the end he sailed away in the direction of New York, happily weighed down by the coat.

Many years later at Westwood, Hugo stayed in the dining-room talking to Eric after dinner. It was ages before they emerged and I could not help noticing that Hugo was grinning like a cat that had got the cream. I knew he was up to something when he announced briskly, 'Well, I think I'll go up to bed now.' Of course I had no idea what he was up to, except that it was sure to be mischief of some kind. That night he began to weave Eric's reminiscences into The Coat. After a few teething problems it turned out to be his most lucrative book. Poppy was unmistakably based on me, though his description was libellous and untrue. It was only forty-eight hours of what he imagined my life to have been during the Second World War. Tim in the role of Peter Ward was given the character of my nephew, Caspar Fleming. 'Lord Bewick' was of course Eric, and a most unkind portrait of him, with all his bad qualities and none of his good ones. In 1966 Collins sent the proofs down to my then husband, Michael Canfield, for our scrutiny. 'We do not want the Earl of Dudley plunging into our offices like an enraged rhinoceros,' they said. We spread the proofs out on the floor and began to prune. I did not care what Hugo said about me and I wanted him to succeed and make money, but Eric was unlikely to think the same way. Being director of so many companies he had his reputation to think of. In fact he was livid and tried in every possible way to prevent the publication of The Coat, but I was the only person who could have done that. Finally, after the cuts had been made, I let the book go. A while later Hugo sent me an inscribed copy and I was touched by what he wrote on the fly leaf:

Darling 1% Poppy
Without whom at
no stage would it have
been possible –
with
LOVE
from
Hugo

The 'love from Hugo' was surrounded by dots which I took to be tears for the things he had said about me. Many people were angered by the book, but some were amused. Eventually all was forgiven and forgotten.

On Hugo's all too rare visits to London he never failed to have what he called 'a long look into the eyes of Guy the Gorilla'. Sometimes I accompanied him on this pilgrimage to the harmless prisoner of fate in the London Zoo. The lonely, thoughtful gorilla's eyes seemed to tell all. In many ways human, he expressed through those liquid pools what he could not actually voice – that he was sad and miserable. Hugo loved animals as I do and he would be glad to know that Guy's solitary days are now over.

My father did not mind being parodied by Hugo in his books, but my sister Ann took a very different line and once succeeded in putting a stop to a book Hugo mentioned to her. It has not appeared to this day. At times Ann and Hugo fought like cats, and when Hugo tried out some ideas on her in relation to a character that might have depicted her, she said, 'If there's one word about me, I'll put the matter in the hands of Arnold Goodman.'

I was devoted to Ann throughout my childhood and until 1945 or so never a day went by without us meeting or talking on the telephone. What went wrong I do not know, but certainly ever since then she has made it clear that she has no love for me. Ann never approved of my marriages or lovers, whereas I have always respected her choice of husbands and men friends. Her second marriage to Esmond Rothermere, after the death of Shane O'Neill, suited her well as she loves entertaining, and in this has both talent and enthusiasm. Certainly Warwick House and Esmond's powerful position in the newspaper world was a great help to her in creating a suitable atmosphere, and she had the necessary money to cope with that scale of hospitality. After the

war she left Esmond for Ian Fleming and continued to entertain
but in a more modest way. When she married Ian, Noël Coward
was a witness and he wrote this calypso, which he sent to me
in London shortly afterwards:

Mongoose dig about sunken garden,
Mongoose murmur, 'Oh my – Oh my!
No more frig about – beg your pardon,
Things are changing at Goldeneye!'

Mongoose say to Annee,
Mongoose say to Annee,
'Your man shady as mango tree,
Sweet as honey from bee.'

Hey for the Alka-Seltzer,
Ho for the aspirin,
Hey for the saltfish, ackee canja, booby's
            eggs, Gordon's gin.

Mongoose listen to white folks wailin',
Mongoose giggle, say 'Me no deaf!
No more waffle and Daily Mailin',
Annee Rothermere's Madame F.'

Mongoose say to Annee,
'Carlyle Mansions N.G.,
Goldeneye a catastrophee,
White Cliffs too near the sea.'

Hey for the blowfish, blowfish,
Ho for the wedding ring,
Hey for the Dry Martinis, old goat
            fricassée, Poor Man's thing.

Mongoose love human sacrifices,
Mongoose snigger at Human Race,
Can't have wedding without the Bryces,
Both the Stephensons, Margaret Case.

Mongoose say to Annee,
'Now you get your decree,
Once you lady of high degree,
Now you common as me.'

Hey for the piggly wiggly,
   Ho for the wedding dress,
      Hey for the Earl of Dudley, Loelia
         Westminster, Kemsley Press.

Ian was the great love of my sister's life. In the early days of their marriage they lived at St Margaret's Bay in a house bought from Noël Coward, as well as in Jamaica. Their house was full of laughter in those days and completely lacking in tension. Ian had impeccable manners and great charm, but inside he was an immensely complicated character. Like my sister, he had a destructive side to him and in the later days of their marriage it seemed to me they were determined to destroy each other. For example, my sister was always very scornful about his famous hero, James Bond. It was sad that as Ian's worldwide success grew, so his health failed, and it was when he became ill that he also became melancholy. Ian had a great passion for golf and used to play at the St George's course at Sandwich. Strangely for such a perfectionist, he was never a great golfer. This worried him and he worked hard to improve his game.

My father and stepmother visited Ann and Ian at Goldeneye one winter, a house where the food was well known to be sparse and often inedible. Ian's cook housekeeper, Violet, was handing round a Pyrex dish at luncheon one day, containing what appeared to my hungry father to be a native form of toad-in-the-hole. He dug hopefully deep into the dish with his spoon trying to fish out what he recognized as two sausages lurking at the bottom. Alas he was out of luck as the sausages were in reality Violet's plump brown fingers as she held the almost empty dish, no doubt containing some mashed-up bread-fruit, a much-favoured diet of the West Indian natives. Ian had many of the qualities and foibles that he later attributed to James Bond. When he was ill he was told to cut out smoking, so he had a special little silver box made to hold only five cigarettes (each cigarette, of course, had a gold line around it). But this did not work, unfortunately, as when the little box was empty Ian immediately refilled it. My sister and Ian had one son, Caspar, of whom I saw a lot later on. In Ian's last years, it was their joint love of Caspar that really held them together. Ian died in 1964 and I attended his memorial service with my then husband, Michael Canfield. As we walked from the church, near Smithfield Market, Cyril Connolly turned to us and said, 'Memorial services are becoming the coming-out parties for the elderly.'

14

Russian Dance

By now we were living mainly at Great Westwood. I had some horses, but not enough. Doodlebug was there, as I had bought her in Birmingham. She was a lovely-looking small grey mare, yet when I purchased her she was on the way to the knacker's yard. She lived till she was thirty years old and was about the best hunter I ever owned.

At the end of 1946 Sara went to a boarding school for the first time, a charming house in the Cotswolds run by a lady called Mrs Fife. The children did not have to wear uniform and they could keep pets; in fact, it was run more like a country house party. One winter Sunday when all was frozen, Mr Fife, an old-fashioned type of man who wore a top hat for church, was walking by a lake close to the house and, thinking the water to be frozen solid, he ventured on to the ice. The story at the school was that when time for luncheon came poor Mrs Fife looked and called for her husband, but to no avail. At length the children, led by Mrs Fife, went on a search. When they came in sight of the lake a gasp went up from one and all. There, sitting over a hole in the ice, was a black object, none other than Mr Fife's top hat. I am told that everything possible was done, but it was too late to save anything but the famous Sunday church top hat. Mr Fife was eventually dragged out like driftwood and given a suitable farewell in the local churchyard nearby. A sad story; one might almost say a cautionary tale.

Sara did not stay very long at Mrs Fife's establishment for young ladies; although I thought it a pleasant place, the standard of teaching was not high. I wished my daughter to go to Paris while she was still young, not to a school but to a family with

other girls of her own age where she would study a wide variety
of subjects in an atmosphere of culture and well-spoken French,
which I regarded as a most important part of her education. Sara
would follow the same curriculum as the daughters of the family.
At first she was unhappy and thought me very hard-hearted to
send her into a life where she had few friends and had to use
her brain, for education in Paris is a strenuous business. However, it was not long before she came to enjoy her life there. In
my mind I have no doubt it was the right idea, as her subsequent
career has proved.

With our marriage being somewhat difficult, I now turned to
a new form of excitement. Horses, which I had always loved,
became my distraction. Mine were not all good enough and I
needed real tuition, as I knew full well that to ride and hunt cross-
country is a very different thing from reaching somewhere near
the top in show-jumping. I went each day to Phil Oliver's well-
equipped establishment in the Vale of Aylesbury, taking my
horses over by box. My wonderful stud groom, Proser, had the
most fantastic gift for keeping the horses in perfect condition.
He knew how to feed each horse differently and each one had
a separate diet – hot meals at night, eggs, beer and molasses, all
brewed in a sweet-smelling cauldron in the tack-room. It was a
different life from speech-making and nursing. I learned much
from Phil Oliver. His technique was rough and lacked the finesse
I was later taught by the renowned Colonel Paul Rodzianko, but
I have no regrets about my time with him. He seldom mounted
a horse; all his control was done by various 'click-click' noises,
which had a miraculous effect on horse and rider. He teased me
about coming near his horses for fear they smelt my scent, saying
to me, particularly at shows, 'Once they know you're around they
won't do a bloody thing I expect of them!'

This was the beginning of a short but on the whole successful
show-jumping career. Eric seemed well pleased with my new
occupation, knowing there was money to be won in contrast to
the hunting field which was all out-goings, the only thing coming
in being doctor's bills for broken limbs and other accidents, many
of which came my way. When I was hunting in the Shires or with
the Grafton or Whaddon Chase, I was always grateful for the
knowledge I had gleaned as a child by following 'Chatty' Hilton-
Green, for he was certainly the greatest huntsman of my lifetime.

I was lucky in that when I first hunted from Stanway it was he who hunted the North Cotswold hounds. From this lovely stone-wall countryside he moved on to become better known as hunts-man to the Cotsmore in Leicestershire, in the heart of the hunting country adjacent to the Quorn and Belvoir.

I loved my hunting days and I think the highest point in thrilling pleasure one could wish for was reached on some of my post-war days with the Belvoir and Quorn. There, in the cream of our grassland Shires, mounted on perfect horses, on a still winter's day, I can recall the excitement and the beauty of it: the trees stripped of leaves, stark but sometimes more beautiful than when clothed in green, standing majestically against an often dark but varied skyline, and knowing that my horse was on his toes, trembling with excitement – as I was myself – waiting for the moment when we would be galloping full tilt, jumping every hedge or gate with ease and speed; knowing, too, that my second-horse man was so quick and clever at keeping pace with hounds cross-country and would not exhaust my second horse, a luxury hardly necessary considering my weight. Admittedly, my post-war hunting was done under ideal and expensive conditions. But pleasure it was indeed: returning home on days which were often cold but still invigorating, days when horse's and rider's breath looked like the steam rising from the bath which came as such a welcome sight at the end of the day, to be followed by tea and eggs. Only then would I realize how exhausted I was and, when I had rested my tired limbs in bed, how loath I was to leave it to prepare for dinner. The English winter seemed to pass so quickly in my hunting days. Also it helped me to evade those shooting luncheons and weekends that I found so boring.

The Windsors came to stay frequently at Westwood. The Duchess was very fearful of me taking the Duke out riding, so it happened very rarely, much as he longed to be once more astride a horse. I was always glad to hear of their much-heralded arrival, knowing it would keep my husband in good humour. Inspector Capstick was also a visitor for a short time as the Duke was always hopeful for news of the notorious robbery at Ednam Lodge, which still remained unsolved. By this time the Duke had bejewelled his Duchess with many new baubles of great value to keep her happy, as she had a most extraordinary passion for all precious stones.

When I had done up the stables at Westwood they were really quite enchanting to the eye – the outside all painted in black and white, the horse boxes inside washed over pale green, in my opinion the best colour for horses' eyes. Bay trees stood in painted tubs outside each box. There was an archway, pointed and made of clapboard, dividing two sets of stabling and incorporating a large arched dove-cote full of white fantail pigeons, which seemed on very good terms with the horses. The loose-boxes had music piped through them, an idea I had as a treat to alleviate the boredom which is the lot of horses when shut up and not free to roam at will. Another idea of mine was to give them hunks of grass with plenty of earth attached. They loved this, tossing it about till finally they had eaten earth and grass, both beneficial to their health and happiness.

I had jumped my horses and Sara her ponies and we had won many prizes and colourful rosettes, but I was fully aware that I needed much more tuition. I had a thrilling time at Blackpool where in August they have a week of festivities ending at that time with a memorable horse show. Here I experienced the greatest of my early show-jumping thrills by winning, to my complete amazement, the Ladies' Championship, an enormous silver cup, plus money. The holiday crowd, with their wonderful capacity for gaiety and hospitality, went crazy. I didn't know if I had won or not, only presuming so from the general excitement and applause. When I retired from the ring, there was Phil, a big smile on his face, knowing my victory had been more luck than skill. The crowd surrounded me, plucking hairs from the tail of my lovely mare, Princess, for good luck; cameras flashed and I came close to tears from joy and the sense of unexpected achievement in this exacting sport.

Eric soon appeared, full of emotion, asking many people from the world of show-jumping to join us at our hotel that night to celebrate my victory. Nothing pleased him more than success. We ended the day with a large ill-assorted party of rough but gay and enthusiastic types. My cup of happiness was full in every sense, for Eric, bursting with pride in me, filled and refilled the huge trophy with champagne for everyone.

After Blackpool I went show-jumping at Frankfurt where I rode extremely badly and had a cracking fall, which dislocated my neck. I was lucky it was not more serious but I still suffer

from that fall. My recovery was greatly assisted by a brilliant
Rumanian called Madame Lizica Codriano, who instructed me
in exercises which are a mixture of her own ideas and yoga.
She had lived in Paris since the First World War. Later she stayed
with me in England and for a time I went constantly to see her
in Paris. She was once a ballet dancer, then she became very interested in the way the human body and mind function. She told
me that in Rumania, when the peasants had finished reaping their
harvest or any arduous physical task, they would lie upon the
ground and a tame bear would walk all over them. The bear's
strong and heavy pads would remove all tiredness from their
exhausted limbs. Madame Codriano studied hard in Paris and
had a very successful practice in the rue d'Anjou, also doing
work in hospitals. Finally she was accepted by the medical profession, who had used her for many years themselves but had never
sent any of their own patients to her!

The only important outcome of my show-jumping at Frankfurt
was meeting the famous horseman and instructor, Colonel Paul
Rodzianko. Eric, using all his powers of persuasion, talked Rodzianko into agreeing that he would live at Westwood and teach
me his particular art of riding which he had taught many eque-
strian teams all over Europe. He didn't really want to take on
this task; he was getting old, and he found my riding deplorable
from the point of view of jumping horses in a confined space.
Fortunately, he liked me; for that matter, he was much attracted
by the female sex generally. He arrived at Westwood on the
understanding that he would instruct me for six months, and my
daughter Sara in the holidays. His first demand was for an indoor
riding school adjacent to the stables. Eric thought he had found
a bargain in the shape of a disused school somewhere in the Midlands, and this appealed to his very astute money sense. But he
was wrong over this; in the end it would have been cheaper to
build a new one at Westwood.

The Colonel was a great character, a tall and fine-looking man,
very Russian in every way. He had been in the entourage of the
Czar and managed to escape at the time of the Revolution. Then
he joined the British Army as a 'Tommy' and progressed from
there. He was nearly always 'broke', or, if he had money, he spent
it freely or gave it away to some undeserving cause. His appetite
could be compared with that of Henry VIII and he married fre-

quently. (One of his wives was the writer, Anita Leslie.) When he arrived with us he had a new young wife, who was related to the Mitford family. He said he was seventy years old, but he was a vain man and in fact his real age was nearer eighty, which was amazing. In the two books he wrote he pretty well gave away his age. He had reason for his vanity as he was a striking figure, especially in uniform. He would often wear the uniform of a pre-Revolution Russian officer for dinner, with medals and other decorations for grand occasions. He obviously enjoyed being dressed up in what looked to me like theatrical costume.

When I say he ate like Henry VIII I mean he ate like nobody I've ever seen; he would devour an entire chicken or leg of lamb by himself. He never drank anything alcoholic. He smoked small cigars almost like brown cigarettes. I became used to his habits, and my cook grew accustomed to the quantity of food needed so that everyone should have at least a morsel to eat after the colonel had taken his fill. Another of his habits was somewhat tiresome. His regimen for keeping fit included doing a Russian dance in his bath, filled with cold water, at about six-thirty every morning. His rooms and bath being over my bedroom he awoke me at this hour every day, and when I mentioned it to him he just said I should do the same and it would help my riding. Before he came to Westwood he had always trained an entire military team so if I claimed I was exhausted he would only reply, 'When you are tired you will fall off.'

Our teaching hours were long, starting about 8.30 a.m. First I had to do exercises on a horse with the stirrups swung to each side, in other words using only the saddle, almost as though bareback. After half-an-hour of this we went into the riding school to do at least two hours *haute école*; then home for a short rest before luncheon. In the afternoon I really longed to finish for the day, but oh no – back to the school and endless teaching, till at last I was allowed a little jumping. He always claimed, and it is true, that to have complete command of one's horse was of paramount importance, then the jumping became much easier. Being coached by Paul was certainly an experience I would not have missed. He was never cruel to my horses, indeed he scarcely touched them, having a kind of Svengali effect with his voice. In the evening he would walk round the stables with me. Each horse hated him and put back its ears till I went into their boxes

with carrots and all the things they looked forward to. Paul said
I shouldn't do this, but I would not listen. He could be harsh
but he had a certain charm; like the horses, I found myself doing
whatever he demanded. He was good company at meals once
his belly was full, and got on well with Eric, for often there were
just the three of us. But when bedtime came, I was truly glad
to rest my body.

Six months of this gave me a real idea of what international
riding was all about. It also kept me away from trouble, because
I had many men at this time who professed great love for me.
Gerry Koch de Gooreynd continued to write endless letters;
mostly unhappy and full of love, always asking me to see him
for just a short while so that he could be sure that I was as well
as I said I was. He was a man of rare qualities and I was lucky
to have been loved so deeply by such a man. After Rodzianko's
six months were over I took up show-jumping seriously. This
was in the spring of 1950 at Nice. Eric was given the title of 'Chef
d'Equipe' to please him. Also there to watch, dressed almost in
disguise, was Gerry. I was delighted to come second on a vast
course, a Puissance, and in third place was Pierre d'Oriola, who
the following year won the gold medal at the Olympic Games
for France. It was almost an honour to be pipped from first place
by such a rider as Colonel Corry, who was Irish and a beautiful
rider. Paul Rodzianko, having accompanied me to Nice,
announced that I had learned enough, and he departed.

After Nice I had a tragedy because my horse called Come
Closer became lame. He was my Puissance horse and my other,
Princess, was of a lighter build and though fast was not very dependable, being brilliant on some days and temperamental on
others, dropping her shoulder just as she was about to take off
and usually dumping me on the ground or, once, in the water
jump, which was full of frogs – a typically French touch – and
equipped with a miniature boat and fisherman. Harry Llewellyn
and I were the only competitors from Britain and when we travelled on to Brussels, which was a lovely show with all the jumps
except the uprights banked with flowers, Harry insisted on riding
Princess. But he fared badly as she just stood and bucked, refusing
to go through the starting line. When he was disqualified I quickly
took Princess away and gave her sugar as Harry was extremely
annoyed. However, I too was disqualified after winning one of

the fast against-the-clock competitions. I had two saddles, one light and the other weighing two and a half stone, the extra weight built in for international shows. Proser, my groom, thought that here as in Paris they only weighed competitors once and, wishing to save Princess the extra weight, changed saddles so that unknown to me I rode in the light one. When I was weighed again, up went the red flag!

It was the Gala night followed by functions and parties, with the ambassadors and other grand people there, which did not please Eric. In Paris his hotel bill was paid, which was unusual because the rule at that time was that the host-country paid everything for horse and rider once on their soil, but that was all. In Brussels they made Eric pay for his first meal. The next day he went back to his old ways and created a terrible scene at a ball that was given to celebrate the horse show. He made me return to England upset and furious with his behaviour. Another occasion I remember well was in Paris when we jumped at night in a covered arena. Eric had brought the Windsors and other friends, which made my nerves even worse than usual. Harry Llewellyn suggested I took one of the early tranquillizer tablets he had brought from America (I had never taken anything of that kind then). Harry said the one he gave me would do no more than calm me down. The obstacles were placed in such a way that it was very difficult to remember the route and Harry's idea proved a disaster. I jumped a quick clear round, but halfway I lost my bearings; the bell rang out loud and clear but I didn't seem to hear, or was so slap-happy that I just continued to jump every fence, but in a slightly confused order. This pleased no one, least of all Eric. The Windsors were just amused. Even when I left the arena for the collecting ring I continued to be delighted with myself, so whatever Harry gave me worked, although in the wrong way.

Eric was always very frightened when I was jumping. Once, during the July International Show at the White City in London, I was completely knocked out while riding one of my young horses. I was hit by heavy poles from every direction. I remembered little (apart from being taken from the ring on a stretcher) until I was being taken back to Brook Street by someone I hardly knew. I asked in a rather muzzy way where my husband was and this kind person, whom Proser had asked to take me home and *not* to hospital, clearly had no idea what I was talking about. But I did remember that Eric had been watching me with some friends from White's. So, on arrival at Brook Street, I asked my maid where His Lordship was. To my astonishment, she didn't know. I was put to bed, feeling hurt and angry with Eric for not being with me; for all he knew I might be dead. Eventually he turned up in my bedroom. He looked most upset and was very soon in tears. When I asked him why he had not come to see if I was badly hurt he explained, through his tears, that it was from fear; he didn't want to know, so had gone back to White's.

This fear of facing realities does at least explain his curious behaviour on many occasions – but that was little help to me because when he did things like this I was hurt by his seeming callousness and looked in the direction of other men. Also I knew that Gerry Koch de Gooreynd was waiting for our marriage to split up again; though, fond as I was of him, I would never have married him because I was not in love. I think he realized this but he still continued writing, and when he became ill again I went to see him frequently. The Hodgkin's disease had returned; I became frightened he might die.

I jumped just a few times in Europe with Come Closer and it was always funny when strangers asked his name and I said 'Come Closer'; they looked completely bewildered. Even in England it was a strange enough name and caused many rather ribald jokes. Sad to tell Come Closer never recovered in spite of the best veterinary treatment. I even sent him to the research institution at Newmarket which has done some wonderful work, but no one ever found out what was wrong.

In all I only show-jumped from 1948 to 1951. I enjoyed much of it, and I took pride in my horses. Their rugs, saddles and everything they wore were beautiful and mostly came from Hermès in Paris. The saddles were of nearly white, creamy doeskin. They were certainly the best-dressed horses I have ever seen. But certain aspects of the show-jumping world sickened me. I witnessed what I consider cruelty to horses behind the scenes, and my groom reported worse things, much wrappings – this means that a pole (sometimes covered in hedgehog skins) is put up at a low height, then as the horse takes off to jump it is raised. The pole hits the forelegs. Other and worse things I understood took place out of the public eye. I am not sure I would have gone on as long as I did but for the fact that it was a form of escape from the difficulties at home. Even when I was show-jumping Eric's ghastly jealousy was very trying, especially over an attractive French rider, the Chevalier d'Orgeix, at that time a success in the team for France; though it is true that he was good-looking and his eye was on me quite often. But apart from anything else, I did not like the way he treated his horses.

15

Lady Boy

I was be⟨...⟩ ⟨...⟩o concentrate on my riding. I began to ⟨...⟩ d men always around, everywhere I w⟨...⟩ ⟨...⟩ers. In my innocence I thought at the beginning ⟨...⟩ performance that perhaps they just liked me! But soo.. ⟨...⟩ on me that Eric had hired private detectives to follow ⟨...⟩ ut it to Eric, and he confessed; he did not trust me, and, yes, they were 'private eyes'. I was utterly astonished, for this was a complete reversal of what I believed to be Eric's attitude. My life had become so unhappy that I had many times asked him to divorce me – citing anyone he accused of so much as looking at me – but he always said flatly, 'I will never give you a divorce under any circumstances.' So why these very expensive detectives? Eric's was not an easy mind to follow.

Bobby and Freda Casa Maury came to stay more and more. Bobby was physically attractive and we had a short love affair. He always told me that Freda was bored with him and that she now wanted to marry Eric, but I will never know whether this was true. He even said Eric would keep my horses round Westwood to annoy her if I should leave him. Life went on. I met Bobby in London but it never even crossed my mind to go off with him – or 'bolt' as Randolph Churchill would have put it. It was a strange, unhappy time. Sara was about sixteen and she hated Eric, which was very sad for him as he adored her. She could do no wrong in his eyes; he looked upon her as his own. I often discussed the situation with Sara and when we did finally leave it was really her decision. He had planned a grand ball to be given for her at Westwood when she was seventeen, but she felt, as I did, that it would be very wrong to accept an enormous

'coming-out' party from Eric when we both knew her feelings
about her stepfather and that my marriage could not last much
longer.

Peter, Eric's youngest son, was still living at home and he was
begging me to stay, not knowing that if I left his father the money
from which I received my income would go to him. Later on we
laughed about this, because though I am devoted to Peter (or
'Wardy' as most people call him) and he is to me, he likes money,
so I often teased him over his wishing me to stay. Would he, I
asked, have minded my departure quite so much had he known
of this potential windfall?

Eric appeared to look no longer at his list of 'Don'ts'. He was
rude to the servants and waiters in restaurants and reverted to
asking people to leave Westwood over the most ridiculous disagreements. I remember one noisy night during a visit from Randolph Churchill – whom, oddly enough, Eric liked. I had gone
to change for dinner when I heard an awful rumpus going on
downstairs. I put on my dressing-gown and went to see what was
happening. Eric and Randolph had decided to play gin-rummy
and apparently Eric was losing, which he never liked at any game.
When Randolph took one of Eric's cigarettes the row started.
Eric flew into a rage and said, 'You drink my drinks, eat my food
and now you even take my cigarettes and my money at this silly
game.' The room looked as though a bomb had hit it; the card
table was broken, chairs were upset and drinks spilled. Randolph
just laughed, while Eric kept ordering him to go. But that was
not in Randolph's nature. He loved a good fight. When Eric met
this kind of response to his behaviour he always recovered from
these mad fits of rage. Similarly, if he knew he had done or said
something awful, he was afraid to open his letters and made me
do it in case there was something in them that he didn't want
to read.

One day, when Sara was about seventeen, we went to London
with the dogs and the faithful Mlle Dupois and decided never
to return to Eric and Westwood, a house I loved. I had no money,
but I realized that Eric could do nothing until something was
arranged; he could not turn my daughter and myself on to the
street. There were terrible telephone conversations but no writing. Freda Casa Maury spent weekends at Westwood; meanwhile she thought that Bobby was seeing too much of me, so

turned him out of their flat in Albert Mansions. He had no
money, so he said, but this I find hard to believe for he moved
to the Berkeley Hotel in Piccadilly and lived there for many years.

Sara was starting to go out to parties with various young men,
particularly at this point with the good-looking Prince Nicky of
Yugoslavia, Princess Alexandra's cousin, who was killed when
his car overturned and he was drowned in a ditch at Datchet in
1954. I was having a gay life and had interesting work – much
needed – as I had become deeply involved with the Christian Dior
organization on the wholesale side in London, which meant frequent trips to Paris. I was well paid and had an office and secretary in their original saleroom in Maddox Street.

I admit I was seeing a great deal of Bobby. I was also sorry
for him. I had gone to a well-known firm of divorce solicitors,
but at first we were unable to make much progress as Eric
would make no move. It was only when I met Lord Radcliffe
that I received real advice, though I was not very happy with it
at the time. His influence and the advice he gave me brought
my predicament to an end. Lord Radcliffe's opinion was that to
get my freedom I must bring an American type of action (mental cruelty) against Eric, which would enrage him, and he would
then probably start divorce proceedings against me, naming
every man he could think of. I would then at the last minute with-
draw my case and Eric would have to go on with his. This advice
was, as one would expect, admirable. I didn't like the 'mental
cruelty' part because it wasn't really true and even if it had been
I would have preferred to be divorced, knowing, as I did, Eric's
horror of being involved in any divorce proceedings whatever.
Also I was legally in the wrong, and the only thing I really held
against him was his behaviour to other people; and I did know
he *still* loved me. Like all things in law it took years of arranging,
and it was not until 1954 that Eric divorced me, naming Bobby
Casa Maury. He mentioned many other names in his petition
– like Gerry and Philip Dunn – but he was persuaded to remove
them before the case came up.

On the actual day of the divorce I fled to Paris in order to escape
publicity. As soon as it was over Eric tracked me down to the
Ritz, where he telphoned me. He asked me to get on an aeroplane
and fly back to London to have dinner with him that very evening.
This I did, and we dined at the Mirabelle – in those days full

of friends, most of whom looked astonished at the sight of us dining together, for some of them had taken sides during the long years of wrangling that had gone on. Some of them looked positively embarrassed, which naturally amused me. When the wine Eric had ordered was served the waiter somehow slipped and to my horror decanted a bottle of claret over Eric and the table. I held my breath, expecting the ghastly outburst this type of accident normally caused. To my amazement, on this occasion Eric smiled and said, 'Dear man, don't worry. Bring another bottle.' Then turning to me he said, 'You see how I've changed. Why don't we come together again?' I was flabbergasted, and changed the subject. From then on we remained the best of friends, except for a short interval in 1966 when my brother's book *The Coat* was published.

A great friend of mine, a farmer who lived near Westwood, Mr Simpson, arranged for the sale of my horses, which gave me some cash. Eric kept my few possessions or destroyed them. Some are still in some distant land with his third wife.

In London I worked and played, both equally hard. Bobby was not in my life for very long. We went to France one year but I was terribly bored. The forbidden fruit, once permitted, was not one bit to my taste, as so often happens. When I realized this I was beset by doubts and my mind became cloudy and filled with gloom at my future prospects. Luckily, this condition soon passed when I remembered that we were just about to return to England. My work, and many other things, filled my thoughts. I suddenly laughed to myself when I thought that Eric had always called Bobby Casa Maury 'that Cuban motor car mechanic'. This was really unfair because Bobby had been quite a well-known racing motorist and, as is always true in life, however short a love affair one usually learns something from it – often something unpleasant about oneself. From Bobby I learned to drive a car exceptionally well. It isn't much, but I am grateful. The real problem with Bobby was his reverence for sex. He treated love-making like going to church – no jokes allowed. I thought his attitude ludicrous, for if laughter and love don't mix, then, personally, I don't begin to understand. Perhaps my sense of the ridiculous went too far for such an ardent and single-minded lover as he was.

The return journey to England by car was nothing, but my

heart was heavy with the many problems that must lie ahead. In spite of unhappiness with Eric I had become accustomed to great luxury of living; the small and tedious things that money takes care of had always been dealt with by a good secretary, two chauffeurs and endless staff. I tried not to calculate or think logically but to summon up more courage than I had ever done in the war. I knew I was behaving badly in every direction. I longed for country life and the smells of outdoor living, not Paris or London where, in the world of *couture*, I was mostly indoors and everything was over-sprayed with scent. The future suddenly looked grotesque and rather frightening, not knowing where the next penny would come from should I not succeed in my work at Dior.

In October 1952 a great friend of mine, the Countess of Derby, suffered a ghastly experience at their vast house, Knowsley, near Liverpool. One night when her husband John was attending a function in Liverpool Isabel was having her dinner in her sitting-room while watching television. She was waited on by the butler and under-butler, who were assisted by a new footman. When she had finished eating the butler returned to ask if there was anything more she required that night. At that moment the new footman entered the room – this time armed with a Sten-gun. He opened fire on the butler and under-butler and killed them in a few seconds. Then he turned his attention to Isabel, shooting her in the neck. But by great good fortune it was a glancing shot, missing her spinal cord by a millimetre. She fell to the ground in a pool of blood. Isabel's personal maid rushed in on hearing the noise and very bravely stood over her. The maniac then ran out of the room and headed for the kitchen quarters. There he encountered the chef and fired again. Luckily the shots went through the chef's tall white hat, riddling it with bullet holes but leaving the chef unharmed. The gunman then sped off into the park that surrounds Knowsley and on reaching the main road found a telephone box from which he dialled the police, telling them he wished to give himself up.

Isabel was soon treated for her wound but the whole affair not unnaturally left her shaken and nervous. The following March she telephoned me and suggested that we go to Val d'Isère, more for sun and rest than skiing. I had just recovered from flu and had arranged to take ten days off from Dior, so I was delighted to go with her. She also suggested that we leave the travel and hotel booking to the charming and capable Mr Gibbs at Claridge's who knew us well. We set off for Paris on the Golden Arrow. In this comfortable dining car we were served by a particularly pleasant and efficient waiter, who seemed to know us both. He was most attentive to our needs, but when he turned away from us at one moment Isabel suddenly said in a ringing voice, 'I suppose the bugger's going to shoot me now.' The dining car had been quite quiet but when Isabel's extraordinary remark rang out there was an all-round gasp and some of the passengers sprang to their feet in astonishment. It was all over in a moment or two and I must have been the only person present who could have given a quite reasonable explanation for Isabel's outburst.

On my return I heard from Gerry that his health was deteriorating and also from his sister Glad (Mrs Jan Ciechanowski), who had lived in Washington since her husband had retired there after the war, having lost everything. (He had been the Polish Ambassador both there and in London.) I threw myself into my work, which was the best thing as well as being a necessity, but I also spent much time with Gerry, whose change in appearance shocked me. However, he made another miraculous recovery, which was a great relief. He made me promise never to return to Eric – a promise I kept. He knew the gossip about Casa Maury, but paid no heed, and he was right.

Shortly after this, Bobby, whom I still saw, told me Freda would not take him back and intended to divorce him, which indeed she did. He introduced me to someone called Anthony Pelissier, who strangely enough had been married for a few months to Freda's eldest daughter, Penelope Dudley Ward. We, Bobby and Anthony and I, frequently played golf and dined together. It was not long before I realized I was really in love again, this time with Anthony. I have been lucky in this way, because to be deeply loved is not so difficult but to love that person as much as they love you is as near perfection as one is likely to get. I have had this happen three times. Eric; now Anthony; and the man I loved most of all, who has not yet come into my story. Without real love between two people, life is very hard to bear; in my case, almost impossible. I know one ought to be able to live without this, but I have never had the skill or aptitude to do so.

Anthony was another extraordinary character. He was the son of Harry Pelissier who was famous for this topical theatre, the 'Pelissier Follies', but subsequently drank himself to death in his thirties. Pelissier kept changing the material in his productions, writing and composing topical songs which would go on to the stage the same night. He was one of the most popular theatrical figures of his time. A picture of him still hangs in Rule's, the theatrical restaurant in Maiden Lane. Many people, such as Eric's sister, Dickie Benson, had all his music and words. She used to tell me how much she adored his songs and she played and sang them very well herself. I'm glad to say that I was able to take Anthony to see her many times, and when she was dying he was able to cheer her enormously.

Anthony's mother was the actress Fay Compton, whom Pelissier married when she was sixteen. She was the sister of Compton Mackenzie, and though they were both fond of each other they were exceedingly egocentric about their respective careers, acting and writing. Fay used to accuse her brother of not attending her latest first night, while he maintained she never read his books. This led to many arguments. Compton Mackenzie was a difficult character anyway. At the Savile Club he liked to sit surrounded by good listeners and in his later years he spent the winter months in Edinburgh, where he never left his bed. Surrounded by books and papers, he held his own form of court for those who visited him.

Anthony and I loved each other almost instantly. He had too many talents; he always said it was hell because he never could decide which one of the arts to settle for. He painted, composed music, wrote and acted in early life. Later he directed films and plays. I tried my hardest to get him to settle for one of his talents, which might have brought happiness to him and others. He would not even try to like any but a few of my friends – my aunt Kakoo, Patsy Ward and Dickie Benson. Otherwise, for about five years he cut me off from everything. I did not mind because we were happy together most of the time; also he educated me in many ways, telling me what to read and enlightening me about many things of which I knew nothing. He had left his second wife, a charming woman, so he had three children, the eldest being Penelope's daughter Tracy, whom I was never allowed to see. In fact she changed her name to Tracy Reed, as Penelope's second husband was Carol Reed the film director. (Tracy married first, Edward Fox, then another actor, Bill Simpson, who played 'Dr Finley'.)

Anthony's life had really been a disaster when I met him. He rarely went home, except to see the children. I talked often to his wife; she said she had loved him deeply but was 'over it' and couldn't face going through that ordeal again. Perhaps fortunately for me, there was no divorce or I might well have married him. Instead we spent nearly five years living together. I do not regret it although he practically destroyed me. He was always making different plans for living, but worse than this he constantly disappeared for a few days or sometimes weeks to his club, the Savile, or worse still, said he was going to kill himself. He was a mercurial character of great brilliance but everything he loved he seemed in some curious way to destroy. This seemed true also of his many talents. There were times, even for so much as a year, when all was bliss, then something changed and he would leave me, or say he wanted to live in a barge on the Thames, or on top of some distant Welsh mountain. I think our happiest times were in France where we spent many months.

Sara was fond of Anthony and he loved her, but when she married Charles Morrison in 1954 he wouldn't even attend the wedding, though Eric did. I was in love with Anthony when Gerry was nearing death. I told Gerry all, and he seemed pleased that there was someone he thought would look after me; little did he know how it would all end. Gerry went into the Westminster Hospital sometime in 1953 and his sister came over from Canada. She was a very sweet woman. Gerry then insisted on coming home to his house in Buckingham Street with a nurse. He was a shadow of his former self, as Hodgkin's disease had turned into leukaemia, so there was really no hope of a further lease of life. His sister, Glad, begged me to spend all the time I could with him, though she was living at Buckingham Street and I was still in my flat at Bryanston Court with Sara and my ever-faithful maid, Mlle Dupuis. Glad said to me, 'He doesn't really want me here, or indeed to see any of his old friends. He only talks of you, so please be here most of your time.' So I went there at lunchtime and when my work at Dior finished, and towards the end of his life I stayed with him most of the night although at times he was scarcely conscious, but even then from time to time he would call my name, or my dog's name, Beany, asking if we were comfortable. It was an agonizing time and there was so little I could do except that, from my nursing experience, I think I made him more comfortable than his own nurse by the mere fact of being there.

Suddenly on 19 October 1953 at around six o'clock in the evening he started to try and talk, but it just made him cough. The nurse and I gave him oxygen, but nothing was of any avail. He clutched my hands and all in a second his agony had ended. I was terribly unhappy and went down to the sitting-room to tell his sister. She was kind and tender and also desperately sad. She adored Gerry. She was practical about all the horrible things you have to do when death occurs. Straightaway she said, 'You know Gerry was a Roman Catholic, although he never talked of it or went to Church.' I said I did, but I knew nothing about the Catholic faith where death was concerned. She said he must not be left alone till he was taken back to Belgium where all the family were buried. He had apparently told her this was his wish and that I was not to go. A requiem mass was to be arranged at the Farm Street Church in Mayfair. She then said, 'You must get some rest now but would you come back about ten o'clock and sit in his room all night.' In a kind of exhausted way I said, 'Yes.' All through that long but rather wonderful night, with candles round his bed, I watched his face. It gave me some comfort for the peace and tranquillity transformed him into a young and happy man again; all the lines of pain and misery just seemed to vanish, and I experienced that feeling of having no fear of death. Indeed I was almost happy that his in many ways unhappy days on earth were finished. It reminded me also of my mother and the way she looked in death.

I have never heard anyone say an unpleasant word about Gerry. Speaking for myself, he gave me true and devoted love for many difficult years. After his death I missed him quite dreadfully, having always been able to tell him everything. He left me in no way a fortune, but I was for the first time financially independent. He had never liked his work as a stockbroker with the firm of Panmure Gordon but he was very shrewd and well informed and he left me some shares in a private company called Pyrotenax. It seemed hardly enough to cover my divorce expenses which came soon after, bringing with them my freedom.

(When Pyrotenax became a public company my shares were suddenly worth £80,000, but this did not happen for many years.) He also left me the remaining eighteen months of his lease on the house in Buckingham Street and its contents. He had two brothers, one of which he did not like, but the other he left well off with the residue of the estate. The Farm Street requiem mass for Gerry was short and rather beautiful. The church was full, and I felt, quite objectively, that everyone who came really cared. Their faces showed great grief.

My work with Christian Dior was now of even greater importance, and also of great interest, as I was allowed to choose at least five or six dresses or suits from each collection as one of the many 'perks' – and I don't mean from England; my dressing was all done in Paris. My most important work was handling the press, getting as much free advertising as possible, and, better still, the colour photographs on the covers of the monthly 'glossies' such as *Vogue* and *Harpers* – not so easy to achieve! Next in importance was my selection of the model dresses, coats and suits from the Paris collections in August and January to make up our English collection – the ones most likely to attract the British buyers. Being a wholesale business, I had to remember we were selling to all the large stores in London and the provinces.

To begin with, I loved my work and was devoted to Christian Dior himself, and the managing director, M. Rouett. Of course, the whole French side of the business was owned by M. Boussac, the big textile industrialist. As Christian once said to me, when there had been some trouble over a dress, 'I can do little to help you, I have even sold my *name* to M. Boussac.' The trouble I refer to was quite serious. There was a lovely, romantic evening dress, designed, I thought, for the very young, and called 'Fête en Village' – a froth of very fine Swiss broderie anglaise, with masses of delicate wild flowers embroidered on it. In London it sold, with identical material from Switzerland, for about £100; in Paris it was being sold for £500. That year there was a wonderful ball given by the Pembrokes at Wilton in Wiltshire. Unfortunately, some elderly ladies who dressed in Paris had chosen this very girlish dress at a high price; meanwhile, many of the same dresses had been bought in London (for a slightly different price!) for girls as their first ball dress. I think there were something like six of these dresses at the party, and my own daughter made things worse by borrowing my model from the stockroom. All hell broke loose and I was sent for to go to Paris. There was nothing I could do because 'Dior London' sold the dresses to the big stores, therefore we didn't know the destinations of individual models such as 'Fête en Village'. The discrepancy in price made matters worse!

From then on, poor Christian had to make another collection for London as he was already doing for New York. In fact, I think this extra burden contributed to his early death from overwork. After he died the Paris side of my work was neither so interesting nor so much fun, except for the presence of Lillia Ralli, a most elegant woman. My work at Dior was spasmodic; at times one was dead-beat, as when the winter or summer collections were being shown. One bitterly cold January, while the winter collection was being shown to buyers from all over the world, the lights were on at the Maison Dior for twenty-four hours a day. In other words we worked day and night for about five days. I usually minded the August collection more as the crowded rooms became stiflingly hot. One night it was arranged I should have a working supper at 2 a.m. with the managing director, M. Rouett. I was already feeling ill and during the meal I almost collapsed. I had to tell M. Rouett that I wasn't well, but his reply was, 'No one becomes ill at collection time.' For once he was wrong. I staggered out of the restaurant and somehow reached the rue de Lille where Diana Cooper had lent me her flat. Anthony was there and I remember little except finding myself in bed with a high fever and pneumonia. The doctor who attended me used that old-fashioned but successful treatment of 'cupping' (egg-cup type receptacles were dipped in spirit then lit and placed round back and chest – not painful but leaving red rings for several days).

Anthony was always at his most thoughtful and loving when I was ill. It was curious to find that a man with so many other talents could also be a good nurse. Perhaps he loved me more when I was confined to bed! My ten days at the rue de Lille flat were in some ways very happy; when I returned to health Anthony resumed his old games of hide-and-seek!

Sometimes in England we would take the whole cavalcade of model girls and trunks of clothes around the larger towns of England. It was rather like a travelling circus or theatre. This was

enjoyable as we met many different people. Though they were
often dull, something funny always seemed to happen. Occasionally one of the mannequins would disappear, leaving my secretary and me not knowing what to do with one girl short – but
knowing full well she had gone off on some date with no intention
of returning in time for the show. In desperation (and feeling very
elderly) I would take her place, having no idea how to walk up
and down what was known as the 'cat walk'. But it was all amusing experience and I regret none of these frolics into a world I
knew less than nothing about; by the time I decided to do other
work, I really had learnt a considerable amount about *couture*
and the 'rag trade'.

Anthony was a joy to be with and, at the same time, quite a
taskmaster. He would say things like, 'You were born with a
good brain but you've never used it, preferring to play in so-called
Society. So you've wasted your life, mostly from laziness.' This
sounds pompous and school-masterish, but I didn't mind because
there was so much love behind these lectures, and also truth.
Before one of his maddening and often heartbreaking departures,
with no reason given except something like, 'We come from different worlds,' he left me a charming poem. (I must explain that
he always called me 'Lady Boy'.) When I found it on my bed
I really did think he meant this to be the end between us:

For Laura

Dear Lady Boy, had we not met
I never could have been in debt
To you; Sensibility,
Trust, Humour, Flexibility;
The Urgency of carping fact,
The Confidence I ever lacked;
True standards and a deep Disdain
For Bourgeois Sentiment. Again,
I owe for Health; for what you are –
My own imperishable Star,
By whom I navigate the seas
Of sometimes feckless miseries.
How pay you back? I owe far more
Than this – but my diminished store
Of Qualities holds no appeal –
How could we ever make a deal?

Already on a larger scale
You own what I'd put up for sale;
Music and Words; Colour and Light;
The intimate and gentle night;
The Love of Animals; the wry
Laughter; the sharp enquiring Eye;
The Grass-green countryside;
Talk, wit; a proper Pride
In roots.

But as I breathe and live
They're all I'll ever have to give
And so it is with secret Joy
I stay in debt, Dear Lady Boy.

I was desperately upset. He had so often gone off into the blue, but somehow I never thought he would not return; this time seemed different. But I was wrong and he did come back, though to a turbulent way of life and my constant worry about what he might do next. I was therefore always in doubt, perplexed and robbed of my self-confidence. Yet he had so much to give. I still have much of his work, paintings, plays, music and lyrics.

Had Christian Dior, or rather the very commercial Boussac set-up, realized that I was leading the life of a recluse, seeing scarcely anyone but Anthony, I feel I would soon have lost my job. They thought I was always out at parties showing off their clothes, which was very far from the truth. After work during those years I either cooked dinner or we would go to some Soho trattoria. I lost touch with all my old friends. When the lease of Gerry's house came to an end, I rented a charming flat in Eaton Square and found a wonderful maid, an Austrian called Prisca Ellis, with whom I am still in touch to this day; she even has my two parrots, Porgy and Bess. My London flat had a garden at the back and I made it most attractive, and when Anthony was settled at one of his many works life was happy, too good to last. I was always wondering what his next idea about where to live would be. He never left me for long enough for me to pick myself up or see my friends. Occasionally I would go out with other men. This was always the moment he rang up, expecting me to drop any plans I might have made and continue life with him, which (quite unlike my normal character) I would do.

Once at least we dined with other than our own company, and

for me it was a memorable evening as our hosts were Laurence Olivier and Vivien Leigh who was the heroine of one of my favourite movies, *Gone with the Wind*. I knew her already as I had arranged her clothes at Dior, not always an easy task as she was petulant and hard to please. However, the result was so good that it was worthwhile. That evening at L'Etoile, though, she was divine with her youthful 'pussy cat' face. He was charming too but still very much the actor, and I sensed an unhappy tension between them. My theory is that he was the survivor as after their parting she always looked strained and unhappy. I felt she continued to love Larry. Harold Wilson later made him a life peer – the tribute of one great actor to another?

16

Contessa

I was growing rather bored with my work at Christian Dior so in 1955 I decided to leave and fulfil my real ambition, which was to have a shop of my own. Anthony was very much opposed to the whole idea, but at this time he was being extremely difficult himself; anyhow I wished to explore this new field.

I opened my first shop called Contessa in 1956. This did thrill me. It was in Rayner's Lane, on the outskirts of Harrow, not grand in any way. I started by letting someone else do the cheap buying, which was a field I did not know well and which didn't interest me, but having little cash behind me I had to go easy on the dress materials and stuff for the curtains. I also had to have the cabinets that contained the paper patterns, Vogue, Butterick, McCalls and Simplicity. All this cost money. I was continually doing sums to see how things were going. I enjoyed decorating the windows, putting in among the cloth the most weird and, I thought, attractive things to catch the eyes of the passers-by. I loved selling, doing up parcels and telling the most awful white lies, such as pretending to the inhabitants of Harrow that I made my own clothes when in fact they were still all the things I had from Dior, Paris. I named the shop Contessa to tease Eric. His coronets even appeared on my wrapping paper.

On Fridays I stayed open until eight in the evening to give the girls who worked in London a chance to visit Contessa on their way home. My idea was slowly to upgrade the shop, both in appearance and the stuff we sold. To make any money, I also had to keep my eyes on the prices of John Lewis, who were then, as now, both competitive and fair, giving the best possible value for money. All went very well, so much so that within six months

I was able to open a second shop, at Borehamwood, a new town not far away. Soon after that I leased a shop and workrooms at Radlett, my idea being to make up people's curtains and upholster chairs, etc. Though this was a minor decorating establishment, I was commissioned to refurbish one of the fashionable London clubs.

The press were most helpful, giving me the most flattering write-ups, and I took full advantage of the publicity, knowing that people of those north and north-west suburbs of London were likely to be fascinated by the idea of a Countess running a shop, which did me no harm at all and indeed was a useful and simple way to success. At one time I had seven shops. I thought of the old days when we English had been called a 'nation of shopkeepers' and I was happy to number myself among such people. In the last century my daughter's in-laws gathered a great fortune from haberdashery. I have been told that they also made a 'corner' in black crêpe at the time of Queen Victoria's funeral, thus furthering their riches.

I worked hard and conscientiously, firstly to make a profit and, secondly, because of the need to take my mind off Anthony's (to say the least) eccentric habits. Otherwise I feared for my own sanity, leading a lonesome life, cut off from friends, and with Anthony so often missing. He was rarely far away, but during these disquieting times he certainly made me very unhappy. Yet he was such a wonderful person to be with – charming, witty and, strangely enough, of great understanding.

About 1958 Anthony seemed to become almost impossible to live with, and when he was absent I saw no one; all social life had gone and, worse still, the situation began to affect my health. I lost confidence and often found myself in disillusion and dismay about the future. My work suffered and I left more and more to other people who were not financially involved – a dangerous situation. When Anthony returned, however, all was forgiven, however hollow his reasons had been for leaving me. This was because of his gift of gentle sympathy for the unhappiness he had caused, making it sound, in a really ridiculous way, as if it was all my fault.

Lady Glyn was still alive and Eric kept pestering her to influence me to return to him. She was a wonderful woman and I must have been the cause of a great deal of trouble to her. She even lent me some money for the Contessa shops. Fortunately, I was able to pay her back. I usually told everything to my brother, whom I adored, but over Anthony I kept certain things from him. I really do not know what he felt about Anthony, except that he called him 'his Frothship', and once got furious because Anthony 'preached' during dinner.

By Christmas 1958 I was less inclined to think life impossible without Anthony; by this time, many big changes had taken place, brought about by him. He decided, quite suddenly, that he needed country life, large rooms and space; no more barges or cottages on Welsh mountains, follies which, luckily, I had managed to avoid. This house of his imagination sounded lovely, but very difficult to find as, according to him, it had to be near London. Another frightening factor was money. I only had a leasehold on the Eaton Square flat, and a short one at that. Nearly all of Gerry's money had gone into the shops.

However, I found the house through John Derby's youngest brother, Hughie Stanley, who was then working on the forestry side of Alfred Savill, the estate agents. He told me it was near Amersham and Beaconsfield and that it was called Hertfordshire House, although in Buckinghamshire. All this filled me with gloom; the local fox-hounds, the West Buckinghamshire, hunted around there about once a year, and I knew the country was dreadfully built-up; in fact, the odd day I graced this pack with my presence I used to call them the 'Watford Jockeys'. Hertfordshire House was owned by a man called Burman, who was more than half German. During the war he lived in the gardener's cottage. The moment I saw the house I felt certain somehow that I was going to buy it, but Mr Burman would only let me have the house with two cottages more or less attached, and fifteen acres, while he kept a four-hundred-acre farm with quite a big house and several cottages. This didn't worry me at the time as it was a lovely Georgian house with bow-windows facing south, but apart from finding the purchase money I realized there was much to be done which would have to wait a while. Coutts Bank was most obliging and lent me a considerable sum against the shops. So, with Anthony's approval, I decided to go ahead and buy.

The reason for Hertfordshire House being called by that name when it was situated in Buckinghamshire was connected with the

Quakers, the Society of Friends, if one can apply the word 'society' to such a glum institution. There were many Quakers round Birmingham when I lived in that area and I rather admired one of the leading ones, Dame Elizabeth Cadbury, even though every chair in her house was so uncomfortable it nearly broke my back and the food was almost uneatable. It is a curious faith, creed, or whatever you like to call it.

We moved to Hertfordshire House in August 1957 without doing anything to it except to take on a most disagreeable gardener. I remember it was a particularly nasty cold wet August. I put what furniture came out of my flat into the house, but alas some of Gerry's furniture which I had given to Prisca, my wonderful daily lady from London, remained in her London flat. Then I left her alone in the house, as she had always promised to start me off there, and rushed over to the nearby house of Dickie Benson (Eric's sister) for comfort and warmth, as I was more than slightly worried to find that my furniture only filled my bedroom and the sitting-room; all else was bare and suddenly looked a formidable and worrying task to deal with.

The rest of that year I was very occupied. Gerry's Pyrotenax shares became public, giving me more money. Through a great friend of mine, Tony Weldon, I was introduced to a stockbroker, Geoffrey Standon, who was the senior partner of a firm called Scott Goff. He not only did wonders for my money but has also been a staunch, devoted friend, especially during the last ten years. I was not only busy, but other beaux had begun to come into my life, though Anthony was still the only man I loved.

I then began to buy carpets and remove the really terrible curtains left behind by the previous owners. Everything was easier then as I had my own workshops and the facilities for wholesale buying through my Contessa shops. My greatest problem was lack of furniture. I had given Anthony a piano, which filled one of the two really large bay-windows in the drawing-room, but it took years before the house was in any sense completed. The garden also was nothing at that time, though by 1969 it was really lovely.

Through most unlikely circumstances I met Barbie Wallace (now Mrs Herbert Agar) again. I had hardly seen her since before the war, when I had spent many happy weekends in her houses. Her present husband is a true intellectual and the author of many distinguished books. Anthony was one of Herbert's best friends and was at his side when he fell in the Savile Club, permanently injuring himself. But my reunion with Barbie took place before this, when I was in London with Anthony. To my surprise, he asked me one day if I would like to dine with the Herbert Agars. I was delighted at the prospect, knowing whom Barbie had married and all the tragedies that had befallen her. Barbie, on the other hand, wondered who this friend was that Anthony was proposing to bring to dinner, having no inkling it was me. She was not exactly enamoured of the Savile Club and called the members 'the Drones'; with few exceptions she did not know their wives or friends. Anyway, going to the Agars' mews house was sheer joy for me. It was what used to be the chauffeur's flat and other storage space in the mews backing on to the large house they had in Hill Street, Berkeley Square. She was relieved it was the Laura she had known, whatever else she disapproved of (she had got the whole Casa Maury story wrong). And from that day she has been the most wonderful and loving friend. I could ask for no more than she has given me in help, love and understanding.

Hertfordshire House absorbed me; there was much to be done. I achieved a butler and maid, and a new gardener, almost as disagreeable as the previous one but more efficient. After Christmas 1958 Anthony walked out, leaving all behind him, giving no reason other than that he 'was not meant to live in such a house with domestics!' The next night I was alone, sad and filled with apprehensions, when suddenly a very dear friend of mine, Frankie More O'Ferrall, rang up. He had loved me for a long time before the war but fortunately married a lovely girl and wonderful wife much younger than himself. When he rang that wonderful night he said he and Angela were having a New Year's party, but quite small. He mentioned some names that made my heart sink even further, but at the end he mentioned someone called Michael Canfield. I asked who he was. Frankie replied, 'It just shows what your life is like, not knowing him. He is just about the most attractive man in London, but unhappy and alone, his wife having left him for another man.' He also said, 'It's time you came out from hiding with that "actor man",' as he called Anthony. This made up my mind. I changed my clothes and drove to London and his party, little realizing how that short drive would change my whole life and that each mile I drove was leading me closer to true love and happiness.

The Adorable Canfield

The course of one's life is often dramatically changed by a quite arbitrary decision to turn left instead of right at a crossroads. The left turn leads to a casual encounter, a last-minute invitation perhaps, and suddenly one finds oneself swept along a seemingly inevitable path into a new world. Looking back one can but thank one's stars that one did turn left, while wondering a little what (if anything) lay hidden around the corner to the right.

I did not much want to go to the More O'Ferrall party, and it was without much enthusiasm that I arrived in Curzon Street at about nine o'clock. I looked around and realized that I knew everybody in the room with the exception of one man, who had clearly had too much to drink. In fact I accused him of wearing contact lenses, his eyes looked so glazed and unhappy. For years I had not been attracted to any other man but Anthony, yet as I looked at this man and he looked at me, we were instantly attracted. It was love, my heart sang. The man was Michael Canfield.

The party continued and we were going to dine in some restaurant. Suddenly Michael and I decided to go off on our own. I told Frankie and Angela, who didn't mind. Michael had his own car, known by him as the 'Blue Bullet', and at this time I had a fast Alfa-Romeo. Realizing Michael should not drive, we took my car and went to some small bistro. We talked for hours about our lives. All the time he was getting more sober. He then told me of his friendship with Barbara Astor. I told him I knew Michael, her husband, who then rather liked me. He said he was off to St Moritz with a party and not too fond of the idea, as he had broken his leg the year before and Kate Smith (now

Townsend) had pushed him around in a wheel-chair and then fallen in love with him. His life sounded as much of a muddle as mine, if not worse. I took him to his flat in Eaton Square, then returned to Hertfordshire House feeling a much happier woman.

The next day, by pure coincidence, Peggy Munster rang me, somehow having heard the news that Anthony had left me yet again. She suggested I should come and stay with her in Kitzbühel, Austria. All this was confusing. I told Michael I had better go and have a change of atmosphere and thoughts, as he was going to St Moritz anyway, albeit reluctantly. We met each other a few more heart-warming times. We even stayed with the More O'Ferralls again for a shoot, which he hated because he disliked shooting, and then the time came for my departure to Kitzbühel. I was driven to London by my new-found butler to go from Victoria by train. To my never-to-be-forgotten joy, Michael was standing on the platform, looking very handsome and young and, as always, beautifully turned out. William Douglas-Home, a great friend, called him 'the adorable Canfield' – and how applicable! Michael also admired my dressing, something he always noticed and either approved of or didn't! He had an extraordinary natural instinct for all things beautiful and knew just how to dress for all occasions. This sounds feminine, which he wasn't, but he had that most important quality that all men should have – a streak of woman's genes – giving them understanding, usually impeccable taste and making them wonderful company.

When we talked at length he admitted, and it was obvious, that he was very 'tucked up' inside himself and unhappy. Two things had caused this, perhaps even from birth. He was an adopted child and he had a definite 'death wish' (also unknown to me but cured later). He felt rootless, only being in England for a short time as a publisher (his adoptive father, Cass Canfield, headed one of the oldest publishing houses in New York, Harper, now Harper and Row). An unhappy marriage had made everything much worse. He was due to return soon to New York; at that moment he was working in the Hamish Hamilton offices as a scout for his father's firm, and feeling inadequate, with not enough to do.

But on the platform at Victoria all was joy; I did not yet know of any of the complications inside him. I find railway stations, for some unknown reason, romantic and exciting places, and yet sad, for so often they are the scene of a farewell, among all the clatter and noise. That day at Victoria it was a kind of farewell, but I felt not for long. Inside me, I was aware of a new glow of the unexpected and a great happiness to come. Nevertheless we said a tender and tearful goodbye. When I reached Kitzbühel Peggy gave me a great welcome, saying straight away, 'You look more yourself than for a long time,' which was certainly true. Then the telephone rang and it was Anthony, asking many questions. I just said, much to his surprise, that it was my turn to have a holiday. He behaved as though he had never done such a thing! The conversation was short. Soon after, another telephone call – to my delight it was Michael saying lovely things and, best of all, that he had changed his plans and was not going to St Moritz but would come to me. Peggy and Paul had no room in their house so arranged a hotel room for Michael in the town. This was perfection. We did not ski but walked and talked and, for the first time, in his hotel, made love. He was shy but a wonderful lover. On this visit to his hotel he was in the middle of reading *Doctor Zhivago*. He threw it across the room and I don't believe he ever finished it.

We didn't stay long. Soon after this, Peter, the Munster son, arrived and offered us a lift to Munich, from where we took a flight to Paris.

Our stay in Paris was the scene of an unlikely episode in our lives, which amused both of us then and still makes me laugh when I think about it now. It was the more amusing because, apart from being shy and sensitive, Michael had an undoubted twinkle in his eye and an enjoyment of the ridiculous side of life. It is right that I should record it for while everyone happily reveals many details of love affairs, there is still a certain reticence to share some of the side-effects, which, I suspect, have been experienced by more than a few of my readers.

Shortly before leaving London I had had dinner with Anthony. Michael, it appears, went to a drinks party and took some strange Balkan tart type back to his flat. My dinner with Anthony did not go well so I left and went straight to Michael's flat. He opened the door looking unlike himself, half undressed, with a dame who could scarcely speak English lying on the sofa, also not dressed. Michael just said, 'Thank God you're back,' and told the woman to go home. I thought this was too much and said he must at least take her home or call a cab. She lived nearby, so he was finally persuaded to walk her back. That seemed to be the end of the matter, but on the flight to Paris Michael became somewhat preoccupied. His thoughts were far away and he was clearly a worried man. As I observed him I could not but wonder what was, so to speak, 'eating him'. Of course I had no idea that he was in reality being nibbled at by some tenacious mites. Indeed this was the explanation for the scratching that was taking place.

When we arrived in Paris, Michael revealed the cause of his worries and asked me to go to the chemist to get some powder to cure the problem. Unfortunately my French vocabulary did not extend far enough to make myself understood, nor were words associated with sea-food or signs of the zodiac appropriate in this context. Luckily a gentleman in the chemist came to my rescue. I returned to the hotel where we attacked these tiny but multitudinous insects. They did not take kindly to the cure. Small as they were you could see them jumping around in the white-tiled bathroom where we performed the operation. I remembered from my nursing days that they laid eggs in great profusion, so I told Michael his troubles were by no means over. We continued our battle against these jumping mites every day; meanwhile I tried to steer away from possible infection. Alas I was unsuccessful, and by the time we reached England Michael was cured and I was the victim, much to his amusement.

I now decided the time had come to ask Michael to Hertfordshire House, finished or not. He lost his way, naturally stopped at the local pub, and was told the way by locals who said, 'You know who lives there? The Countess of Dudley,' as though I were the local queen. This made him laugh, especially when he saw the mess the house was still in.

That night I gave him a room opposite mine. He had been in the glooms about returning to America, but a letter from his original adoptive mother cheered him up. Soon after the adoption she had divorced Cass Canfield and was now called Katsie Churchill. She adored Michael and was always asking him to return to the USA. This time the letter said she and her husband, an architect, John Churchill, were about to come to London. When bedtime came Michael went to his room and, after some time, ventured across the passage to my room carrying, as a joke, that blasted *Doctor Zhivago* and saying he must finish it. At the same time he jumped into my bed among the dogs, who looked a bit put out, although it was a very large bed. *Doctor Zhivago* soon fell on the floor but, before making love, he told me his age, which upset me; he was nearly eleven years younger than me. It didn't worry him at all because, as he explained to me, he had been told by several doctors in this country and America that he could never have children, and didn't care. I never quite believed this because he seemed to love my grandchildren.

He remained in his London flat, in fact we kept it on for many years, but came to Hertfordshire House for most weekends. An exception was one Easter weekend when we went to the More O'Ferralls. On our return on Easter Monday, as neither of us wished to go racing, we were told by the butler, Faull, that Mr Pelissier was playing the piano in the drawing-room and had just asked for tea to be taken to him. We decided to go into the butler's cottage and await Anthony's departure. This was turning out to be such a long wait that I decided to ring him up, pretending to be elsewhere and not able to return that night. I saw this as the only way out of a possible row. He was not pleased, but after another hour he departed. Michael and I, with great relief, returned for dinner in the house, but it set up doubts in Michael's mind as to whether I was really through with Anthony. I was, for sure, but I could see his point. For instance, when I first told Anthony on my return from Kitzbühel about my love for Michael, he just brushed it aside saying, 'I suppose it's some ski instructor. This so often happens.' Clearly, whatever he may have said in the past about all his uncertainties about life, deep down he had a great conceit. As I have so often said about my long relationship with Anthony, he was complex to himself as well as to others who crossed his path. Later he did meet Michael and they liked each other well.

When Michael's mother by adoption, Katsie, came to London, she and her husband John stayed at the old Cavendish Hotel in Jermyn Street. Rosa Lewis was dead by then but I had met her when taken there by Randolph Churchill years before, in the thirties. She had been a great character, always with a glass of champagne in one hand. She used to feed her dogs – a long string of mongrels – from the counters on the ground floor of Fortnum and Mason's, and even those forbidding gentlemen in tailcoats dared say no word of rebuke whatever delectable morsel she

picked up to drop into their waiting mouths. When Katsie stayed
at the Cavendish towards the end of the fifties they still had open
fires in sitting-rooms and some of the old atmosphere, but one
already felt its days of glory had ended. I suppose Katsie wished
to stay there because of her years in England in the early twenties
when she adopted Michael. She was then certainly a very beautiful woman. By the time I met her she had let herself go; she was
fat and she drank too much. In the end I think she liked me but
at that first meeting I saw a real glint of jealousy come into her
eyes. Her husband was a sweet, kind man – and an excellent
architect – and I was very fond of him. When they stayed with
us at Hertfordshire House she came into my bedroom where
there was a photograph of Sara's daughter Anabel. Her eyes lit
upon it and she asked who the child was. When I replied, 'My
granddaughter,' she said, very pointedly, 'So you have a *grandchild*.' I felt like saying, 'So what?' but kept my mouth shut. Her
remark had already said plenty in the way it was delivered.

After that visit Michael and I discussed marriage, but saw no
point in any hurry. We had really no time; I had my shops and
Michael his work. We were blissfully happy; what time we did
have was spent on the house, which by slow steps we made into
a really heavenly place to live and entertain in. Michael left for
America to see his father by adoption, Cass Canfield, who is
married to a wonderful woman, Jane White. She is a talented
sculptress. I have two pieces of her work, one a head of Michael
when he was about seventeen, the other a bird on the wing.
Michael's real parents remain a complete mystery to me. Eric
Dudley always told me he knew who Michael's father was – the
late Prince George. Where he obtained this information I do not
know. It was not only from Eric I heard this; it was a general
rumour around London, quite rightly hotly denied by the Canfields. There certainly was a resemblance in face. Michael was
tall with very fine limbs and beautiful hands. When I met him
he worried about who his parents were though later this constant
search as to who he really was seemed not to trouble him; but
he always quite liked the rumoured idea and once told me himself
that he was of royal blood because his nanny treated him as
royalty – whatever that meant. The Canfields themselves, whom
I respect and love, have never told me anything. Jane did once
talk of it, when Michael and I had decided to get married. All

she said was, 'Michael is English,' and, as she put it, 'very well-born'; also that when Cass adopted him he had to fulfil certain promises about money and the best of education. If the story is true, Prince George must obviously have been a very young man – and who was Michael's real mother?

An incident that made me wonder occurred when the Windsors asked us to lunch, once in Paris and also at their *moulin* house outside the city. The Duke never stopped staring at Michael, so much so that I said, 'Sir, is anything the matter?' The Duke quietly replied, 'Yes, what Eric has told me I am sure to be true.' I asked, 'And what is that, Sir?' He replied, 'I am certain your husband is my brother's son. Of course, it must have been when brother George was but a boy.' When I told Michael this he was delighted. I think he had heard it anyway as we were few for luncheon. I mention this story because I was thinking about Jane Canfield's beautifully sculpted head of Michael. When it was un-packed at my present home, Gellibrands, the removal man almost dropped it, exclaiming, 'Blimey, it's the late king!' And I remembered my long talk with the Duke of Kent (as Prince George became) all those years ago when he stayed at Himley, so soon after which he was killed.

18

Life at Hertfordshire House

For the first year after I met Michael, Anthony continued to write and did not accept the situation even though he knew it had come to pass through his own behaviour – unforgivable but always in the past forgiven. None of this worried Michael or me, except perhaps in the first few months when possibly there was doubt all round, about Michael's work in England and the difference in our ages. The only thing there was no doubt about was that we loved each other and that we both adored Hertfordshire House.

Even before we married we spent hours planning the things we wanted to do to it. A major idea was to build on what we called the 'loggia'. This was part-designed by Katsie's husband, John Churchill, but soon after he made his rough drawings he had a heart attack and died. Eventually we followed his plans and had it built with glass and lead domes, with pigeons made of lead perched on top. This was my idea, and complemented the hundreds of real white fantail pigeons we kept. The rest was what most people call a sun room or conservatory, but ours was always full of flowering shrubs and in the high bow-windows beneath the domes there were window boxes full of whatever flower annual we chose for the season of the year. Michael had a passion for the sun, so this room was ideal as it seemed to catch those few glimmers of sun that fought through the English cotton-wool skies. When the loggia was finished (after we were married) we spent more time here than in the rest of the house during our so-called summers.

When we did decide to marry the formalities were achieved very quickly. Michael's one fault, if you can use that word for something that never bothered me, was not taking any responsibility or actually arranging anything. So when he said to me, 'How do we get married?' I had a good idea. Faull, the butler whom Michael disliked, always knew everything. So we agreed that just this once we would let him make the plans. We also told him to tell his wife, who was by way of being my maid, to be sure to call us in time to get to the register office in Amersham! He asked us for the various documents he needed, and then he arranged everything except the flowers in the house which of course I always did. We asked a handful of people between us. We cabled Katsie Churchill (who had become less difficult) and she came all the way from Martha's Vineyard, the island near Boston where she lived with her husband. We also asked my aunt Kakoo Rutland, my daughter, her husband and my granddaughter, Anabel; my father couldn't come and the Canfields decided to let Katsie have this occasion to herself. Apart from anything else, we only wanted a few people because it seemed to us we had been 'married' for so long. My darling brother, Hugo, turned up and took some very funny photographs in the register office itself. If this makes it sound rather like a joke wedding, that was not the way we felt.

One thing I hated – being superstitious – was the date the butler chose, 13 June 1959, but Michael seemed to think nothing about being married on the thirteenth so I soon forgot my qualms. That day started badly for me. I was on the verge of being felled by a migraine, so I went to Amersham doped with various pills and looking awful, as one does under these conditions. I had started getting true migraine headaches about 1955. They are a dreadful affliction, which only the people who have suffered these blinding headaches and vomiting can fully understand. There was a time when I would have only one in about six weeks; later in my life, perhaps brought on by unhappiness, they would sometimes last for four days in a row. There is only one cure for me, to be 'put out' by some injection, which not all doctors will give. To describe real migraine is almost impossible as every sufferer has a different kind. All I can say on this subject is, as regards myself, it nearly always happened when there was something important to do. When we were having friends for the weekend and I had done the flowers, arranged the meals, and the house was looking lovely, Michael would say: 'Now tomorrow you will be in bed with a migraine.' This he dreaded as much as I did. Being of a shy nature, he feared being left to entertain the house party. But he was so often right. I will say no more of these ghastly attacks which have ruined about twenty years of my life, and turn back to that beautiful June day of our wedding.

The ceremony in a register office is very brief, so in no time we returned home. Somehow it made a difference knowing that Michael was my husband. We said this to each other almost simultaneously as we drove home, for he felt as I did. We had a delicious cold luncheon out of doors with our relations. There were many telegrams to open, many jokes and much gaiety all round. My father cabled: 'Michael is the first son-in-law that I am fond of.' Not long afterwards we met Nancy, Lady Astor, staying with Nancy Lancaster. Nancy Astor swept into the drawing-room, took one look at Michael and said to me, 'I'm so glad you have married a man so much older than yourself again.'

One very special thing between Michael and myself which nobody else knew about was that I always called him 'Crumbs' or 'Crumbo' while his name for me was 'Snail' or 'Snaily' (he said that at any sign of real disagreement or trouble I would disappear into my shell). We only called each other Michael or Laura if one of us was upset. The only snag about our pet names was that Michael had a beautiful golden labrador which I had given him, also called Crumbs. He was by nature quite obedient so if we were walking in the garden or the woods and I said, 'Oh, do look Crumbs, darling,' (talking to Michael) the poor labrador would look bewildered, imagining I was calling his attention to a rabbit or squirrel.

That lovely June evening we flew off to the Ritz in Paris, happy but exhausted. We only spent two nights there as Philip Dunn, one of my old beaux, had lent us his delightful farmhouse in Majorca for as long as we liked. In Paris Michael bought me the most beautiful things at Boucheron – a gold bracelet and a wristwatch, also a basketwork evening bag in gold, all chosen with his impeccable taste. In later years he would tease his father, Cass, by saying things like: 'Not bad on my wages.'

Majorca was heavenly. Michael gloried in the sun and very soon became so brown I could hardly believe anyone could take such a grilling. There was no house for miles around. Also there were good, pleasant maids, delicious food and excellent light local wine which I had to stop Michael from drowning in! On the two occasions that we went out in those three perfect weeks, we took one of Philip's boats. Time passed very swiftly. My Crumb would think nothing of reading an entire book stretched in the full heat of the day; it never seemed to harm him. He never suffered ill-health, even when he drank too much. At one moment I wished he would have some ill effects, even just a normal hangover, but he never did. Parties or having people staying with us were the dangerous times. When we were alone I had no problem. Certainly he drank, but not more than many other people do. He had so many inner complications to deal with and yet was able to give me and his friends a loving sense of security. He was quiet by nature, and then suddenly he would change from being quite withdrawn and give out his very special and marvellous laugh, which was never far away.

Neither of us minded leaving Majorca, except for leaving the sun. We were always pleased to return to Hertfordshire House. We felt more settled and contented now that we were married, and all the plans we had made about house and garden became easier to realize. Though I had many ideas I was very ignorant about the garden, and so was Michael. I bought endless books on gardens, but it was not till Lanning Roper came into our lives that things took real shape. Gardening and writing about gardening is his life, and instead of just telling one what to do, as some experts would, he loved to work in the garden himself when one was lucky enough to persuade him to spend a weekend – a rare joy as he was then, as now, in great demand.

Gardens take a long time to reach fruition; hedges and shrubs have to be tended for many years. The house was far less of a problem, as there I knew what I was about; it was more a question of money. Both of us had what my grandmother Wemyss used to call 'furniture mania' so we often stayed up late at night changing everything around. Also we had a particular friend called Frank Wigram, who lived a couple of miles away and had a small but fascinating antique shop. He was the only neighbour whom we saw constantly and he helped us greatly in finding reasonably cheap but attractive furniture. Pictures we found for ourselves, with luck and for little money; I still have them with me, an odd but interesting collection, for the most part dogs or horses. There is nothing of great value but they certainly go a

long way towards making the house warm and comforting to
the eye. Even after we had changed the fireplaces and built many
bookcases the house had too little furniture; the drawing-room
seemed rather barren. But having to decorate and furnish slowly
and with great thought was, I'm sure, to the advantage of the
house. For years we would search the countryside for some particular piece of furniture we had set our hearts on, and we loved
every tiny object. In many ways we led a rather selfish life, except
that I think we gave many people enjoyable and relaxed weekends.

I began to breed Shetland ponies, quite seriously, till it became
too much work. Our first stallion was called Grock, after the
clown, and well-named he was. Fearing he would be lonely we
found him company in the form of a donkey called Donk, and
a charming but destructive goat, Daisy. She had to be disposed
of eventually to the pets' corner at Whipsnade Zoo, because I
hate to see animals tethered and however high we made the fences
in her paddock she climbed them with the greatest ease and proceeded to do untold damage to the garden. Grock hated his nur-
sery-maid donkey and was always escaping under the rails of his
large and comfortable field and hut. He would either come into
the house and eat everything in sight or wander up to the village
and drink the milk outside the cottages in the early hours of the
morning. When he reached marriageable age we found him two
delectable lady friends that we named after Michael's two
mothers, Jane and Katsie.

We also had a tame chinese goose that I hatched under a
chicken. Later I reared her myself as the companion egg was
addled and the chicken took no further interest in the gosling
once it was hatched. To begin with I thought it was a male, so
he was christened Oswald, but the following spring he was
revealed to be a she by laying countless eggs and was from then
on known as Ossie. Nobody but I really liked Ossie. She was
a wonderful watchdog, better than the dogs, but it was nonsense
to suppose she would eat the grass. She tapped on the kitchen
door at least once an hour and ate two loaves of Hovis bread
a day. In the spring she laid quantities of vast eggs, after which
she became sulky and broody, not even wanting to use her own
swimming pool.

At the beginning of our married life we only had Michael's

labrador and my old pekinese Beany, and a lovely-looking snow-white tiny pekinese called Oliver. Alas, Oliver died very young of some type of jaundice and Beany died of old age; she must have been quite fifteen. So Michael and I decided to have a complete change and, from a *Times* advertisement, bought two Jack Russell terriers. The third one in that litter was bought by Randolph Churchill. He called his Lord John Russell. Michael's was called Jack and mine was Russy. They had great charm, but were completely mad in their different ways and by the time they were three months old they never stopped fighting. Jack could do no wrong in Michael's eyes. He was always leaving his mark, just a few drops, everywhere he went. This was hopeless to cure because, if reprimanded, he bit one; therefore over the years a yellow fringe developed round the edges of carpets and curtains. He smiled, as all the dogs did, but Jackydoodle (as Michael called him) was constantly talking or rather grumbling to himself. I have never known a dog with so much to say.

With that picture of our animal population it will be obvious that our country walks were full of incident, involving ponies, donkey, goat and all the dogs. Even Ossie joined us at times.

This was country life at its most enjoyable, by our standards. The first three Christmases we spent at Hertfordshire House were fun but most exhausting, as is the way in one's own house at this season of the year. Apart from my father and stepmother, a small and incongruous group took it for granted that they would share Christmas with us – Jubie Lancaster, Ava Waverley, Randolph Churchill. I remember one disastrous Christmas when Randolph kept Ava up all night reading Evelyn Waugh to her. The next day she was completely exhausted and asked the fine-looking elderly ladies' maid I then had, Mrs Milne (whom Diana Cooper nicknamed 'The Ghost'), if she could perhaps have a key to her door. To me it seemed very funny, especially as we had no keys! It reminded me of Himley during the war and the way she used to lock her husband out on their honeymoon!

One Christmas, when I went into the sitting-room to get someone a drink, I found Randolph on the telephone saying the most awful things about the food, the people, the cold and a whole mass of other rubbish. He continued as if alone. When he finished his conversation I asked what it was all about. He just said he was talking to a lady who didn't like him being with us. This was a woman called Mrs Bevan who lived near Randolph in the country. She was devoted to him and looked after him most wonderfully during his last ailing years. I am sure this talk was quite unnecessary. She knew that Randolph was an old friend and that I was blissfully and happily married. Much as I always loved Randolph, he had a great talent for 'trouble bubble' where possible.

In the evening of Christmas Day we asked many farmers and other local people, plus children, to come to us for drinks and food. This was sometimes overdoing things. Most of our friends staying in the house retired to bed till comparative peace returned.

Ava and Katsie seemed to hate each other on sight, much to the amusement of Randolph. One year Randolph arrived straight from Nassau (I think it was about the Bay of Pigs period) after spending time with Jackie Kennedy and Lee Radziwill, and had nothing suitable to wear for an English winter. I took him to a local shop but it wasn't a great success, as all we found was a suit which, although at least thick and warm, was in loud, bright 'bookmaker' checks! At luncheon that day I joked about his peculiar appearance. He turned to Michael and said, 'How can you tolerate your wife after those sweet gentle whispering sisters?' – a reference to Michael's ex-wife Lee and her sister Jackie, the President's wife! Randolph was for ever enamoured of the Kennedy clan. So be it!

Hertfordshire House was a delight to decorate for Christmas. I loved making swags of holly and yew intertwined with red ribbon to frame each doorway on the ground floor. In the drawing-room the Christmas tree stood tall and shapely. To decorate it I used only red and silver balls, small at the top then gradually growing in size till they became larger than tennis balls on the lower branches. I then used fine, silver tinsel looped around the tree as simply as possible, going from bauble to bauble. The presents were piled around the base, done up in plain red tissue paper and tied with silver. On the very top there was a single silver star. The house looked warm and festive and even 'Old Grouch' was usually in a pleasant mood; I think he enjoyed helping me make and then tack up the prickly and heavy swags round the doorways.

One of our favourite guests at Hertfordshire House was Robert Heber-Percy. Strange to say I had never met him till sometime in the 1950s as he was a great friend of my ex-sister-in-law, Patsy Ward. He owns Faringdon, a very beautiful house, much of which he has cleverly turned into flats, done in such a way that one would never suspect he wasn't living in the whole place himself. He keeps the front entrance with its lovely double staircase and the long but wonderfully proportioned drawing-room, over-looking the park and lake. Robert is one of my craziest friends, much loved by me, and he encourages his own eccentricity. For example, the pigeons at Faringdon are dyed a multitude of different colours. Robert also has an unlikely but lucrative sideline – he is an undertaker. To prove this job to himself and others, he one year attended an undertakers' conference at Blackpool. When staying with us it did not matter if the house was already full, as he travels light; usually his luggage was no more than a rucksack which contained a few pills and a velvet dinner jacket rolled in a ball. In this way he needed no cupboard space, so more often than not he slept in Michael's dressing-room. He appeared to enjoy this as there was a door through to our bedroom and in this way he could overhear every word spoken by us or our rather talkative dogs.

As in childhood, when one is really happy one just takes it to be the natural way of life, which is so very far from the truth. So it was at the time I am writing about. The making of a house, with a husband who has good taste and is equally interested, is as enjoyable an experience as I know, and probably few people have revelled in this creative amusement as much as I did. Each day there was some new idea or excitement. Sometimes both Michael and I had the 'glooms', but the mood passed rapidly. No two people can possibly not quarrel about some trivial matter when they are together so much. Even at breakfast Michael ate on a tray in my bedroom, so the daily newspapers sometimes provoked ridiculous arguments. Michael would suddenly become a socialist or very American, to irritate me. I would do something similar, but it was a sad and rare day that didn't end in laughter. When he went to London, which he preferred to do by train, he would think about whatever had gone on between us, and meanwhile I went through the same process. So it was never long before we were on the telephone and all was well.

Many people must have had similar experiences, though personally I think few men have as many different attributes as my

Crumb. There were so many sides to him. Some faults are necessary, as we all have them, and how often one loves people for
their weaknesses and worries. If Michael was in a quiet, preoccupied mood he had the capacity to reach my heart and tear it apart,
giving me much to ponder and try to puzzle out. I knew that
he was often exasperated with his work, which might be the root
of the trouble. Now that I really knew true happiness, the smallest
frown on Michael's face made me search for a way to ease him
out of his worries. I would walk those impossible, adorable dogs
for miles, thinking and thinking what would be best to do; my
mind ran on, telling me that nothing is impossible, or as bad or
good as you expect, therefore the answer could not be far off.
I knew only too well that his work did not give him the fulfilment
he sought. We often talked of our love and our life together, but
Michael for some time avoided talking of his work. He liked his
office at Hamish Hamilton's in Great Russell Street, and he also
liked the Garrick Club, not far away, where most days he had
his midday meal, much enjoying the company and the atmosphere.

I would willingly have gone to America, but Michael objected
strongly to this. He always had a strange fear of New York,
except for short visits which he enjoyed. By now nothing would
have made him leave Hertfordshire House; therefore for long
periods we just did not discuss his work, apart from the minor
day-to-day goings-on. Michael's 'fear' of New York did not
relate to muggings and that sort of thing, but was something he
really scarcely understood himself. I find it an exhilarating place
but Michael found the rush and speed too much. He seemed to
lose his assurance when there alone; his letters suggested panic
and made me worry about his slight drink problem. Fortunately,
these occasions came but rarely and I was sure to write each day.
This was his wish and my pleasure. He was so precious to me
that each day apart seemed an eternity. Without realizing it he
gave me a great deal of anxiety, even from the early days of our
relationship. He would say quite out of the blue, 'One thing I
do know is, thank God I will die long before you.' This was
always a puzzle and a worry to me, as he was so much younger,
and what he called his 'death wish' had passed. It was Ali Forbes,
a great friend of ours, who told me about this 'death wish' and
said, when he visited us at Hertfordshire House, how happy he

was to see Michael content with his life with me, even if his work did not fulfil his hopes or stretch his brain.

When he was with me there was a togetherness which made time go by like a streak of lightning; at other times I had that sensation that deadens one before a thunderstorm. Even if I stayed in the country and was busy while he was at work in London, at the back of my mind I longed for his return; towards dusk, in winter and often summer too, I would light a huge log fire, in front of which we had our dinner. We seldom watched television; there was always so much to talk about. This was our very precious private life and during those magical years if we spent a weekend elsewhere we rejoiced to return home, always saying the same thing: simply, how much more fun we had alone together in a house we loved and with all the 'Woggins', as Michael called our dogs.

Enough about our own very special life. I certainly feel it all over again in my heart and body just by writing down a mere sketch upon paper. Each sentence makes me relive every moonlit or sunlit moment that is now really only a ghost, but a ghost that will live with me forever.

19

A Sinister Picnic

On our return from Majorca we had domestic troubles with the butler, Faull, and his wife. Michael loathed the sight of the man, but at the same time admitted that he knew all about his job and did it. This, of course, was a blessing for me, even if it had to end sometime – and end it did, in a sad and dramatic way.

One day as we approached the house in my car Mrs Faull came rushing out in a crazy state. She kept repeating over and over again that her husband must have killed himself. Would we take her to the police without delay? Naturally, we were surprised and asked questions. It appeared he had gone out without the little Mini we kept for errands, taking only a gun. But he had been gone only two hours, so why all the hysteria? There was more in this than met the eye, we decided. So we told Mrs Faull that if by 6 p.m. (it was then only soon after luncheon) there was no sign of her husband we would take her to the police station. When we did the police were slightly sceptical, but came to our house with tracker-dogs. There were a few terrifying moments while we put our own dogs under lock and key, so enraged were they at this invasion of their territory. Nothing could be found except the gun. Finally, with great effort on all sides, we put Mrs Faull to bed with sleeping pills. By now, in spite of Michael's intense feelings against the butler, he as well as I began to have forebodings. Around 4 a.m., when we were fast asleep in bed, the telephone woke me. To our amazement and to my relief, it was Faull's brother ringing from London to say that Faull himself had just walked into his house and seemed to have no idea what he was doing or where he was. Michael's reaction was quick: 'I always knew there was something weird about that man.'

The next few weeks turned out to be hard work and worrying. Faull was returned in an ambulance. He seemed dazed and very far from his old self. My maid, Mrs Milne, helped me in the kitchen where we had a rather hopeless Italian girl. I can cook and, given time, take great pleasure in my culinary achievements. All this went well; in fact the change was imperceptible to Michael as far as his comforts, which he enjoyed, were concerned. To me it was a catastrophe. I did not know what to do next. The doctor said Faull must not be moved; Mrs Faull became very unpleasant, saying her husband had worked too hard, which was nonsense. She also told us something we had never known – that in the war Faull had been blown up and spent months in hospital in a state of severe mental derangement.

There appeared no way to free the cottage, which we wanted for another gardener. 'Old Grouch', the head gardener, needed help. In the house it was quite easy when we didn't entertain, but this was seldom the case. After some very arduous weeks, when I neglected my Contessa shops to my cost, the Faulls took off and left the cottage without a word. To this day I have no idea where they went, nor did I ask, for although I knew I would miss his undoubted efficiency, Faull would anyway have had to leave because of Michael's very real hatred of the man he called 'Mr Know-all'. Finally, we were lucky to find a wonderful Italian couple with the most beautiful child I have ever seen. When they came this little boy was only two years old, with the biblical name of Ishmail. We both adored him, and five years of peace in the house followed. We bought more land and another charming 'gingerbread' type of cottage from the new owners of the farm; it cost nothing compared with the prices of today. Now we felt rejuvenated, with new hope for the garden, and not always beaten down by the domestic worries of too large a house.

Neither of us being too content with our work we proceeded to make matters far worse by deciding to have an antique shop, named Charteris. I thought at the time it would give Michael the outlet for work in London that he really sought. We found a manager with the experience and knowledge we both lacked, but he proved to be a difficult character. He had knowledge and used it to his own advantage. Michael was not helpful. The whole idea was for him to spend some time each day in the shop, and not just go around buying, which we both enjoyed. This venture was short-lived. We sold some most attractive things but no money came our way. So with little fuss or recrimination we closed down!

Then came a really fantastic take-over bid for all my shops from a rich man in Manchester. I had agreed with Michael that we must accept when, to my horror and dismay, the wife of a man who was concerned with the running of the shops came to see me, saying that her husband would shoot himself if I accepted the offer. Here I was a gullible and utter fool. I told Michael all about it that night, and he quite rightly said, 'You can't believe that kind of talk. Take no heed and go ahead.' He was right and this is what I should have done. But, because of a lurking fear that the man might take his life, I turned down this magnificent offer. Not long after this the shops ran into severe financial trouble. In haste and fear Michael and I, with much sound advice and help from Frank Wigram, sold all the shops with the exception of the original one at Rayner's Lane. The shops ended by being an expensive venture, but while they lasted and I gave them the attention they needed they had been profitable and made many of my expenses deductible from tax. When it was all over I was greatly relieved; it had all been too much.

The one remaining Contessa shop I kept for many years, having a wonderful and totally dependable woman called Mrs Baily to run it, with me to help her over the choice and buying of the stuff. Here I could always go and spend a day selling over the counter and making my usual mistakes in giving wrong change for money taken! I gave up doing the windows and many things that had pleased me in the past.

When we went to New York I saw a greatly changed aspect of that city from my previous experience. The Canfields had an enchanting house way down on 38th Street in those days. It was an unlikely house to find there, tucked away, with a little garden back and front, almost hidden by the surrounding skyscrapers. It was a happy house. Here we had a small bedroom on the top floor, with a bathroom well equipped with everything we could possibly want, something that civilized Americans are much better at achieving than we are in this country. This house was very much part of the world of books, and was frequented by the Canfields' friends from the arts. It was with great pleasure that I found myself neither amongst Eric's jet-set friends nor the very interesting but rather distressing seamy side of New York which had been shown to me by my medical friends. It seems to me that in New York it is easier than in London to gravitate towards whatever interests you most. I would not want to live there, but nonetheless it is a city of many fascinations.

Life with the Canfields was comfortable and interesting. They have a lovely country house, the inside of which is very like the best of our Georgian manor-sized houses here, although built in the 1920s. The atmosphere is also very British except that there is no garden, though they could have a lovely one if they so wished. But Jane is very busy with her beautiful sculpture and, as for Cass, it would be hard to think of anything he has not done in his interesting and overflowing life. He has retired from being the chairman of his publishing house, where he showed an almost unique talent for the financial side of the business as well as finding an exceptional list of outstanding authors. Perhaps that was why Michael found him so difficult to talk to, for Cass was always working out some new project, either on paper or in his head. They had a lovely escape hide-out on Fisher's Island, where Jane could relax and Cass could play his abominably bad golf. This was more of a therapy than a sport to him, as he is good at all other games. His golf drove him to distraction because he could not master it. I think he would admit that, in spite of all the varied things he has done successfully, golf has and always will evade him.

His son, Cass Junior, is quite unlike his father. When my brother met him, he said he had at last met a 'Nancy Mitford American'.

Katsie, the first Mrs Cass Canfield and Michael's 'other mother', and her husband, John Churchill, led a very different life. Their life revolved around Martha's Vineyard, and here we spent many hot mosquito-ridden Augusts. Some people adore the Vineyard; I am not one of them, though I was much taken by seeing it once in the autumn, the celebrated Fall when all America is a perfect and beautiful blaze of colour. A couple who really seemed to love Martha's Vineyard were the author John Marquand and his wife, Sue (a cousin of Michael's who sadly died recently and very young). They had a charming piece of unspoilt land and many amusing and intelligent people from New York, such as Lillian Hellman, the author and playwright, came to stay.

John and Katsie Churchill had some enjoyable qualities but their capacity for drink was quite something to behold. Whisky, gin and vodka all arrived in giant-sized bottles. They both drank from the morning onwards. While John was alive I was staggered by this foolishness. When Katsie was not only alone in life but also ill it was more understandable, but I was very sad for her. Also, I was annoyed by her constant efforts to encourage Michael to keep her company with endless nightcaps. I had to become a tiresome governess while trying to put a stop to this both boring and perilous habit.

On one occasion, the August before Jack Kennedy's horrifying assassination in November 1963, Randolph Churchill was staying with the Kennedys at Cape Cod when he decided to pay me a visit at Martha's Vineyard, a short distance away. On arrival he realized he knew no address; he thought Canfield would be sufficient information, forgetting that Michael had two mothers in America. With his usual determination, he asked all the oldest inhabitants up and down the island if they knew anyone who had once been called Canfield. By evening he found his way to the house and, to his surprise, he also recalled Katsie's name, having met her at several Christmases at Hertfordshire House. The name, of course, was the same as his own, Churchill!

When he arrived I was out playing croquet at a nearby house. Eventually he turned up there in a broken-down old taxi. Michael was elsewhere playing tennis. Before I had time to think Randolph had whipped me away. He was angry with himself for, as it were, forgetting his own name and he went on grumbling about this, complaining that he had had a wasted day and going on to insist that I go with him to an evening picnic which was being given by Bobby Kennedy (and every other kind of Kennedy except the President and Jackie) on that ill-fated river estuary of the Chappaquidick. When Randolph and I arrived at the picnic spot, Bobby Kennedy met us. I am sorry that he too died by an assassin's gun, but I must say I didn't like him. There was something about his manner and his eyes that make me think of pictures I have seen of young Gestapo men.

Michael knew all the Kennedy clan, having been married for

some years to Jackie Kennedy's sister, Lee. He told me that J.F.K. had suffered a serious back injury in the war so he had to have cortisone treatment of some kind. As a result of this he was not allowed alcohol. In order not to put a damper on the party he used to have a bottle of champagne in a wine cooler at his side, but the contents of the bottle were, in fact, milk. I only met Jack once, but Michael knew him well and liked him. I had known and liked the eldest Kennedy son, Joe, who stayed with us during the very early period of the war at Himley; also Kit, who married Lord Hartington. Joe was killed in battle and Kit was first widowed by the war, then died in an air crash in France. Whatever has been said and will continue to be said about the Kennedys, their burden of almost unbelievable misfortune and tragedy has certainly been savage in its weight of destruction, especially for a family who thought they were all-powerful in every conceivable way. Randolph was a great Kennedy fan, I was not.

Night had now fallen and the picnic (which appeared to me to consist almost entirely of the Kennedys and their many noisy children) was lit up by barbecues. For some unknown reason I was filled with an acute foreboding and wished to leave as soon as possible. I also realized I had no way of communicating with Michael to tell him where I was. Randolph was not much help, as he wished me to stay to enjoy the frolics. As luck would have it some late arrivals turned up in another of those old taxis. As they got out I nipped into the cab without a further word to anyone, and asked the driver to take me back to the other end of Martha's Vineyard with all speed. At the time I obviously had no idea of the dreadful happenings to come, yet I was unbelievably relieved to escape from what appeared outwardly to be no more than a rather large and noisy but harmless all-night junket. But as I jolted home in that most welcome taxi I couldn't understand my feelings; there was something thoroughly sinister lurking below the surface of that party. And when, some years later, the Mary-Jo Kopechne tragedy occurred, that evening returned to my memory very vividly and I recalled with a shudder my determination to get home.

I had the same feeling in 1961 when I visited my dentist and he recommended me an osteopath, whose consulting rooms were above his at 19 Cavendish Square. Thus that very evening at five-thirty I met Dr Stephen Ward, who ushered me into his sitting-room and offered me a drink. He was too pleasant – unctuous is the word – and I felt 'I must get out of here.' Then I fled, saying I'd make a proper appointment another day, but with no intention of doing so.

That particular August we had asked our great friend Frank Wigram to stay at Martha's Vineyard. (By this time John Churchill had died.) When I finally reached Katsie's house I found a rather cross, disgruntled trio eating their dinner. Michael was annoyed with me, having no idea where I could be. Frank was doing his best to calm Katsie down from making pretty tough remarks about my curious behaviour. When I explained what had happened, Michael's annoyance vanished and he was very interested in the whole story, knowing the Kennedys far better than I and, furthermore, being quite fond of his ex-brother-in-law, the President.

Both Michael and I looked forward to returning home. Katsie loved Michael too much, and in a very feline way which he resented; therefore when she was almost on her deathbed it was with great difficulty that I persuaded Michael to go to her. He arrived too late, which meant that her real son, Cass Junior, was with his mother during her last hours and showed great love and tenderness towards her at a time when she was much in need. However, one thing is quite clear to me in the rather complex character that Michael was. He always enjoyed any visit to America, whether for business or pleasure, once Katsie was no more, whereas before he had been loath to go.

20

Voyage through France

On our return to Hertfordshire House in the autumn of 1963 we still had many plans for the garden, which was just beginning to take some shape and form, and the loggia was at its most exciting stage of near-completion.

There was a sad moment, however, when we decided to stop breeding Shetland ponies, though we took our time about disposing of them until we found them good homes nearby. This didn't happen till the following year, but the decision was made and my darling Grock, plus wives and foals, eventually departed while poor old Nanny Donk was delighted to leave us for a farm next door where she joined another donkey for a more peaceful life than she had been subjected to with us, particularly in view of Grock's ceaseless and uncalled-for attentions. This treatment I was then also spared, for when spring came his loving arms often threw me to the ground when I was least expecting such demonstrative behaviour. The hundreds of useless chickens also went; they made a lot of mess and, even more tiresomely, never laid more than a few eggs. They gave us no pleasure. The white fantail pigeons remained, with two dovecotes and Ossie's ceaseless talk, either to herself or her reflection in some car that stood near the house. We still had two terriers and two labradors – the original Crumb and a son of his called Harry. So, from a rather muddled animal life which took up too much time, all our concentration was now directed towards creating a lovely garden.

Michael, being of a very tidy nature, loved doing the sweet-peas, tending them twice weekly once they started to flower, trained on canes – a long and arduous task which he enjoyed though it seemed to me a rather tedious job. He usually did this around six in the evening, with a glass of whisky and soda at his feet and his beloved Jack or Jackydoodle watching every move he made. Michael found pleasure in doing all the most methodical things that gardening necessitates, edging the lawns and generally tidying up all round. This was fortunate as I am rather untidy in a garden. I love the flowers, their names, and the real excitement of seeing things grow. There were times when our ideas would clash, mostly because I like shrubs rather under-pruned. I sometimes trembled when Michael was too free with his secateurs. He was quite determined not to learn any but the well-known and obvious names of plants and simply refused to read about flowers other than the ones he personally loved. Here he had his own personal running battle with 'Old Grouch', the head gardener. On Sundays in particular Michael had a free hand in the greenhouse, tossing away many horrible cacti and other great favourites of most old gardeners. This left me with a more than usually disagreeable 'Grouch' on Monday mornings, especially when he suffered from indigestion. I always knew when he had this complaint because he sucked some white tablets which left a thin film round the edge of his lips. Then I avoided him as much as possible.

The end result was that we succeeded in having a very beautiful garden, but to reach that point we had many disappointments and heartaches. Even when we quarrelled over some utterly ridiculous and trivial matter it was short-lived, ending in laughter. This was the perfect way to clear up some unimportant mistake one of us had made; always we were working together towards our mutual objective. As in everyday life, if one is in a position to discuss the irritations, large or small, the burden is at once halved and seen in the right perspective.

I am far from careful or cautious by nature; somehow I have always felt that all will become as I expect it to be. Life isn't like that, and Michael was fortunately able to pull me back from many follies, interceding on my behalf with his better judgement, not seeing life with that glint of sunlight I sought to find even on an unpleasant winter's day.

It was an evening such as this when in November 1963 I went to the kitchen, having remembered that we were going to have dinner at Great Westwood, my old home, with Eric, who had just married again – to Grace Radziwill, whose husband had once been married to Michael's first wife. It was quite a merry-go-round as this diagram shows.

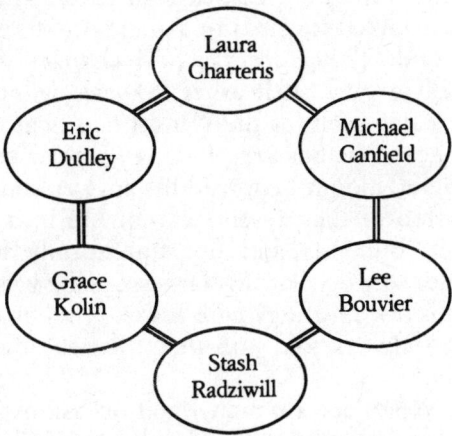

As always in the domestic quarters, the television was on. I could barely take in what was being said, but what was soon both clear and ghastly was that the President of the USA, Michael's ex-brother-in-law, had been shot. From what I understood he was dead, his wife sitting by his side, unhurt but spattered with her husband's blood. Having only met Jack Kennedy once it was no personal grief to me, nonetheless I was stupefied that such a truly horrible crime could have been perpetrated in cold blood on a crowded road surrounded by a motorcade of police and all the protection that is routine in America for any President. My first thought was to break this almost unbelievable news to Michael. He could scarcely believe my account of what had happened. It was a special shock to him as he had spent much time in Jack Kennedy's company. Then we both listened to the radio. It was all still somewhat confused, except that this horrific crime against what many people thought was youth and hope for all mankind had in fact happened.

Life must go on, so we proceeded to change for dinner. We knew that the Duke and Duchess of Windsor were to be the only other guests at Westwood that evening. Somehow they had not heard the news, and even when they did they thought it must be some ghastly rumour. But the butler, Balance, confirmed the story, so it was not long before it was being discussed.

I had not visited Westwood since Eric's marriage, so, before dinner, I was both intrigued and surprised to see a table in the sitting-room laid out with a vast dish of caviar and champagne in buckets. As I walked towards this unexpected sight Eric came towards me. I said, 'Things seem to have changed in this house,' meaning the caviar and such other luxuries, which had never appeared in my day even for the Windsors. It was at least some light relief to hear Eric answer, 'I know, isn't it vulgar?' On a night of death and gloom I enjoyed his answer and needed little more explanation of the present way of life in a house I had admittedly left, but was still not unnaturally interested in. Michael was not surprised at this largesse as he was accustomed to it through his few meetings with his ex-wife, by then Princess Radziwill, who always told him that this was the way things should be done!

We went to Westwood on many later occasions and they also came to us. One night we took Randolph Churchill with us. After dinner Eric disappeared upstairs. He came staggering down again, carrying a full-sized portrait of me painted by Anthony Devas, which he presented to Michael. Before Michael had time to accept this not-much-wanted gift, Randolph said, 'Surely you're not going to give Michael the frame as well as the portrait!' Eric made no comment, Randolph roared with laughter and the picture was put in our car. In the end we had three portraits of myself. However, the one thing I should have enjoyed to own was the sketch of me by Augustus John. I had some pretty long sittings in a very cold studio, but when Augustus John's interpretation of me was shown to Eric, he didn't like it. I must say I saw his point, but at least I found it an entertaining drawing, if unlike me. Augustus John, who did not like his work criticized, said to Eric, 'Paint her yourself.' I never saw this work again but was told by a friend of John's that he destroyed it. To sit for Augustus was quite an experience, for he was often feeling ill from over-indulgence the night before, or feeling too well, which ended in one having to be very acrobatic round the studio to avoid his unasked-for attentions! These sittings with Augustus baffled me. He was the most unexpected of men. He had, if he so wished, great charm and was well endowed intellectually, and yet at times showed himself to be a character of great instability and even with something sinister about him.

In those blissful years I noticed that I became more vulnerable, perhaps the inevitable result of growing older. Not that I ever thought of or feared age; it was more an almost unconscious ebbing of a joyous way of life that by some unpredictable, remote possibility might be seized and taken from me. I felt like a dog with its bone, or a child who screams even before its precious toy is snatched by an older person or a stronger, more masterful child. These black, thoughtful, sometimes abject days did crop up, like a tiresome weed that seems to grow again a few hours after one has spent endless and what appears to have been fruitless energy pulling and scratching. The most tenacious and resolute of such species is bindweed, and I have wondered when gardening why we fight this common, wilful flower, for if it weren't for the damage it does to plants of a more delicate nature, left to itself it is a pretty thing, every bit as attractive as Morning Glory, the seeds of which are no longer on sale in America on account of the possible LSD content. When a day of gloom and lethargy comes upon one there is no better therapy than to use one's hands to eradicate some tiresome troublemaker; to force oneself into doing a boring and uncreative but useful task. They are not the days to dream up some new idea for house or garden.

I am talking of the 'self-employed' such as I was at Hertfordshire House, with only too much that needed doing but nothing to force idle hands when I felt uninspired. Sometimes a sense of duty motivated me – a duty to have something to show Michael which he would approve of when he came home in the evening. Michael was born to have many melancholy moments, making it all the more essential for me to show no sign of gloom. When alone together life was seldom anything but perfect, but always I was on the watch for the times when something in the course of his work in London would send him home to me full of sadness. This usually happened on what I came to call 'black Mondays'. We only spent at most two to three nights in London, so that on Mondays he always came back to Hertfordshire House. If I had also had a troublesome day it was then the more difficult to make his sometimes sad eyes fill and overflow with laughter, which was what I longed for; otherwise I felt inadequate.

It was during the so-called summer months, when the sunlight that one expects so often hides behind grey cotton-wool clouds, that we most blessed the loggia. Here we sought warmth from the sun that was there even if it played hide-and-seek high above the cloud; even on a cold, grey day the glass and leaded domes made it possible to eat our luncheon there and very often dinner, too. In some ways Hertfordshire House, after many years of work, became a very English, warm and comforting dwelling. Of all the many friends that came to stay, Diana Cooper pleased me most by calling it 'the house without fear'. Another compliment came from that charming writer and poet, Laurie Lee, who while walking in the garden with his most attractive wife once said to me, 'In your house I really could write.' When the Laurie Lees lived in London, before their much-longed-for child arrived, they used to come to stay. After dinner his wife would sing to his guitar accompaniment in the most lighthearted and enchanting way.

In the early 1960s it was a must for both of us to explore some country in Europe and search out objects for the house and loggia. We pretended the furnishings were complete, but every now and then we laughed and decided not to try and fool each other about the scarcity of those necessities that make a house *look* comfortable as well as being so. Having a new and powerful Mercedes, which was my wedding present to Michael, we discussed such a trip. Portugal was our choice, because we hoped to find rugs and pottery at more than reasonable prices. We must have forgotten, or just not taken in, how terribly long the journey would turn out to be. We decided that we would each drive for about three hours, then change over. From Buckinghamshire we drove that unpleasant and dull road to Kent, took the ferry, and crossed the Channel to Calais. In France there is always a thrill in just looking at the *Michelin* guidebook, even if not intent on a stop (except for a pee behind a tree) for some four hundred kilometres.

This journey through France was not unfamiliar but it was now new and exciting because Michael was by my side. We travelled along the old Route 1 to Lyon, then on to the coast at Narbonne. From there we zigzagged along the coast till we reached Barcelona. We did no more than *touch* the Spanish food, and found it quite repellent. Not only was it ugly to look at, but everything seemed to float in fat. How could a boiled egg be impregnated with this loathsome grease? Before this I had only been to Madrid, staying at the best of all Ritz hotels and scarcely going out, except the tiny distance to enter the Pravda and feast my eyes on the many beautiful pictures or else to the houses of Eric's rich and grand friends.

From Barcelona down to Valencia it was not enjoyable – long, straight roads with many potholes. One real danger was the odd donkey, either burdened down with packs upon its back or pulling a thing on wheels that could hardly be called a cart. The poverty seemed very real; bent men and women laboured on dusty earth, and it was only early spring. In summer's shimmering heat I couldn't imagine that crops would grow, however hard the peasants worked. The only fat and prosperous Spaniards I ever saw were the priests, pink and white in the face, their long black robes slightly grubby at the feet. Suddenly, emerging from a succession of those bleak villages, we found ourselves in a dream world of white blossom and overpowering scent amid the beautifully tended orange and lemon groves which seem to surround Valencia for miles – not really an accurate description because Valencia is very near the sea, but all approaches to the town are one huge orchard. It was a beautiful sight – to say breathtaking would be too near the truth, for the scent of orange blossom is overpowering. The vivid green and the porcelain-like flowers made us feel glad we had chosen to go to Lisbon the long way, right round the peninsula of Spain.

By this time we were both fed up with driving along these dusty roads so we decided against sightseeing of any kind, and took the coast to Malaga. In those days the southern coast was being developed for tourism in a big way. We didn't have the energy to leave the coast and look at Granada, which we much regretted; instead, if various people were to be believed, the hotel at Marbella was good. When we reached Marbella we felt we had earned a rest from the driving wheel. Then the sun came out. To mention the sun as far south as this seems strange; maybe we had been unlucky but it really was the first time we had seen it since leaving England. We had all the dust and lustreless grass that one associates with constant sun; we had suffered, as it were, its ill-effects without its warmth or glowing shadows.

We stayed two nights at Marbella. Then we telephoned to David Herbert, who lived near Tangier. He was most welcoming and suggested we should come and stay with him. We postponed our shopping spree in Lisbon and went to Gibraltar, crossing over by ferry to Tangier. Whether it was more important to visit David or look at Granada is a moot point; the former, I'm sure, was the more entertaining. David Herbert's house and garden were charming. He is one of the few self-imposed exiles from his own country that I know who seems completely happy. He has made a life for himself within its (metaphorically) rather limited walls. He is, as he always has been, gay and amusing and loved by the natives as well as the small collection of people from various countries who have settled in Tangier. He keeps many strange 'mutt'-type dogs and a monkey. The garden is a tangle of colour, which I enjoyed. At that time of year his orchard was full of arum lilies instead of being daffodil-strewn like ours. One of his dogs, tiny and pathetic, had had boiling water accidentally spilled over it. I christened this sad sight 'The Burnt-Out Case', after Graham Greene's book which had just been published.

After our visit to Tangier we went back to Gibraltar to collect the car, and continued the journey to plunder the shops of Lisbon. Alas, we had to stop a night in that unattractive garrison town for I was smitten with a bad migraine. It was a fierce attack, so Michael found medical help. After one night's sleep I had more or less recovered enough to continue our journey, for we still had quite a drive ahead and we were now behind our timetable; besides the scenery was not something we wished to linger over.

Lisbon was very pleasant, and we found so many rugs and blue and white pottery-type china that we had to send most of it home by ship. We also more or less ran out of money so we telephoned Xan and Daphne Fielding, who invited us to a sumptuous meal in their house nearby.

The next day we faced up to the long trek home; we took the shortest route out of Spain, having already had enough disgusting Spanish food. We could have gone home via Madrid, but instead we made straight for the town of Valladolid, a long drive from Lisbon. By now we both rather disliked Spain so we spent the night at Valladolid and decided during a late and pretty nasty dinner that it would be our last meal on Spanish soil. In the early morning we headed for France and we must have driven at terrific speed because we had a delicious luncheon at St Jean de Luz. Here we really patted the car like some trustworthy horse and once more thought we could take a rest by staying a night

1 Ann (*top*), Mary Rose (*left*) and
me, 1923

2 A portrait of my mother aged
seventeen

3 Jane and me at Stanway

Three Generations of Weddings

4 David and me, 1933

5 Sara and Charlie, 1954

6 Anabel and Michael, 1979

7 Sara and me at Himley, 1944

8 Eric Dudley

9 Himley on the day of
my Red Cross Fête, 1944

10 Auctioning two chickens for the Red Cross Victory Shop in Wolverhampton, 1944

11 Listening sceptically to Harold Wilson, then President of the Board of Trade, 1947

12 *From left to right:* myself, Anthony Eden, Little Winston, Randolph, my sister Ann at a party at Warwick House, 1949

13 With Virginia Gilliat
(later Lady Sykes) at
Himley, 1942

14 Colonel Paul Rodzianko (the photograph
is inscribed: 'To Laura, with love and
admiration for her bravery. Paul, 1949')

15 Me competing at Windsor Horse Show, 1949, on my horse Princess – with
a suitable background

16 At my desk at Dior, London, with secretary and dog

17 Me decorating the windows of my first Contessa shop

18 Michael Canfield at the Frankfurt Book Fair, 1969

19 Michael and me at Hertford-shire House with Crumb, Daisy, Grock, Oliver and Beany

20 Gerry Koch de
Gooreynd, 1950

21 Lady Diana Cooper,
Christmas 1977

22 The Duke and
Duchess of Windsor

23 With my nephew Caspar Fleming and my dog Russy at Hertfordshire House, 1967

24 My aunt Kakoo (Kathleen, Duchess of Rutland), 1967

25 My brother Hugo shortly before his death

26 My father bird-watching in Spain in the 1950s

27 Bert Marlborough with Ben in the Temple of Health at Blenheim, 1967

28 Gellibrands

29 Pat and Jenny Duncan, dogs and me at Gellibrands, June 1979

or two with friends. We had in mind Tanis and Teddy Phillips, who lived just outside Biarritz.

I went off to telephone them but couldn't find their name in the directory. I came back to Michael to report my failure and as I was saying I found it strange, because they had lived in this house for so long, I suddenly had one of those twists of memory; I had often stayed at their house, La Domaine de Migron, which reminded me that as a joke they were in the telephone directory by the names they called each other: she was Lion and he was Bear. On remembering this, back I went to the directory and, sure enough, my memory had not misled me. I found a Mr and Mrs Bear and a Mr and Mrs Lion. Once more we rested from a long drive, at the same time enjoying being with Tanis and Teddy and for me, particularly, it was lovely to see Tanis's maid Selina who had been such a friend in New York in 1946.

On leaving La Domaine de Migron, we had had enough of travel so with a minimum of overnight stops we made a bee-line for Hertfordshire House, the car bursting with our Lisbon booty, and some attractive knives and forks with bamboo handles which we had bought in France. We had been away for three weeks.

Our first telephone call when we arrived home was to one of the few neighbours we saw much of – Frank Wigram. He and his mother lived in charming houses in Penn, where Frank had his very successful antique shop. We asked him to come over to see our spoils from overseas and I recounted a funny moment which had happened at the Customs when we reached England. The car was full of things under a hundred years old, and therefore not technically antiques. I told Michael to leave the Customs Officers to me. When they opened the boot, they naturally asked about the rugs from Lisbon. I asked them solemnly not to pull them about as these rugs were so ancient that I was afraid they would fall apart. To my amazement and joy, they believed me and, after a chat about antiques, we passed on without paying a penny.

We enjoyed our first visit to Tangier and so returned the following year with my brother Hugo, his wife and children. We found the Casbah rather depressing. It was amidst the sad sights of the Casbah that Barbara Hutton had a luxurious house. The Woolworth heiress had a new lover. He was a good-looking Guardsman who liked to play polo so she provided ponies, a field and other polo players from England. He also liked to serenade his loved one on a guitar. Miss Hutton was still very pretty, although she was now drinking pretty constantly and rarely left her own house where many parties, lasting till morning, took place. There was a dearth of males so Miss Hutton summoned six of his Guards officer friends, and ordered suitable evening clothing to be flown over with them from Harrods.

For some unexplained reason she would not invite me. I do not know the reason for her attitude as I recall meeting her only once, and that years before and quite uneventfully! So Michael and I were excluded from these lavish junkets while Hugo and Virginia went, as did all the others from the English colony, plus their guests. Their hostess took rather a liking to Hugo. On one of these occasions, knowing her to be well wined, he sat cross-legged at her feet hoping that one of the vast precious-stoned jewels would fall from her and that when he retrieved the valuable bauble for her she might say, 'Keep it.' This was a daydream on his part; at least the 'keep it' part was, for a jewel did fall right into his lap, but to my brother's great disappointment Miss Hutton grasped it back and pinned it to her dress without a word.

One evening when the children had gone to bed the four of us went to a night haunt, having it in mind to try smoking 'pot' or marijuana, which was in plentiful supply. Someone told us where to go, as many places sold you cigarettes saying they were marijuana when there was nothing in them but ordinary tobacco. We each lit up our pot cigarette, which none of us had tried before. On me it had an electrifying effect; after one puff I was laughing madly about nothing. The more Michael, Hugo and Virginia dragged away on their cigarettes, the glummer they looked because they got no kick or whatever you are supposed to get, and the more I giggled away. They then bought more cigarettes. I shall never forget their enraged faces as the second helping, so to speak, still had no effect. After a while we walked back to the hotel, I feeling very happy and they looking pale under their sunburn and gloomy with disappointment.

That reminds me of something strange which happened at Hertfordshire House, one weekend during the summer of 1966. A young man of great brilliance and charm, Roger Klein, was staying with us. He was spending a few months in London, but his real work was as one of Harper and Row's most promising editors in New York. As he had plenty of money of his own he was gaining as much experience as he could by travelling abroad. On this particular Friday-to-Monday, those present were only Michael and I, Kate and Ivan Moffat and Roger. I'm sorry to say Sunday was, as so often happens in English summers, a rainy and dismal day. Soon after breakfast Michael came back to our bedroom, saying, 'Roger has quite a number of LSD capsules. Ivan and I have already swallowed ours and of course Roger has probably taken even more. He says he's well acquainted with this drug. There is one for you and another for Kate.'

I knew nothing about LSD beyond what I had read of its effects on different people – that those who indulged in this drug could have good or bad 'trips'. I immediately told Michael I wouldn't dream of taking it. I then went upstairs to Kate's room. As I expected she would have no part of it, at the same time warning me of possible consequences, as she had witnessed the effects of LSD on previous occasions and knew they were long-lasting. She said we must keep an eye on those that had gone on a 'trip', good or bad. During that morning Michael kept saying he felt no different, but he was. For instance, he was by nature a sun-lover, yet he looked out of my window and re-marked on how beautiful the rain was. He then went into the garden where a young under-gardener we had at this time was working. As they walked among the sodden flowers, Michael said how well the Mercedes was growing! Then, as luncheon time arrived, neither my husband, Ivan nor Roger had even glanced at the Sunday newspapers, of which all three of them were normally avid readers. When luncheon was actually ready Ivan was missing. I found him lying in the pouring rain in the orchard. He was quite unlike himself, almost rude when I told him he would catch a dreadful cold and he must come inside and eat. He then rushed through the house and upstairs and locked himself in his bedroom.

We had a silent, dreary luncheon. Those on a 'trip' ate nothing – I'm sure at this point the servants were bewildered! The after-noon passed without drama, but equally it was an unhappy situation for Kate and me. Towards tea-time Michael, to my great relief, seemed normal; Ivan on the other hand was still silent in his bedroom. I banged on the door saying he must come down and have something to eat and he eventually let me in, but he was far from being himself. 'I've been in a tormented state,' he said, 'thinking I was encased in a red marble ball, with no way of escape.' Then he came down and asked for a hearty tea. After demolishing food he appeared better, but still strange. Quite unexpectedly my daughter and her husband called for a night on their way to London. Strangely enough, they talked of nothing but a programme on LSD they had seen on television the night before. No one else spoke much – and they naturally did not realize they were witnessing the real thing! This was my first and I'm glad to say last experience of a very alarming and unpredictable drug. The sad sequel to this weekend was that Roger killed himself some eighteen months later towards the end of a long course of psychoanalysis in America.

21

Barbados

In 1964 we were much tempted by an invitation from Peggy and Paul Munster to go and stay with them in Barbados, where they had rented a house during January and February. As Michael craved sunshine, having lived most of his life in America where at least the summer is certain to be summer, I was all for going to the West Indies; having given up hunting I had long since found little pleasure in the English winter. So about mid-January we set off to an island in the sun. After a long flight we landed in Bridgetown, and made our way to Glitter Bay Beach House on the St James coast. It was 8 p.m. Barbados time.

Here on the Caribbean Seas, not so far from the equator, night falls swiftly around 6 p.m. The moon looked unbelievably large, lighting up the pretty house which was perfect in design. The only sound seemed to be the ripple of soft waves mixed with that delightful 'clicking' of the crickets, a sound I always associate with hot climates. That night we sank into bed knowing we were on an island that we loved and would come to love more deeply.

The following day was one of exploration. We soon discovered the island's temperature was ideal, both night and day. Having been almost unknowingly beckoned into the sea at an early hour, we found the balmy water sheer joy; no question of a quick pre-breakfast dip, for when the sea was in good humour one lingered in its weightless warm arms for an unexpected length of time. Then we had a delicious breakfast and a vague look at the local newspaper, which was little more than three or four pages of island news. Sometimes the news suffered at the hands of local printers. One day a queer friend, who was staying at Ronnie Tree's, came in very amused by an account of a recent wedding: 'The bridegroom looked lovely with a hibiscus in his bottom-hole.' I was more amused by the antics of the common sparrows, which are almost identical with our sparrows at home except that they have much larger feet for clinging on to the coral-built walls at any angle. They seem to have complete trust in humans and no fear of them. The houses are all open to the gentle warm air and the birds come and go with ease.

At Glitter Bay we ate on the large pillared terrace or below it in the dining-room, equally open in design. This was one of many enjoyable things about Barbados – one was in the open air all the time and there were no mosquitoes or other tiresome insects to avoid. I was surprised to find the island kept green by welcome showers of soft rain and instantly dried by the gentle trade winds wafting by.

The natives of Barbados seemed as warm and kind as their climate. They love each other and very soon you are made to feel that they love you, too. They have a natural elegance and sense of colour in their dress, unlike some other poor and distant countries. I never remember seeing an animal ill-treated, and indeed it was rare to see a child cry. On Sunday, a charming and surprising sight was to see a mass of children pour out of their shacks, all spotlessly clean and laughing, their dresses starched, wearing irresistible little hats and bonnets covered in ribbons and bows, often with pigtails plaited to perfection. How they appeared from these primitive huts so beautifully turned out for church was to my mind an object lesson to more developed civilizations that have many more facilities.

Barbados is by no means the most beautiful island in the Caribbean, being mostly flat and covered with sugar-cane plantations which are the main source of revenue, apart from the tourist trade. On the other side of the island from St James is the Atlantic coast, which is much wilder, with usually more turbulent seas; it is known as 'little Scotland'. Barbados is quite small and lacks the varied and more lush vegetation of other islands; even the bird species are limited. There are humming-birds (but the rather dull ones, drab in colour), many grackles, and a greedy yellow-eyed and rather unfriendly type of blackbird. But my first love were those common sparrows, with their big feet and cheerful, cheeky fearlessness. Their impudence is half their charm. From our first breakfast I encouraged them to hop on to plate or cup, stealing one's food. Their favourite treat was their own home-grown sugar, for which their appetite never seemed to be satisfied.

Lizards and chameleons are much in evidence around the houses, mostly at night, when they either fight for minute insects or remain immobile, usually in pairs. The lizards did not have the capacity to change colour and become almost invisible like the chameleons, which could be found draped around a lamp, taking on the same colour as the object they laid themselves upon, lying in wait to gobble up any fly or midge attracted by the light.

A special feature was the new hybrid hibiscus that grows in every imaginable colour – either in the garden or for picking, not for flower arrangements but for just the heads to be gathered in the evening and strewn on the dining-table. They do not wilt till the morning, and as they flower in great profusion this seemingly wasteful way of treating them has no ill consequences. One large majestic tree – the bread-fruit tree – serves two purposes; it gives sometimes welcome shade and at the same time is laden down with fruit which is the basic subsistence food of the natives. Some of them grow as large in circumference as our oak or beech, the strong healthy branches dangling low from the main trunk. To the natives it is the tree of knowledge and they have good reason to respect it for it serves them well.

The sea is not always gentle, but there is no real danger except when a strong underswell develops. Then drowning accidents are not unknown. Also on leaving the sea it is easy to get scratched by the innocent-looking coral stones, and any small abrasion is apt to go septic. Most houses are prepared for such minor casualties having sulphonamide powder to anoint these cuts, which then give no further trouble. On rare occasions there could be a truly angry sea, not to my liking. Michael, being a strong and beautiful swimmer, revelled in these monstrously large high waves for he could spend hours surfing happily; few other people took pleasure from these boisterous days.

On our first morning as we strolled along the beach I felt thirsty and seeing some little green apples piled in mounds near native dwellings I picked one up without thinking and took a bite. It seemed natural that they must be edible. The taste was bitter but no worse than that. Fortunately we met Peggy Munster and

Ronnie Tree and almost before I realized what was happening they whisked me off to the nearest doctor, pushing me into a car in my bathing dress with no time to change. They then explained that these little apples are almost pure acid, therefore very dangerous to bite, let alone swallow. I was lucky; the juicy bitter mouthful did me little harm. The doctor gave me a lecture and a large bottle of something alkaline to take several times a day. The slight burning sensation in my stomach had disappeared by evening. Even the leaves from these apple trees are to be avoided; some people have been badly burnt by sheltering from rain beneath them as the drops of water filter through and burn your skin. Someone staying in Barbados the year before had done no more than I did, yet finished up in hospital for several months. Nature is very thoughtful in one way; next to the acid apples there always grows a white wood tree, the leaves of which, if crushed and placed on skin burns, are the best and almost only cure. I was only informed of this later by one of the natives who became my friend. The natives know many cures for ailments. I do not mean 'witch doctoring'; it is mostly common sense or trial and error from the days when they first worked, or rather slaved, in these parts.

Life on this dreamy isle was not all lying about; it is full of activities. One did not need much sleep and for a tropical climate felt full of energy. The mornings consisted of bathing and reading from an early hour so that at twelve-thirty most people, including ourselves, were ready for a delicious rum punch followed by lunch. Then I nearly always played golf; the course was very moderate but I can think of nowhere else that golf has been so enjoyable. I had a musical comedy type of caddy called Dale Levine to whom I was devoted. Michael played tennis in the afternoons as he did not enjoy golf. I usually rushed back from my game to change and play bridge. When staying with the Munsters, naturally our lives, particularly in the evenings, were the same as theirs, so we either went out to dinner or they had people in.

It was hard to get to sleep – something about the air. This was not difficult to remedy as there was a hut on the way to the golf course which was a chemist's shop. Here you could buy any form of sleeping pill without prescription. I remember later buying a vast bottle of Mandrax and if anyone who came to dinner bored us, I laced their coffee with these white tablets. It was never long before the unsuspecting guests started to yawn and long for bed! I must add that such drastic measures were used only in rare and exceptionally tedious cases.

The great centre for entertaining talk, bridge, croquet or just delicious food and meeting anyone of interest was Ronnie Tree's beautiful Palladian style of house at Heron Bay. It was situated close to the sea on a bay from which the house derived its name. It appeared larger than it was, being long and narrow with lovely tall pillars and double stairways outside the house both back and front, all in perfect proportion, perfect in its land and sea setting and giving an impression of age and tranquillity. When I first saw Heron Bay I could scarcely believe it had not been built many decades ago. Ronnie was the uncrowned king of Barbados. Before he left Britain, driven away for the usual tax reasons, he had owned and lived in one of the most beautiful houses in England, Dytchley in Oxfordshire. It became well known in the war for there Winston Churchill spent time for security reasons, particularly when the moon was full.

When Ronnie decided to abandon the English way of life and tax, he selected Barbados on which to build a little empire, consisting of his house, the Sandy Lane Hotel and a golf course, all done with impeccable taste. Heron Bay gave an impression of the best and happiest side of colonialism; plenty of smiling black servants always to hand, though perhaps not quite enough by Ronnie's standards. When his two sons were staying with him and all three came in from golf they expected their shoes to be removed by butlers – and there were only two servants of that rank in the establishment! Ronnie owned one of the only two electric golf carts on the island. Since he was not the best driver of an ordinary car he found these small vehicles quite impossible. He often overturned on a rickety wood bridge that crossed a small ravine, but fortunately never came to much harm.

Victor (Lord) Rothschild also had a house in Barbados. His idea of relaxation after golf was quite strange. One wall of their mostly open-air sitting-room consisted of a large aquarium, which contained a mixed collection of different fish, some innocuous, some predatory. He used to sit for hours, alone or with friends, watching the predators hunt and eat the other colourful sea-creatures. This was, I imagine, his own private 'Think-Tank'.

We spent two or three weeks with the Munsters for two suc-ceeding years. Towards the end of our second visit we met a little old American called Mr Porter who wished to sell his house called Prudence. I was fortunate to sit next to him at a luncheon party. Michael and I had seen the house, which was nothing to look at, though it was at least built of coral stone and lay some hundred and fifty yards back from the sea at the end of Ronnie's garden. In our view it was ideal, being small and having a secluded garden. It certainly had charm and it was easy to see what could be done with it without too much expense. Michael completed the deal with Mr Porter before we flew off to New York that evening. It was a most happy decision. Before this happened we had considered buying the Avons' house. In fact, Mr Porter's little place gave us much pleasure and laughter for several years, and it was no financial burden as Michael, coming under American law, could rent it and put most of the upkeep down against taxation. He also said he would do the housekeep-ing and shopping to give me a real holiday from everyday chores. This I always thought an unlikely possibility.

As things turned out, everything was taken care of by Mrs Mason, an excellent cook-housekeeper whom we inherited from Mr Porter. She also arranged other domestics for the duration of our stay. She was a large lady, competent and with a warm ever-welcoming personality which turned Prudence into a house without worry. The size was just right, giving us three bedrooms and bathrooms, a large hall for dumping things in, and a most charming living-room which bowed out into the garden and, as they say in advertisements, the usual domestic quarters.

There was an adjoining piece of land that I was most anxious for Michael to buy as it was the home of some monkeys which are not to be found in great numbers on Barbados, as in the so-called rainy month of November they suffer many chest com-plaints which keep their population down. Clarissa Avon would not agree with me; she actually tried to get the monkeys shot because of their playful ways and the odd bite they took from the Avons' fruit. I was afraid someone would build on this plot of land, thereby scaring the monkeys away. We succeeded in buying it and for thanks the monkeys came into the sitting-room and proceeded to take all the stuffing out of our chairs and sofas!

Many people we found interesting to meet used to come to Barbados, even for a short time. For instance, one day I remember meeting that wonderful lady, Princess Alice, Countess of Athlone, Queen Victoria's last surviving granddaughter. For many years she was a regular visitor to Ronnie Tree, being chancellor of the University of the West Indies. That same day we had the still beautiful Greta Garbo for luncheon and in the morning I warned one of the Beatle songsters against taking cover from rain under those innocent-looking acid apple trees. I don't pretend this was a typical day, nor would I have loved Barbados as much if it had been, for we didn't go there to meet people that had been or still were in the public eye. I just give this day as an example of how varied the visitors to this island are.

The Canfields and Jane's sister Babs and brother-in-law, Dan Caulkins, for some years rented another very pretty house called Heronetta, so there was much *va et vient* between Prudence and there, also many golf engagements with them, all of which was most enjoyable. I suppose we wintered there for about five or six years. Returning home soon made my face and body turn from a healthy brown to the pale yellow of the daffodils that were about to carpet our entire orchard; Michael somehow kept a lovely brown for some weeks.

Randolph Churchill, to whom we lent Prudence one year for Christmas when his health was failing, 'liked it very well' to use his own words. Incidentally he thought it the most unlikely name for a house of mine. We had quite a few friends to stay there, preferably two at a time. One year Adrian Daintrey, the artist, to whom we were both devoted, stayed one whole winter through thick and thin. He painted by day and in the end there was no place for him to sleep except what I referred to as a dumping room. That winter Liz and Billy Wallace were with us, so at night when Adrian had finished his dancing activities, which he and I did each evening to the hi-fi gramophone, and Billy and Michael had about exhausted themselves with various cabaret turns (which I admit they did extremely well), we then put Adrian to bed on more of a table than a bed; not that he minded where he slept as long as he knew Mrs Mason would be there in the morning. Adrian gave us a painting for Prudence on his

departure. It was a surprising work of art to find in Barbados –
very large and done in bright blue and white chalk, depicting
Windsor Castle. I'm sure by now Mrs Mason has taken it to her
own house.

Dear Daintrey was a charming guest, except at dawn when he
always had trouble finding his bathing shorts and succeeded in
waking up the entire house. He did well financially, demands
being made on his artistry by visitors who wanted him to depict
them as looking seventeen when they were nearer seventy. Most
of his remuneration came in dollar cheques and he was always
worried by this, doing little sums to translate dollars into pounds
for fear he was being tricked in some way. I'm sure he must love
his memories of Mrs Mason and the tropics. Of the few months
we spent at Prudence, none were as noisy or amusing as when
Daintrey danced.

Once, in March 1967, Michael had to return to London on
business and so I decided to visit Bert Marlborough in his
attractive house near Montego Bay. He was surrounded by a
great number of friends and relations. One evening we seemed
to be waiting a very long time for dinner, so Henry Porchester,
who was overseeing culinary matters, went to the kitchen to see
how a suckling-pig was doing. He feared he would find it burnt
to a cinder, but on the contrary nothing was happening at all.
The cook was in the throes of childbirth and all the staff except
Bramwell, Bert's valet, were attending to her needs. On hearing
that we were to be denied the suckling-pig, Bert commented,
'We'd better eat the baby instead!'

It was a different world we faced when we returned home.
Michael felt guilty about taking any other holiday from his books
than the few weeks of winter we spent at Prudence. I feel if
there had been more for him to do, and of a more exacting and
absorbing nature, he wouldn't have had the very real guilt complex that his office gave him. I am sure I'm right about this for in
1968 when we were in Barbados he was very serious about the
idea of working there, so much so that we even went to see their
Minister of Education about the possibility of a teaching post.
Fortunately the man we saw turned out to be not only charming
but extremely truthful and frank, unlike so many political people.
He told Michael that he could certainly find him a post in the
University at that time, but it would be temporary as it was

Barbados government policy that eventually all such work would be carried out by coloured people, whenever possible natives of the island.

Apart from our winter holidays, most years we escaped to the sun for a brief two weeks in August. Some summers we went to the Aga Khan's house in the South of France, a most delectable villa called L'Horizon. He lent it to Primrose Cadogan (the Aga's aunt) and Robert Heber-Percy. Once we arrived at the villa we seldom ventured out, the roads on the Côte d'Azure having become impossible during summer months. We gobbled up the chef's wonderful food and bathed in a vast pool that also had a chute going into the sea. Robert and Michael both drank too much and, though not admitting it, felt pretty awful after ten days of rich food and excellent wine.

Another year we stayed in Sardinia with Peter Ward and then flew in a dangerous little butterfly aeroplane we had to charter to land in Nice, where we visited Peter Wilson of Sotheby's fame and a relation of mine. He was just settling into his newly bought estate not far from Grasse. The entrance to his château had a tiled floor designed by Picasso, who was still alive and living nearby. There was a lake which we used as a swimming pool. Peter was always good company and the visit was full of laughter.

One year we visited Anne and Michael Tree on Spetsi, and made an interesting and alarming trip to visit Paddy Leigh Fermor in the heart of Greece. We were taken there in two shifts in Niarchos's jet-propelled helicopter. It was a rough day to navigate the mountains; thunder and lightning caused the helicopter to drop very suddenly every now and then, and I felt sure we would crash on some mountain peak. Michael and I took the second trip, giving us a chance to look round Niarchos's island. It was an incredible place, staffed by Germans dressed in white with soft rubber shoes. They spoke little and always seemed to carry out their duties at a silent trot. Game birds and stags in their thousands awaited slaughter in the autumn, with no escape once imported, and also bred on the island. It was an eerie feeling. I asked Stavros whether his ideas took inspiration from my brother-in-law Ian Fleming's books or were his own original rather frightening and cruel planning. I received a guttural and unintelligible answer to my question. The set-up gave me the creeps; at the same time one could not but be fascinated in a macabre way. It forced one to think of the devastating aspects of having money in such quantity, the power that it brought and the lengths its owners went to for amusement. In this case, admittedly, tragedy came in its steps.

Paddy had turned architect–builder and was in the final stages of building his new house, which explained to Michael why his last book had hung fire, Paddy being one of Harper's most successful authors. We landed on a sun-dried piece of land in front of the house which was to become an olive grove. His architectural abilities were very impressive. The large mahogany doors looked as if they had been hewn in another age and not built by local craftsmanship under Paddy's supervision. His library was charming; books in shelves at a low level went right round the room. An ancient peasant woman served us a sumptuous meal. Our little party consisted of Diana Cooper, who had made her own way there by bus the day before, Anne Tree, Nancy Lancaster, Niarchos and ourselves.

The journey home was even more hair-raising. The pilot made me sit alone at the back of this fast-whirling helicopter as he wanted weight in front. Michael felt no fear as he was sleeping off a long-drawn-out, well-wined luncheon. I was relieved in many ways that I could see little, owing to low cloud and the gathering dusk. We landed safely and were taken home in one of the many speedboats tied up in Niarchos's private harbour. As we walked up the hill the short distance to the Trees' house, the scent at night of a particularly large white variety of jasmine was intoxicating (not that Michael needed any help from flower power).

I have already mentioned Michael's tendency towards the bottle and the fact that this slight weakness of his only rarely bothered me. I admit that the ouzo in Greece did cause me some concern. He was in no way an alcoholic; sometimes months went by without him overdoing any form of drinking. My policy was not to nag but every now and then to come out with a sharp attack, always to good effect. When we were alone there was never any problem and if at parties (when I'm sure his natural shyness had something to do with it) he felt he had yielded to the temptation he would often simply say he wanted to go home. In Greece I was forced into a minor row with him, really because I minded so dreadfully the prospect of him looking and being foolish. None of this made the slightest difference to our love. Till this phase passed, though, I have to confess to some anxiety.

Back home again, and as always delighted to be so, we returned to our rather cocoon-like way of life. I have often thought, looking back, that we were far too self-sufficient to each other. Friends were most welcome but we made little social effort. I have learned to my cost that to depend on happiness in this way is a dangerously sublime existence with the very real possibility of losing acquaintances and leaving oneself alone in an often unfriendly world; people just fall away into non-existence if one makes no effort to keep in touch; they have their own lives to live and work to do. One thing Anthony Pelissier was always telling me – but to which I wouldn't listen, thinking his words like some of his actions to be destructive – was 'Life has to be lived alone.' Even now I don't agree.

Our move to Portman Towers in 1969 was a great excitement. For furniture we dismantled one entire room at Hertfordshire House, deciding to leave it empty for the time being as it was mostly furniture that we had removed from our old flat in London. The only things that never seemed in short supply were books; we always needed more shelves in the country so that was no problem. What perplexed me in our new establishment was how to make a room look cosy and attractive without a fire-place. These modern blocks are really no more than overheated concrete squares with too many doors with atrocious-looking hinges, so there was much work to do. I realized I could do no more than make it quite agreeable, having no good structural bones to build upon.

It was now late November and we had planned on spending Christmas at Crowfields with the Canfields. The year before we had also promised to go but I had been ill, and having told the the staff at Hertfordshire House they would be free from us over Christmas we ended up by going to Blenheim. Bert Marlborough was more delighted than Michael, as he had been an admirer of mine since I was eighteen. Christmas at home would not have been Christmas anyhow for by now, sadly, Randolph had died. When he was so desperately ill I went down to his Suffolk house, which he called 'Country Bumpkins Ltd'. It was there he tackled the mammoth task of writing his father's life. When I went to visit him he had told me on the telephone that he had not raised himself from his bed for weeks.

I went by train, and on arriving at the small station of East Bergholt, where Randolph had said one of his secretaries or young gentlemen would meet me, I found nobody in sight. I was just about to search for a telephone when to my complete amazement a car appeared, drawing to a stop in an alarming and crooked fashion, attended with much noise of brakes hastily applied. At the wheel, attired in his pyjamas, was my host, looking deathly ill. We had our usual argument about who should continue driving, but this time it was short-lived. I soon became aware of what a vast and touching effort he had made in meeting me himself, typical of his bravery when facing death.

I drove him back to his house where we had a long, sad talk, knowing he had but a short time to live. Already he was finding it impossible to work and his greatest concern was to find a good biographer to continue with his father's life history. His closest friend in the country, Mrs Bevan, who fortunately loved him dearly and took care of him for many ailing years, came to dinner that evening and Randolph insisted on making a pretence of eating. When Mrs Bevan went home I persuaded Randolph to give in and return to his bed, which he did more than willingly.

I stayed two sad days and nights. On leaving him in Mrs Bevan's capable hands I knew I would never see him again. It was not long before he died, leaving quite a blank place in my life. We had corresponded or seen each other for so many years. Michael and I attended his memorial service, and as we left St Margaret's, Westminster, I commented to Ali Forbes how well Randolph's mother, Lady Spencer-Churchill, looked. Ali said to me, 'You must know what a tonic it is for a mother getting on in years to attend her own son's memorial service.'

Michael was sad, as he had grown fond of Randolph over the time he knew him. On many occasions he had reluctantly answered the telephone if I was out or in the bath and it was so often Randolph on the line (or else Bert Marlborough) that Michael used to say, 'Those Churchills always ring when you're unobtainable, and you never ring them back, which makes them call again.' Michael had a real phobia about the telephone at home. In the office he told me it was different, and anyway, something that had to be done. 'An invention for communication', he insisted on calling the telephone, as if it was something new in our lives. He had little love for it, unlike me, who spends far too much money on the telephone's diabolically expensive accounts.

22

Michael's Death

My brother Hugo's health began to break down in 1962–3. He was living near Perth, still in Scotland but not nearly as far north as he and his most devoted wife, Virginia, had lived before. This was a way up in the north-west tip of Scotland at a lovely place beside a loch called Little Ferry in Sutherland. Here they had a great tragedy. Their eldest son was drowned. They loved Little Ferry but in the end the memory was too much, making this house untenable, so they moved to Perthshire. After the real Highlands of Scotland, the other children thought Perthshire little more than the suburbs. They took some time to settle in their new home.

It was here that my brother had his first bout of ill-health. On one occasion he was taken to the hospital in Perth and from there on to the Royal Infirmary, Glasgow. He was then suffering from an acute form of pancreatitis. He was operated on and a large abscess was found to be causing the trouble. I visited him in Glasgow. The Royal Infirmary is one of the gloomiest buildings I have ever been in, but I believe medically it is advanced and then it was well equipped and had many excellent doctors, although I thought they and the nursing staff were grossly overworked.

Hugo was first in one of the many-bedded surgical wards; later he was in a side ward with one other bed, occupied by a rather meek man who was a civil airline pilot. Hugo always said that I entered his room and, without looking round me, flung off my fur coat, completely covering this already rather invisible man. This wasn't true, but my darling brother enjoyed making a perfectly ordinary situation into what he thought was a funny story. His version went: 'Quite unexpectedly, the side ward was filled with the smell of exotic scent and my nice meek companion patient was enveloped in mink.' My scent I will not argue about, as I have always used Balenciaga's Le Dix and therefore can't smell it myself. The mink was rubbish, as I would never wear mink by day except as a lining to a coat. I know too much on the subject of dress. Apart from anything else, a mink coat wrongly worn is the height of vulgarity and nearly always a sign of the *nouveaux riches*. (I remember with horror the sight of two women draped in mink in the West Indies in a temperature of eighty degrees.)

After my brother's illness in Glasgow he was, and looked, a very sick man for a while, although he did much work, writing both his novels and also television plays which he found an easier and quicker way to turn the pennies than the long arduous task of writing a book. I often wonder if that time in Glasgow wasn't the beginning of the deathly grip of cancer which caught and devoured him in 1969–70, but this is probably not the case as although the unpleasant abscess was slow to drain and heal, he appeared well for several years.

By the Christmas of 1967 Hugo and Virginia had moved further south into their first owned house, Elvington Grange, near York. We spent that Christmas with them and it was most enjoyable. Michael and my brother were much the same age and were devoted to each other for many years. That year my brother gave me for a present a large leather donkey, big enough to sit on. Round its neck it had a vast red label with the words, 'One of the few of your four-legged lovers that will not kick you.' Unlike Hugo, Michael was blessed with remarkably good health and I only once remember him having to go to bed with what I thought was flu. When the doctor arrived to see him I was almost too ashamed to take up his precious time for by now Michael was eating a hearty meal on a tray, accompanied by a bottle of claret.

My own health was far from good during the summer of 1968, mostly because of worsening migraine; any investigations I underwent seemed pointless as nothing could be found. The miracle that Dr Felix Mann had performed with his acupuncture needles and skill some six years previously no longer had any effect. I myself remained convinced that it was something wrong with my liver, having suffered the misery of hepatitis, or jaundice, twice. I was to prove right, but not for many years.

As I was ill in London at a time when I was due to interview a second gardener and his wife, Michael, who had never gone through such an ordeal, was very helpful. We were lucky that Pat and Jenny Duncan, with their baby, came to us and, though Michael never volunteered any details, their version of this interview was that they were terrorized by the dogs, particularly the two terriers. These made such a noise that both Pat and Jenny were transfixed, wondering if they would be bitten or even eaten alive. When I asked Michael how the afternoon had gone he passed it off as, 'The dogs did all the talking.' The true fact was that the interview had given the Duncans no idea about anything, but by good fortune they liked Michael and as for the rest they would just hope for the best. For over a year this proved to be hell, what with 'Old Grouch' on the one hand and, below stairs, a rather unpleasant Italian couple. There was still the ghost-like figure of Mrs Milne, my very ancient ladies' maid, but she was soon to depart to join her sister in Australia. This was one relief, as Michael couldn't stand the sight of the poor woman. The Italians, having proved how nasty they could be while we were in Barbados the following winter, departed, and I decided to get some Filipinos. One of them, Marcela, is still with me. The man borrowed money, then cried a good deal before leaving.

In the summer of 1969 Michael's brother, Cass, spent the weekend with us at Hertfordshire House. Cass had never seen Blenheim, and since Bert was always inviting us we decided to take him over to see the *son et lumière* at the palace. Bert was alone there and so he invited us to an early dinner. There was just time for me to show Cass Jr around before dinner, thus leaving Michael and Bert alone together for a short while. Michael later revealed that no sooner had we left than Bert pressed him for £20, the price of our tickets and his own. Michael agreed to pay but added, 'I do not carry the money with me, so I will ask Laura or send you a cheque.' Bert's response was, 'Oh! please don't ask Laura. She would find this rather strange. Send me a cheque.' I was somewhat surprised to hear this and when writing to Bert I added: 'Your thrift is well known and that is a kind word.' Bert was curious about money. Food and drink were freely available at Blenheim and in large quantities, but he always attempted to make me pay for the smallest pot plant or cutting from the garden. Of course I never did!

All being well at Hertfordshire House we planned on spending Christmas at Crowfields, flying to New York about mid-December. There were to be a few festivities and Michael felt he must attend the Harper and Row Christmas beano, which he hadn't done for many years.

One weekend in early December the telephone rang and it was Virginia, my sister-in-law. I knew my brother had not been well and I was anxious for news. She was calm, as is her way, but I could hear by her voice she was near to tears. To my horror and misery, she told me the worst one could possibly hear – that Hugo had been operated on in York and the surgeon had found cancer all round the liver ducts and that area, and had done nothing to eradicate this grave situation; furthermore, he had told Hugo how seriously ill he was, and why. I asked her if there was any hope. She replied that the only chance was to move my brother to London when possible and that she was already making enquiries through the doctors in York as to whether the famous surgeon, Sir Rodney Smith, if given all the necessary information, would be willing to re-operate in the hope of finding some way of removing the cancer-affected tissues.

There was little else to say at this deeply depressing moment. I then told Michael the ghastly news. I simply didn't know what to do with myself. Although by now it was nearly dark, I flung on a coat and took the dogs out, my mind in a haze. As I walked, the implications of Hugo's illness became ever more horribly clear; knowing as much as I did about medical matters made my fears grow and I could see little hope for my brother's recovery. On my return Michael looked as miserable as I felt; there was not much to say, and up till then I fear Michael had not accepted the cold hard fact that there could be little hope.

There were more immediate plans to discuss, as we both intended leaving for New York around 14 December. I suggested that Michael should go as arranged while I would await further developments and anyway join him for Christmas, never then believing Hugo would undergo further surgery. But Virginia telephoned quite unexpectedly quickly to say that Sir Rodney Smith would undertake performing another operation if Hugo was brought by ambulance to St George's Hospital in London when considered strong enough to withstand the journey. Some few days later my brother was able to endure the long and bumpy drive; he was most valiant about it, even making jokes when the ambulance driver lost his way. Yet all the way Hugo was on a drip and a continual blood transfusion.

Michael left for America and we had many transatlantic conversations all inside of one week. In the last talk we had I was forced to say I could not join him in New York on account of my brother's condition and the pending operation, to which Michael replied that he would take the evening flight home. I do not remember many details of that catastrophic time but I do recall that he told me to meet him at London Airport on the morning of 21 December and then rang again a few hours later to give me his flight number. By now Virginia and I were at the flat, taking turns to visit St George's Hospital where Hugo looked a mere grey shadow, the rest of him being skin and bone. I told him Michael was returning home instead of my going to New York, which seemed to bring a smile to his ashen face.

All now seems blanked out by what was to come, but I remember wondering on the morning I was to meet Michael if I should check the flight to see if it was on time. Then the telephone rang; there was much confusion and talk of Nova Scotia on the line, when amongst these strange noises a voice asked to speak to me. I have no idea how long this impersonal and unknown voice spoke, telling me that Michael was dead. He had suffered a massive heart attack in the aeroplane that was to bring him safely home to me. I could scarcely take in this heartbreaking news; I was completely stunned. My young, strong and so beloved Michael, my own darling Crumb, had died in the very way he often jokingly said he would – suddenly, without warning and without me.

The flat was empty, Virginia being at the hospital. I could not cry or ask any questions. I was alone and robbed of all I loved. Instinctively I knew what must be done. I rang America to break this ghastly news to Jane and Cass. By their time it was the middle of the night, so I gave them a terrible shock.

Soon after this, as always when I am in trouble, Barbie Agar arrived. To this day I haven't asked her how she knew. Various people seemed to turn up offering sympathy and help. Ivan and

Kate Moffat were both around. Ivan took charge of the practical things that had to be done. I remember few details of that day, except that Cass and Michael's brother went to Nova Scotia to bring Michael back to Hertfordshire House, where he was buried in the churchyard near to our house on Christmas Eve. His tomb bears the simple inscription 'The Adorable Canfield' which are the words of William Douglas-Home. The day before my daughter Sara was very sweet and came home to me.

Further kindness was shown to me by my ex-husband Eric Dudley who, immediately that he heard the news, telephoned me from Paris and was most sympathetic and understanding. He continued to do this for several days, then suddenly there was silence. Then Peter Ward, my stepson, rang and told me his father had died, six days after Michael's death. He asked me to accompany him to Paris for the funeral. This was a further shock and misery as Eric and I had remained close friends after the divorce except during the *Coat* incident. It seemed that all that had been vital to me in this life was being taken away at the same time.

I guessed that, although it was Christmas Eve, some close friends would come to the funeral so I was determined to make the house a bower of foliage and flowers, the way Michael liked to see it, even if he never would again. I was terribly alone and the memory of my mother's sudden disappearance from this earth came flowing back to me from over the years. The finality of death is the hardest part to bear, for there is no point in looking for hope. The death of someone as much loved as Michael is worse than any physical form of pain. So it was to be for me for a very long time; anything I did or any word I spoke was mechanical, like some wound-up toy. The days were bad enough, the nights often sleepless, however many pills I took; nothing closed my eyes from looking into a hopeless bleak future.

The Canfields brought me back to our London flat. I went to see my brother at St George's Hospital and Virginia and I had a quiet sad dinner later with the Canfields at the Connaught where they were staying. I could not swallow a mouthful of food; even now eating remains a pleasureless must.

Christmas Day was grim. All the decorations and festivities made me, if possible, more desperately unhappy. This is the way I still feel about that season of the year and I doubt if my attitude will ever change. I grieved, wondering how much grief my heart could endure, knowing myself to be far less resilient than when young. I was the one that felt deprived of all real life, although it was Michael who had died. I spent the day with the Canfields, who wished to visit St Paul's Cathedral, which I do not believe I had seen since it stood out alone among all the surrounding buildings which·had been blasted by air-raids.

At tea-time I visited my brother, who had undergone a further operation. He was a pathetic sight. All he could say to me by way of comfort was that while I must look upon Michael's death as a tragedy how much worse it would have been if he had died a lingering and painful death as he, Hugo, was about to face. At this moment in his desperate fight against cancer he saw no hope and longed for an easier way out of this harsh world. I had no idea what hope, if any, Rodney Smith held out. Looking at him as I did then on that very cruel Christmas, there seemed to be more tubes and bottles than flesh. Now I know that all the operation did was to allow an outlet for his bile, which was otherwise certain to poison him, in other words, his agony was prolonged and he was enabled to live another seven months.

After he left hospital he came to my flat. Never again did he look anything but a dying man. Virginia's courage was in some ways as remarkable as my brother's. Between them, they put up a very brave fight until the end. While still in hospital Hugo had some accountably fearful moments, when he told me I must help him by obtaining some pills, such as secret agents were equipped with. He kept telling me he knew they existed as he had written a short story about their use, going on to say that otherwise he must become strong enough to drive a car and find some deserted spot to shoot himself, as he had no wish to let his children see him run downhill anymore than they had already, nor did he want Virginia to have to nurse him endlessly to no avail.

I never heard him talk in this way again, although when visiting him in Yorkshire on many occasions I had no doubt in my own mind what he was feeling and when writing he would refer to himself as merely a husk. Towards the end I went more frequently to Elvington. It must have been his last letter to me in which he says 'I live in a half haze of omnipon and try not to brood on what the next phase will be. Please God, let it be short. There is now no point at all in being alive except now and again for half an hour – a pleasant talk with one of the children or Virginia. So I say good-night darling, love, Hugo.'

In many ways, my brother's death when it eventually came made me feel my own existence had little further point, for in some peculiar way his long and painful illness concentrated all my thoughts on him, therefore dwelling less on myself and on what to do about my own shattered life without Michael. I neglected all work, and found Hertfordshire House devastated by happy memories of days gone by, never to return.

During the winter of 1970 the Canfields and Babs and Dan Caulkins persuaded me to fly to New York and go with them to a hotel called Del Charro, in the town of La Jolla, which lies on the borders of California and Mexico; they wanted to do some health cure in Mexico. It was very sweet of them to invite me on this trip, and I accepted. After Michael's death our favourite neighbour, Frank Wigram, was my only solace before leaving for the USA and also on my return sometime in early February 1970. He lived only a stone's throw from Hertfordshire House and had shared so much of our contented and happy life there and during the last few months in London. All I remember of those weeks before leaving for America was certain people, like Anne and Michael Tree, taking me out to dinner, which can have been no fun for them. I could not be anything but heartbroken. There were others who tried. Anne Tree said something to me on the telephone I shall not forget, as it was so true: 'When someone like you is suffering from Michael's unthought-of death, your friends might leave you to grieve alone – treating you as a leper.' I now realize how difficult it is to know what to do with someone in the state I was in then.

One old friend who played his cards too soon and, for such an excellent bridge player, all wrong, was Bert Marlborough. He had always loved me but did not appreciate how much I needed to be alone and how little I would welcome any suitor. His well-meant behaviour made me angry and for quite a year I refused to see him.

With deep unhappiness came more ill-health and my migraines seemed to attack with a constant fury. On the flight to New York I was smitten with one so awful that I crouched in pain and sickness in the loo for the greater part of my journey. There was worse to come; when I arrived at Kennedy Airport a

formidable black man informed me my visa was out of date. I
visualized myself being sent to Ellis Island. Fortunately I telephoned Cass Canfield, who rescued me. Now I have a permanent visa, arranged by David Bruce when he was the US
Ambassador in London.

The Canfields had just sold their house in New York and
moved to an apartment in the UN Plaza. There was no room
for me, so it had been arranged I should stay at the Colony
Club. Here I collapsed for two days and nights from pain,
misery and utter loneliness. Then there were lawyers and bankers
to be seen, all the horrors attendant on a husband's death. After
this I spent a day or two at Crowfields. I remember little of this
visit except one incident, when Jane said she was going to a
monthly luncheon with some dozen local ladies in the Bedford
district. They each took their own sandwich lunch and met to
discuss a current and popular book. She didn't think I would wish
to go, but when she told me that the book (which they had all
supposedly read) was Antonia Fraser's *Mary Queen of Scots*, I
thought it better to go instead of brooding alone at Crowfields.
It seemed to me that few of the ladies present had really read
the book, so I suggested I might tell them something of Antonia's
personal and rather hectic life, married to a cousin of mine, Hugh
Fraser. This I proceeded to do. They appeared to be fascinated
by what I told them, and finished up more intrigued with the
author than with her book!

Soon after this I flew with the Canfields to Los Angeles and
motored to La Jolla. At the Del Charro Hotel I found that my
in-laws had a pleasant enough bungalow for four, while I had
another bedroom with a door like a loose-box for horses. For at
least two weeks I was mostly alone during the day while they
went off for the mysterious cure in Mexico. At moments at La
Jolla I was in complete despair, passing the time answering the
hundreds of letters of condolence I had received from people. It
was at least a way to fill the time but even then, try as I would,
I remained engulfed in my own misery.

Many people of interest lived at La Jolla, all quite advanced
in age. I think I am correct in saying there were something like
ten Nobel prizewinners. They found this place, with its wonderful climate, agreeable for life in retirement, knowing they would
find congenial company almost in their own back garden – one

man gave this as his reason for living in such a hideous spot. For this it was, with a vast six-lane highway running through it, on each side of which stood giant-sized advertisements or huge gasoline stations, ruining what once must have been lovely country. There were clearly no laws against total defacing all natural beauty. It was also very built-up, leaving one no place to walk.

We made some outings of interest, such as having luncheon at the world-famed medical centre, Salk, where the vaccine against poliomyelitis was discovered; doctors and students came there from all over the world. Jacques Cousteau came all the way from Los Angeles for dinner one night. I had met him before, and found him a man of considerable charm. I have always admired his underwater work and his literary abilities. We also went on several occasions to San Diego, which claims to have the largest and best-kept zoological gardens in the world. It certainly has an immense variety of animals and the bird sanctuary, with lush foliage and an artificial river running through it, was a wonderful sight, although I am not happy about zoos in general as I hate to see caged animals, even if in the bloodthirsty world we live in this may prove to be one of the few ways to preserve many species of wild life from extinction.

The hotel at San Diego prided itself on keeping up a Victorian atmosphere. A few times I went over the border. The poverty there was striking in its contrast to California. I would have liked to know more of Mexico, had I had the heart or health, but both had deserted me at that time. Otherwise I most certainly would have done this, for I had little to hurry home for – only my dogs and a much-dreaded empty house without Michael's longed-for presence. But there was one more urgent thought: to see my brother, knowing he could not linger much longer in a world that had left him, to use his own words, a mere husk, or in my words, not more than a shell where life once was.

I decided to leave La Jolla, where, although Jane was her usual sweet self, she was worried by Cass, as he was not in the best of health, and though Dan was fine and continued his obsessional golf, Babs, Jane's sister, was not too well. In my present state I feared I could only be a depressing influence. I flew to New York and spent a night or two at the Canfields' apartment, which was unoccupied except for one maid. I saw a few friends, but nothing seemed to have any purpose; everything I did only made me recognize more clearly my own despair. So I returned to England where at least I could see my brother in Yorkshire, for he had now vacated my flat and gone home to Elvington.

When I arrived back at Hertfordshire House it was cold in every sense. The house seemed bleak, the garden covered in snow. The dogs were noisy in their delight at seeing me, and Jenny and Pat did all they could to alleviate my loneliness. Frank Wigram was a wonderful help, so much so that there came a time when we briefly contemplated marriage for the sake of companionship. But the seeds of rumour were sown and blown up by William Hickey's column in the *Daily Express*, much to Bert Marlborough's rage, as he always remained in hopes that I would one day marry him. So soon after Michael's death it seemed natural to be with Frank, as we had known each other so well over many years. As to marriage, it would not have worked out, for he actually enjoys the privacy of living alone and is very busy with his work so that he has no fear, or even feeling, of loneliness. His mother lives next door and he also thrives, when at home, on the constant if not always welcome sound of the bell coming from his antique shop. He derives interest and amusement from his customers and we remain great friends.

23

I Burn My Boats

The following two years I spent in an attempt to make myself believe that it was possible to live at Hertfordshire House alone. Friends stayed at weekends but usually left on Sunday night, throwing me back on the fact of my own inadequacy and never-ceasing memories of happy days gone by. When summer came I would try to exhaust myself by working long hours in the garden, sometimes as long as the evening light persisted. This proved hopeless, ending in more sleepless nights often to be followed by a migraine. I spent more time in my London flat because it scarcely had time to remind me of Michael, whereas in the country, at the place we had both loved and created between us, I found life hard to bear.

I did stay, reluctantly, one or two weekends at Blenheim, and Bert remained constant in his wish to marry me. I was fond of him but, as I frequently explained, Blenheim was so terribly gloomy. This was not only my view but that of the first Duke's Duchess, Sarah. It was built as a monument, not a house to live in. At times Bert would try to counter this statement by quoting the many thousands of paying tourists who flocked to Blenheim each year. But he did not see that this made it even worse than gloomy by turning him and his friends into exhibits, like freaks or animals to be gazed at. I felt this most acutely when playing croquet in the public eye, surrounded by a chain to keep the not unnaturally inquisitive visitors off the lawn. I thought at any moment they would throw us stale bread or nuts as in the zoo. The park was always open to the public and the palace for certain months in each year.

Secretly, I believe, Bert was in agreement with me. His reason for continuing to inhabit Blenheim – or as he came (through me) to call it, 'the Dump' – was a real fear of being the first Duke not to reside there. For despite being a wonderful example of workmanship, it was a mausoleum. The private quarters were situated in the north-east corner of this monstrosity in stone, for the rather beautiful and interesting long library runs the full length of the south side, giving an aspect to please the eye: formal gardens and, beyond, the lake and park which have an undoubted magnificence and beauty. The library, when in normal use before the war, was never exactly cosy but it did have virtues such as sunshine, and there were usually many house guests to bring some life to this vast room, unlike the present day when, at different times, it gives the impression of being dead, or slightly musty, or crammed like a sardine-can with a polyglot mass of tourists.

The park has many beautiful aspects, with lovely avenues of trees and a very fine bridge crossing a long stretch of water, which is seen at its best when one arrives at the gateway in most constant use. Bert, his guests and the public approach the palace this way through what is historically called the Triumphal Arch. The private entrance has a sepulchral air and, even given money and a free hand, I always felt it to be beyond my imagination to see how this only entrance to the private part could in some way be made more cheerful. Arriving visitors had no choice but to descend a few steps into what appeared to be a dark dungeon and from here to be confronted by a lift which deposited them on to what was really the ground floor. Here were a chain of sitting-rooms and intercommunicating doors, a dining-room, and Bert's own bedroom adjacent to a larger bedroom, ill-proportioned and dark, which had a particularly melancholy air, the walls being hung with tapestry relating to the first Duke's military glories. The overmantel was huge and heavy in design, one of Vanbrugh's worst efforts in my eyes. Above this was a larger-than-life portrait of Queen Anne surveying the room with the distaste it so well deserved.

Having given my view of Blenheim, it is understandable that when Bert and I resumed our long-standing friendship, I preferred him to stay at Hertfordshire House, or more frequently saw him in London. We often discussed my feelings about Blenheim and I left no doubt in his mind as to how I felt about the palace and, if at a later stage I should ever consent to marriage, as to the many changes I would insist on making. To everything I said he acquiesced, saying I could do as I pleased so long as I would marry him. I knew this would then mean that I must take on the onerous task of improving many things and all the other duties entailed in helping the people who live and work on an estate of this size. I took for granted the long-overdue redecoration and the total changes I would make in the private rooms in the north-east corner where no sunlight ever seemed to penetrate, with the one exception of the Grand Cabinet, a room mostly used for playing bridge. On the floor was a very beautiful Savonnerie rug and there was some very good furniture, including a beautiful Reisner desk worth many thousands of pounds. The adjoining room had a lovely painting by Stubbs, not of a horse as one might expect but of a recumbent lion.

During the years of 1970 and 1971 I continued to battle with life alone at Hertfordshire House. The house appeared too large when by myself; even the garden needed more labour. Michael had done so much towards its general upkeep. Another factor was that the heart and enthusiasm were no longer in me. I know Pat Duncan felt the same, for although he had not known Michael long and his feelings were obviously not as painful as my own, nonetheless he had already become deeply fond of Michael, as had his wife Jenny. As time went on, the dice seemed loaded against my being able to remain in the only house and garden I had ever really loved, as it brought back so many memories. My life became no more than an existence; I seemed to be, at best, half alive, but I decided I would make no decisions over Hertfordshire House for the time being.

I made many journeys to visit my dying brother in Yorkshire. He looked dreadfully ill, but had not as yet taken wholly to his bed. He continued to write television plays. He even did some gardening and played childish tennis. This was the most pathetic of all, for before his illness he had been a strong and excellent player of the game. I think he suffered much pain. Not that painkilling drugs were ever withheld, but he had a strong desire to feel clear-headed, not muzzy or unlike himself, till towards the end of the summer of 1970, when he knew there was little time left. He was anxious about the welfare of Virginia and his four children; although Frances, the eldest, was grown up he was fearful over money and their future when he, the breadwinner, had gone.

He entered for a time a rather charming nursing home situated by the beautiful York Minster Close. There was nothing the medics could do; the cancer within him was growing apace. These were tragic times for all his loving family. Bert Marlborough took pains to send bunches of home-grown muscat grapes, and grouse from Scotland when the shooting season began, although he only knew Hugo through me. It was both kind and thoughtful and I was grateful to him. My brother's life just petered out that autumn. It was a mercy for him, though a terrible loss for his family. The last time I saw him, not long before his death, I secretly hoped his agony of mind and body was nearly at an end.

After my brother's funeral, which took place at a little village church near his wife's home, Skipworth in Yorkshire, attended by a few people but with mountains of flowers, I returned home to my London flat to ponder on my own loneliness, having been robbed in under a year of the three people closest to my heart.

It was only now that I began to wonder whether at some time in the future I should not perhaps accept Bert Marlborough's proposal of marriage. I knew that he had loved me for a long time and that he was lonely. I was fond of him and saddened by the way his hospitality was taken for granted by many who cared little for him. Blenheim, gloomy and out of date as it was, would be a worthwhile challenge to take on and, as Bert continually reminded me, I could make him happy.

All through that heartbreaking year of 1970 I saw much of my friend Ivan Moffat, a successful film script writer here and in Hollywood. Then to my great sadness he returned to America, because of the lack-lustre film situation in England. Life became even lonelier when Ivan was gone. I often thought of extracts from my brother's letters. Once he wrote saying,

Loneliness – which is no joke – and probably hell for you – as it is for me. Indeed I would go into the streets if I were a lonely woman – even at 80. Frances [his eldest daughter] sometimes reminds me of you; start *showing her* where the hairpin bends actually lead to crashes – and where they don't! And teach her that she (like you) has been born with blinkers, fangs and a heart as soft as butter. I do my best!

Sometime late in 1970, still deeply unhappy and ill, I entered an international backgammon contest run at Aspinall's Club in that one remaining beautiful house in Berkeley Square. At these highly professional competitions which take place all over the world, the evening before the play begins there is an auction for the prospective competitors and the well-known players are 'bought' for high prices. Being someone unknown I fetched just £100 and then only because Robert Heber-Percy bought me! I believe Robert was offered a high price for me, which I begged him to accept, being by now a mass of nerves and certain I would lose. He would have none of that, treating me like a highly trained racehorse, bringing me back to my flat to rest, saying, 'Lie down and try to drink some tea. I will pick you up when you are due to play the next contest.' In spite of all his care I failed him and lost, though I reached the semi-final to everyone's amazement.

I spent the summer of 1971 at Hertfordshire House. From time to time a car would arrive from Blenheim with instructions 'to collect Mrs Canfield'. Sometimes a member of Bert's family was part of the delegation, in which case I invited them to lunch and then despatched them back to the palace without me. But once or twice I did go to stay at Blenheim and Bert came over to Hert-fordshire House, which he enjoyed, though he complained that my croquet lawn was not as billiard-table smooth as his.

I recall his many grunts when playing bridge; he looked at his opponent's hands, which I appreciated, having watched my grandfather cheat so many years ago. But there was a difference; although Bert's eyes certainly wandered from his own cards, he was also an excellent player and nearly always won. This was where my grandfather came to grief. If people must cheat at bridge they should do it well; there are many methods, such as tone of voice, or counting points by lip movement. A beloved friend of mine does this. His name is Colonel Miles Reid and not long ago he wrote a book called *Last on the List* – for most people he would be last on their list as a partner for a game of bridge. I love to play with him; it takes only a trice to know every card he holds!

In August 1971 Barbie Agar persuaded me to go with Herbert and her to Venice. The plan was to stay at Hotel Cipriani where she said I could bathe and lie about in the sun, and where there would be plenty of people we knew to play bridge with in the evenings, leaving time for sight-seeing if I wished. I decided to accompany them and Miles Reid, my favourite bridge player. We did meet many people, including Tom and Diana Mosley. Strange to say I had not met them before. I found Diana enchanting company and still very beautiful, and Tom fascinated me by walking up and down the terrace, deep in thought, taking his daily exercise. Sometimes I saw him returning alone from the Piazza San Marco in the evenings dressed in a mackintosh and a trilby, after dinner with Prince Clary or some other meeting. He always entered the hotel by the swimming-pool entrance, paused, checked his watch by the clock and then marched up to bed. Robert Heber-Percy was then staying at the Villa d'Ariolla with Kit Lambert, who was enjoying the success of his pop group The Who, though now I fear all the millions he thought were his have gone with the wind.

On this first of several post-war visits to Venice, I met, or rather introduced myself to, someone called Colonel Alexander Young. On arrival at that rather shabby and unattractive airport for the millions who throng this beautiful city I found myself both amused and surprised to see, amidst the crowd waiting to claim their luggage, an upright military type of man collecting from the mass of tatty present-day luggage two immensely large suitcases, almost of the vintage type long since vanished. I remarked on this to the then unknown man, who was, I noticed, travelling with Loelia and Martin Lindsay (Sir Martin and Lady Lindsay) and Colonel Reid. When I reached the hotel Barbie asked me if I had previously known the man to whom I had spoken about his luggage. I replied, 'No,' although by then the Lindsays had introduced him to me formally. The Cipriani *vaporetto* was waiting for the Agars, Miles and myself and it also transported the others, who were staying at a small *pensione*. Alex Young soon left there for the Gritti. I should think he had to, as I doubt if his luggage let alone his person would have found accommodation there.

The holiday started badly for all of us. Loelia took a frightful tumble over some ropes as she was embarking on the *vaporetto*, damaging a knee and nearly landing in that brackish water near the airport. My head was giving pain which meant, I knew, that at any moment I would be laid low with a dismal migraine. Loelia I had known all my grown-up life; I remember her coming to

Innes, my Tennant grandparents' house in Scotland, when she was Miss Ponsonby, before she became one of the many merry wives of Westminster by marrying Bendor, Duke of Westminster. By the time we met in Venice she had recently married Martin Lindsay who, it transpired, was a cousin of 'the mysterious military man', as some friends of mine have described Alex Young without having met him. He is not remotely mysterious; in some ways military, yes, if only from being a colonel and having been educated at Cheltenham College, which, until I knew Alex, I had always thought of as an academy for young ladies.

I spent two weeks or more lapping up the sunshine, spending the mornings round Cipriani's Olympic-sized swimming pool and doing a certain amount of sightseeing in the late afternoon. The colonel appeared to take a liking to me, in spite of introducing me to a word in the English language that I have little use for – decorum! We ended those two weeks by becoming great and lasting friends; he has been kind and generous ever since, through much illness on my part, which has been difficult and tiresome for him and isolating for me.

In Venice Loelia and Martin overdid the sunbathing, particularly Martin, who was born with a skin unable to withstand the penetrating rays of the Italian sunshine. There came a day when the Lindsays' small room at their *pensione* was so unbearable that they had to change their clothes one at a time for fear of touching each other, their skins being so burnt that the slightest touch produced a scream of agony. There was always a group of friends for the pre-luncheon drink most of us indulged in, though Tom Mosley did not join us nor indeed did Herbert Agar. While Tom took his morning exercise, Herbert, having bathed, preferred to enjoy his own special drink inside the hotel where the barman, having known him for years, just named it 'the Agar'. I was frequently taken to the mainland to Harry's Bar, which I personally think to have the best food in Europe, with a crowded amusing atmosphere.

Robert Heber-Percy and I had an adventurous night on the town, ending rather disastrously in the early hours of the morning. The regular ferry system between Cipriani's and the San Marco pier ceased its operation at midnight. We could find no taxi *vaporetto*. At last I managed to hail a disgruntled water taxi-man and got Robert aboard. He had given up and was lying half

asleep on the edge of the Grand Canal. I then had to drop Robert
at the Villa d'Ariolla. He was slightly drunk and gave the
vaporetto no time to stop. He jumped on to the slippery paving
stone at the side entrance off the Grand Canal, from where he
hoped to enter the Villa. He felt no pain at the time, so I continued
back to Cipriani's. The next morning Robert was in a bad way,
with many bruises, a damaged back and, I feel sure, a cracked
rib. In his usual way, he insisted that no treatment was necessary
until he returned to England.

I reached home in September; my health was temporarily
better and being very sunburnt made me feel and look less sickly
than before. I was now dining in London with Bert on his brief
visits to his house in Shepherds Close, usually in midweek. For
some unknown reason we always went out to one particular restaurant, the Mirabelle. He was kind and genuinely wished to
make me feel life was worth living. I promised him I would go
with him to visit his eldest daughter, Sarah Roubanis, in Jamaica
after the Blenheim shooting parties had ended in the winter.

So in early February Bert, myself and his faithful chauffeur/
valet Bramwell set off for Jamaica to stay with Sarah at her house
overlooking Montego Bay and not far from Bert's own house,
which was let that year. Sarah was bubbling with high spirits
when we arrived and the house, garden and swimming pool
seemed very inviting. Unlike Barbados, there were endless long
and late dinner parties; some of the social round I enjoyed, but,
my health being far from good, I stayed in bed many an evening,
well looked after by the faithful Bramwell. The mornings were
a delight, bathing, reading in the sun by the pool and talking to
David Green, the great expert on Blenheim, who was helping Bert
write a book of memoirs which have never seen the light of day.
Sarah was always busy with her farm and taking quite an active
part in politics. She has endless energy. Theo Roubanis played
his guitar and sang melancholy Greek songs for which he has
talent. Bert was in good form, but anxious about me and whether
I would ever marry him. I could only say I had not yet made
up my mind.

After nearly three weeks in the Roubanis's house I felt restive.
Sarah was going off to New York and I told Bert I would leave
with her and pay a visit to the Canfields and other friends. He
was dismayed but there was no argument. David Green was

almost as disappointed. 'You can't go off like that,' he said anxiously. The day before we left, Sarah asked me to accompany her and some other people to look at one or two farms she was debating buying. We drove off in the early morning to prospect various properties. The first stop was in beautiful country, a derelict but wonderfully positioned farmhouse and land. As we all scrambled out of the car I spotted a fine horse all tangled up by a rope he was tethered to. When I had gone to the poor animal's aid and untangled him, I couldn't see where Sarah and her friends had gone. There was a kind of tunnel side entrance to the house. Without thinking I ran into it, oblivious of a concrete beam which crossed above me. The next thing I remember is lying in a pool of blood amongst chicken droppings and pig dung. Then I heard voices calling me. I must have been knocked out by hitting my head on this unexpected supporting beam.

It was some minutes before I was able to stagger out into the gleaming sun and when Sarah found me I was a dejected sight, for my shorts and shirt were bespattered with blood. She inspected my head, which had a nasty cut, and we decided to wash it and then tie a scarf round my head to stem the flow of blood. Feeling somewhat dazed and very stoic, I continued our journey, not returning to Montego Bay till evening. Before ascending the hill to the Roubanis's house, Sarah suddenly said, 'We're very near a doctor's house. I think we'd better let him have a look at your head.' The doctor was in his bath, preparatory to dining out. When he appeared he took a look at my by now blood-sodden head and with a good deal of tut-tutting said he must have a drink before he stitched me up. I felt it was *I* who needed the drink but that was not allowed, for I'm sure he thought, and I knew, that I was concussed. He was very jovial and there were many jokes and laughter in what seemed an eternity before he at last produced his medical kit. He called for scissors and proceeded to cut an unnecessary amount of my hair, much to my displeasure. Then, with a large and antiquated needle, he put eight stitches in my head, prescribed rest, and said the 'needlework' would dissolve!

It was quite late when we reached home. Bert had worked himself up into a state, rightly saying we should have telephoned. When he saw the stitches, which looked and felt like barbed wire, he thought we'd had a car smash. When he had heard the true story he said, 'You're mad and can't possibly leave for New York tomorrow.' But I did just that though I was feeling rather peculiar, and after two or three hectic days there I decided I'd best fly home. Pat Duncan met me at London airport and drove me home to Hertfordshire House. As is always the case after a long flight, the hours get mixed up, but it suited me as I was more than ready for bed. My head was uncomfortable and any long flight was apt to start a migraine. Having calmed down the beloved dogs I retired to my bedroom, not wanting anything to eat. I took sleeping pills, but the telephone rang and as I put my hand out to answer I felt muzzy and exhausted. After a short conversation I replaced the receiver. It was then I realized it was only about 11 p.m. and that I felt hungry. Flinging on my dressing-gown, surrounded by excited dogs, I went towards the back stairs which were very steep with quite a long descent to the area between pantry and kitchen. Somehow I stumbled – either over one of the terriers or just through being dopey from the pills I had taken – and the result was a crashing fall. I landed on my chin, cutting my lip and hurting my jaw. There seemed to be blood dripping from somewhere so with a kitchen towel I vaguely mopped my face which was painful all over.

I was still determined to make the scrambled eggs and so began to explore the kitchen, but I felt too pained to cook and so retired to bed. This accident necessitated an ambulance ride to Stoke Mandeville Hospital, where I was told I had fractured my jaw on both sides. I was given a room there, but after Jamaica I found it very cold. While in the hospital I was much surprised to receive a telephone call from Bert, thinking he was still overseas. He was both anxious and cross, saying he could not keep pace with my accidents or whereabouts! I assured him I was not badly injured, apart from my fractured jaw which made it hard to talk.

The next morning I decided to ask Pat and Jenny to come to my window (which they knew, Jenny having travelled to the hospital with me). I would then discharge myself from Stoke Mandeville without further red tape as I was having no treatment and would recover far better at home with liquidized food under Dr Gibbs's care. This little scheme went smoothly, though the hospital staff may have been bewildered by my sudden disappearance! My fractures took some time to mend and it was over a year before the unpleasant cracking sound on opening my mouth completely vanished.

That summer of 1971 many friends came to Hertfordshire House, but try as I did I could not get over my unhappiness there. I slowly decided the place must be sold. This was the second effort I had made to settle in the house I loved but it was no more successful than the first. In August I went to Venice again, and on my return after long discussions with Bert I finally said I would marry him the following year, but only after he had asked his son, Sunny Blandford, if he would move from his own house and live at the palace. In this way, Bert thought I would be less reluctant to marry him. There was also a brief thought given to us both living at my house, but that I couldn't have borne. I consulted my nephew Caspar about my plans to marry and asked him what I should do. He replied characteristically, 'What does it matter what one does in life?'

So it came about that the word travelled privately that Hertfordshire House might be up for sale. Very few people came to look over my much-loved house. The property boom had not begun, and I had not advertised. One young couple who came were Diana and David Heimann; Diana was Iain Macleod's daughter. They seemed very keen to buy and I asked them to stay for a weekend. Robert Heber-Percy was also present. He thought me foolish to sell so he spent the weekend making derogatory remarks about my house, but his behaviour didn't have the smallest effect; the Heimanns decided to buy.

My last house party was sometime in October. All was arranged and everyone arrived. Alas, I fell ill and was forced to remain in bed from the Friday to Monday. It was then I signed the contract for the sale of Hertfordshire House at far too low a price. I felt my boats were burnt.

24

Blenheim

The following Christmas I spent at Blenheim. It was then that Bert gave me the well-known family pearls, said to have been at one time in the possession of Catherine the Great. The Marlborough pearls are large and perfect as pearls should be. Later I had them re-strung with a pretty diamond clasp Barbie Agar gave me as a wedding present.

On Christmas night there were forty people for dinner. This was the one occasion in the year when the banqueting hall was in use; otherwise it was for the public to gaze upon. To my mind, Blenheim now appeared magnificent in an historical way. At dinner two large fires blazed with yule logs; it really was 'glitter and gold' (Madame Balsan, Bert's mother, who was born Consuelo Vanderbilt, wrote a book called *The Glitter and the Gold* (Heinemann, London, 1953)). The vast table was heaped with a sumptuous feast of highly decorated cold food, boar's head, pheasants with their tail feathers like flags to call attention to their poor aspic-covered bodies, lobsters with their red claws in abundance amongst this culinary display. The dinner plates were golden colour, in reality silver gilt. The chairs were large and comfortable, if cumbersome, but at least suitably regal in appearance for a festive Christmas dinner. I was seated opposite Bert. This was the way, he insisted, the 'place à table' should be whenever I visited Blenheim. Now it mattered no longer, for it was common knowledge that we were to marry. All Bert's children, with the exception of Sarah, went to Blenheim for Christmas, bringing with them their respective husbands, wives and children, so was a real family affair – the way Christmas should be when possible.

It was arranged in the new year that we would marry at Caxton Hall on 26 January 1972. This date was fixed so as not to interfere with shooting parties, the last shoot (consisting mostly of tenants and local friends) taking place on the twenty-eighth. In early January I discussed my wedding dress with two gay and charming French ladies, Madame Nina and Madame Raymonde, to whom I am devoted and who in those days worked at London's Christian Dior, my old stamping ground. Now they are with Hardy Amies. I asked them to make me a simple scarlet velvet dress, which they did. It was essential that the velvet was of the best quality; Madame Raymonde's cutting and fitting were perfect, I made certain adjustments as I always do, and we were all well pleased. I had in mind that this dress would be suitable to wear when I made my first speech in the old riding school at Blenheim, where the annual staff party was held at the end of January.

I became calm and happier than for a long time; having taken the decision I was fully prepared for my new role in life. I even thought of my plans for taking down the tapestries and removing Queen Anne's portrait from my future bedroom. I spent time with Angus Menzies in his department at the General Trading Company, choosing silks and other stuff to cover the walls, having first explored a way of 'battening' the walls of my bedroom to make it smaller, better proportioned, and suitable for my own furniture, the rest of which was to be stored in the Audit room at Blenheim, for it was vast and could with ease hold the entire contents of my house. Another necessity was to find a cottage on the estate that was to the liking of Pat and Jenny Duncan. They chose to live in Bladon, being near the school for their daughter. It was a foolish choice, as I well knew, for the place is crowded with tourists visiting Winston Churchill's grave for the greater part of the year. In such ways I was fully occupied, leaving no time to brood on the prospect of leaving Hertfordshire House, for here I had developed a love–hate relationship.

The twenty-sixth soon arrived. The brief ceremony at Caxton Hall took place at noon, attended by members of my family and Bert's. A register office marriage has no drama, there is little resemblance to a church wedding but nonetheless it is a solemn and serious event. I arrived at this well-known (but now non-existent) place of marriage on the dot of twelve o'clock. There was a large crowd of well-wishers and others unknown to me

outside. Mrs Evans, Michael's and my daily lady from Eaton
Square days, rushed at me when my car drew up, planting a lov-
ing kiss on my face. Then Sunny Blandford and Charles Spencer-
Churchill hastened up to me saying, 'For God's sake hurry.
Daddy's already in quite a state. He's afraid you won't appear.'
I said I was punctual and what was all the fuss about? After the
ceremony Bert and I and a few close relations went to Robin and
Rosie Muir's flat – a sad mission, for Bert's son-in-law was soon
to die of cancer. He already looked deathly ill but wanted us to
have a glass of champagne with him as he was far too ill to come
to luncheon. Young, intelligent and charming, he was dead a few
weeks later.

Then there was a luncheon party in a private room at the Connaught for fourteen relations, including Sara and her husband,
my sister Ann, and Martin and Gay Charteris. It was a heart-
warming feast cooked by a chef who had been my husband's at
Blenheim for many years. His parting gift had been an intricate
and detailed model of the palace, made in icing sugar, and to this
day it is to be seen encased in glass in the centre of the long library.
Our wedding luncheon was not prolonged; delicious food and
wine followed by a cake which was a work of art made by the
same chef. It seemed vandalism to cut it. After this Bert wished
to make a short speech. As he rose to his feet I thought it a mis-
taken idea on his part. On listening to him, however, I found
myself near to tears for, after saying a few words, he fixed his
eyes on me and attempted to sing that old lyric 'I shan't be happy
till I make her happy too'.

When the celebrations were over we drove to my flat to collect
some things before going on to spend the night at Hertfordshire
House. Next morning Bert, aided by Bramwell and my staff,
packed up the contents of the cellar and Michael's cigars, some
of which went in the boot of my husband's Rolls-Royce while
the rest were left for collection another day, like my white Mercedes two-seater car. That evening Bert went to a safe he had
outside the old delapidated study off his bedroom. He returned
saying, 'You thought I wasn't giving you a wedding present, but
here it is.' As I took the heavy package from him, I said, 'I hadn't
given it a thought.' Opening the tissue paper I found two very
beautiful gold boxes, encrusted with small charms made with diamonds and other precious stones. I remembered these attractive

objects well. His first wife, Mary, had collected and been presented with these tiny jewels in England and America. In fact I had given her one of the charms myself. They varied from miniature horses and their shoes to trees, bells and all sorts of things, and they were added to by Cartier's, where the two boxes came from. He then said to me, 'Those are yours forever, whereas the pearls are only for your lifetime' – this because they were heirlooms. I was delighted with his present. One I used for cigarettes, the other as a powder case, making my bag very heavy, but as they were a delight to look at I didn't mind.

The weather was very cold, so I was already beseeching Bert not to shoot during the next two days as he suffered from diverticulitis. At the time he agreed. I also pointed out we had a busy time ahead with Charles and Jane's son, Rupert, being christened on the Sunday. The following weekend was also important, for the staff party took place and another gathering for the tenants. Alas, he disregarded my advice, taking part in the two final days of shooting cock pheasants.

My dogs were a big problem as Bert's boxer, Ben, did not take kindly to other dogs. I had managed to persuade my terrier Russy and Ben to be on speaking terms if somewhat reluctantly. Jack had died the previous summer from a brain tumour. Michael's by now ancient labrador Crumb I thought kinder to put to sleep, but I had bought him a lovely wife, Lena, before leaving for Jamaica in 1971. During that summer she had produced eight puppies which we had reared with some difficulty as their mother, being only a year old, was somewhat negligent. All but one bitch, Linda, which I kept, had found good homes so I was not worried about Linda and her mother moving to Blenheim, knowing Ben would not think of fighting with ladies. Russy went everywhere with me and I thought that, with luck, he and Ben would settle down in an amicable fashion, although there had already been one brawl between them. Miss Hickey (now Mrs Parncutt), Bert's faithful and intelligent secretary, and I had avoided a really nasty incident in the nick of time. Jack Russell terriers have no fear and are pugnacious in character. Unfortunately they never consider the size and weight of an opponent, even of a boxer like Ben, which made me constantly apprehensive.

Bert had undergone an operation for diverticulitis some five years earlier. His surgeon then removed a certain amount of affected gut. Since then, provided he didn't eat foolishly or catch cold, he was in good health. It was therefore with horror I heard he had gone shooting on the Saturday morning in the bitter cold of an English January. Although he would only admit to feeling the cold, I suspect that it was that morning which caused him to have a long-drawn-out illness. He had already arranged to go into Sister Agnes's (better known as the King Edward VII Hospital) for a check-up on 7 February. I refused to let him go out again in the afternoon, but in fact I don't think he had any wish to. During the following days he neither felt nor looked well.

We remained at Blenheim that week. My bedroom and all the other alterations I was to make were planned, but work had not begun. My maid, Jenny, came over to the palace, bringing some of my clothes. Hertfordshire House still being intact, I told her there was no point in bringing many things till there were more cupboards and a total change of my rooms, for by this time I had arranged that Bert and I would have moved upstairs to a suite known as the Tower rooms. I asked her if she and her husband Pat would like to attend the staff party the following Saturday, 5 February, as they were not due to move to their new cottage in Bladon for another month. By this time the removal vans would have cleared Hertfordshire House, and Greggie, my second Filipino servant, the dogs and all else movable would then arrive at Blenheim. It was Marcela's chance to remain in my London flat at Portman Towers where she still is, never having liked Greggie.

As this first week of marriage progressed I became more concerned over my husband's health. When the day of the large staff party came he wasn't really ill, but I fear he felt far from well. Towards evening he asked me if I would mind being accompanied by his eldest son, Blandford, and the estate agent, Mr Murdock, for he didn't feel up to venturing outside to the old riding school where the party was being held. I knew full well how much he was looking forward to seeing me, his new Duchess, meet the many generous people who kept up the palace and the estate and who had given Bert and me a wonderful collection of presents. On thinking back, I wonder if in my speech I expressed my gratitude sufficiently. I wore the dress I had been married in and told all those present I wished it had been possible for them to have attended our wedding. I also said that in future they should bring their problems to me in person and I would always do my best to sort out any troubles they might have; that as yet I only knew a few people in this crowded place but before long I would know everyone individually.

The next day within the palace we had another gathering for the Blenheim tenants. This time Bert seemed better and made a speech, as I did too. He said, 'I'm getting on in years but feel happy at the thought – should anything happen to me, I would leave you in good hands,' looking at me. Everyone I met at these two parties was so welcoming to me that I retired to bed feeling, at long last, there was once more great point in living.

After the parties I turned all my attention and thoughts to Bert. Being due for a medical check-up on Monday had changed his mood. Before he had thought it an unnecessary, tiresome two days to be undergone; now when the day arrived and we were driving to London he was filled with doubts, rather silent and depressed. On arrival he wished to go to my flat for tea instead of going straight to the Edward VII Hospital where he was due at 4 p.m. I was in favour of this, knowing nothing would be done by way of investigations that night. Also, my flat being in George Street, it was fortunately close to the hospital. We reached our destination around 6 p.m. My faithful and intelligent dog Russy came too. I was amazed that no one told me dogs were not permitted, as I knew this was the case! While Bramwell unpacked the few things needed for a short stay, Bert sat in a chair and Russy and I lay on the bed. This was to be the pattern of our lives for many weeks. We brought heaps of flowers from Blenheim which I arranged as best I could with the limited receptacles available. Then, partly to amuse Bert, I replaced Russy's collar with the Marlborough pearls, which not only fitted but became him well. Bert muttered something about me being crazy, but laughed. It took his mind off his surroundings.

During the following days, tests were made but there was no question of Bert leaving hospital. His stomach was still very upset, which I put down to catching cold and a worsening state of diverticulitis. So from 7 February till the twenty-seventh my days were fully occupied. I went to the hospital each morning and stayed on for luncheon (Bert refused to touch hospital food) which Bramwell brought from Bert's house at Shepherd's Close, which by now Bert had given to me to sell or keep. After luncheon

I left Bert to sleep or rest, returning at tea-time, having either taken Russy to the Park or doing whatever else had to be done. Then I used to walk Bert up and down the passage as this was good for him. He didn't enjoy this much until he discovered that he could look through the small windows into the other rooms. After that it became something of an adventure, his curiosity sometimes getting the better of him.

On several occasions I nipped down to Hertfordshire House to see how the dismantling was going and once I spent a night at Blenheim, giving Bramwell a chance to see his family, also to take detailed measurements with Angus Menzies and look at patterns for carpets, curtains and wall coverings. It was the only night I slept away. For dinner I asked Angus, Robert Heber-Percy and Frank Wigram, so we had an enjoyable evening of bridge afterwards.

On 27 February I sent Bramwell home for the weekend to have a well-earned rest. On that Sunday Bert seemed better, so I drove him to a luncheon party at Angus's flat in Eaton Place. Here we found a large and mixed bunch of people. To my delight, Bert enjoyed himself enormously and we didn't return to the Edward VII till nearly five o'clock. He was at his best and most amusing during luncheon. It was a great success and his only outing from hospital. He even derived pleasure from constant criticism of my driving!

Soon after this Mr Dawson seemed worried about the almost static condition of his patient. Mr Dawson sent Bert to a clinic for further unpleasant daily tests after which he returned exhausted to the Edward VII and instantly fell asleep. Shortly after these dreaded visits to other doctors, Mr Dawson said Bert had Crohn's disease and it was decided to call in the surgeon who had operated on him some five years previously, Mr Lloyd Davis, and a Mr Todd. It was now the end of February. I sensed a certain doubt and disagreement between surgical and medical advisers, as I was able to half-listen to their discussions as they studied the X-rays in a room down the passage; my fears mounted.

On 2 March they told Bert and me that they had decided to operate. Bert was still taking his walks up and down the passage. He was not in any pain, just bored. The news of the operation, to be performed on 4 March, came as a great shock to him. I was not in favour of it but there was nothing I could do, except become increasingly fearful of the outcome. Bert only feared the possibility of cancer – the disease from which Mary had died. I did all I could to assure him there was no question of this, which was the truth.

On the day of the operation most of his family had luncheon with me as we awaited news from the hospital. The time lagged interminably. I rang the hospital several times to be told they would telephone me as soon as he returned from the operating theatre. The day before I had engaged two special nurses; one of them, as luck would have it, was an Australian nurse, Rosemary, whom he liked and who had nursed him during his previous illness. About 3 p.m. the telephone at long last rang, telling me the operation was successful but had taken longer than expected. It had, in fact, taken nearly six hours. His family then dispersed.

I waited till evening, then went to my husband's bedside. He had still hardly come round from the anaesthetic. He seemed to be lying too flat and I feared this might lead to further complications, so I decided to order a third nurse so that he would have a nurse constantly in his room. Any other help needed, such as lifting so tall and heavy a man, could be done with assistance from me or from the nursing staff on his floor. I returned very late that night, fearing pneumonia. The following day was a Sunday. I spent all day at the hospital. We talked a little but I was far from happy. All through the following week, apart from going to my flat for a bite to eat, I scarcely left him. On Friday 10 March he seemed slightly better, so under doctor's orders Rosemary and I were able to move him from bed to chair, but only while his bed was made.

In the early morning on the eleventh, at about 1 a.m., I returned to his bedside. I didn't like his breathing or his position in the bed. Having done what I could I returned to my flat, too upset and worried to sleep. At about 9 a.m. I was informed that he had died.

That afternoon Sunny and I saw J. H. Kenyon, Funeral Directors, as they ghoulishly advertise themselves in the daily press. We then drove to Blenheim – Sunny, Bramwell and myself. On the twelfth Barbie arrived, as always near to me when I was unhappy or, in this case, also in dire or deep trouble. Sarah and

Theo Roubanis flew from Jamaica or New York. Sarah was both understanding and helpful. Many other members of the family and my daughter Sara arrived.

The whole of that week is another unhappy kaleidoscope in my life. On Tuesday 14 March my husband was laid in the Blenheim Chapel, the coffin covered in the most dreadful mauve velvet with tassels and the flowers ill-arranged. I managed to get his own flag that always floated in the breeze when he was in residence at the palace. I then replaced the hideous mauve covering with his personal standard, rearranged the flowers and shut myself up in the Chapel; for a while I stayed in silence and in prayer. The following day Bert was buried in the churchyard at Bladon, next to his first wife, Mary, and not far from where Winston Churchill lies. Sunny did one good thing. He arranged for a trumpeter to sound those sad but memorable notes of the Last Post.

There were a vast number of people to luncheon after the funeral. I was lucky in that Paul Maze sat beside me. He was an ancient yet ever-young prolific painter who was truly devoted to Bert, which is more than can be said of many people who accepted his hospitality and did not come near him when he was ill. Another kind friend was David Green, who also used to visit Bert in hospital. In those weeks scarcely a flower had arrived, though one day an enormous golden basket filled with fruit was delivered to his room. 'At last, some token from your so-called friends,' I said. Bert laughed, and then he read the attached card and found it was not from anyone he knew but from Diana and David Heimann, the couple who bought Hertfordshire House from me!

After the funeral I remained alone at Blenheim, having tried in vain to talk to Sunny. I was now sleeping in the Tower bedroom. Greggie was along the passage amongst a mass of my belongings, plus two labradors and Russy. (I realize now that the dogs must have had a wonderful time, hunting and swimming after ducks in the lake and becoming generally uncontrollable.) I was in despair about my future. Bert had said in his will that the London house was mine. He also said a house with land should be given to me on the Blenheim estate. I finally managed to discuss my position with Sunny and it became apparent that there was nothing appropriate for me on the grounds of the estate and I therefore decided to look elsewhere. Barbie had in mind a house in Sussex called Grove Place which Bramwell drove me down to inspect. It did have possibilities, but although I looked at it again, meeting Freddie Wilson of John German and Son and Mr James, who I thought was an architect but turned out to be a quantity surveyor, I decided there were too many dangerous roads and the dogs would undoubtedly be killed. Robert took me to see a house near Faringdon – again hopeless because of too many roads.

Bert's memorial service took place at the Guards' Chapel. The church was full. I noticed many genuinely sad faces from the past as Sunny led me down the aisle on leaving. One of the mourners was Princess Margaret. The service took place on 28 March, sadly followed next day by one for Robin Muir, Bert's charming and clever son-in-law.

I was becoming ill with worry and unhappiness. One migraine seemed to go only to be followed by another. Sarah and Theo Roubanis suggested I should go and stay with them at their lovely newly built house not far from Athens. I discussed with Sarah the idea of giving Bramwell a break, as he was so lost and miserable after some twenty-five years of service to her father, and the possibility of my bringing Pat and Jenny Duncan and their daughter Michelle, who were also feeling lost and unhappy. Sarah agreed to all my suggestions and it was arranged that I should fly to Athens with my 'party'.

But before going to Greece many things happened. I handed back not only the Marlborough pearls, but also, on request, my wedding present, as I was told that the gold boxes had been made heirlooms under the will of my husband's first wife. I also agreed hastily and over the telephone to sell the Shepherd's Close house; by today's standards the price I then agreed was regrettable.

The time at Blenheim before leaving for Athens in April was sad and gloomy, but at least the place wasn't empty or closed down. Michael Waterhouse and his sister Libby, Bert's grandchildren, spent a night and my oldest and much loved friend Didy Holland-Martin brought her youngest daughter Fiona. I was also visited by Diana Cooper and her niece Kitty Farrell, with her husband Charles.

A flat in the palace, not far from my Tower room, was occupied by the Parncutts; he was given the post of chief guide to the palace by Bert, but this was taken from him after my husband's death. They married on 18 March but because of all the unforeseen sadness and general disruption they only had forty-eight hours for their honeymoon. They still have the flat (he continues to work at Blenheim though not in the position he was promised) and fortunately it is large enough to contain many of my documents and letters, and Mrs Parncutt does much work for me in her spare time, away from working for a consortium of doctors. She somehow manages to keep many intricate and changing situations in order, a great blessing for me during troubled times.

We departed on 12 April as planned. Sarah and Theo met us at Athens airport and we were driven to their beautifully situated house. I fear I was a terrible bore; I seldom felt anything but dreadfully ill, both in their charming, hospitable house and worse still when we went to one of the islands, Hydra, on their yacht. Sarah fetched a doctor but he gave me nothing to relieve my migraine. We stayed in Greece nearly three weeks, but considering how miserable, worried and ill I was, it was long-suffering and kind of Sarah and Theo not to send me home much earlier. Dear Bramwell developed a liking for that desperate ouzo for which Michael also had a weakness, and the Duncans enjoyed themselves; but I was no asset to the party.

We found no car from Blenheim at London airport when we arrived back, although a telegram had been sent. This was the first experience I'd had of such treatment. However, we hired a car and reached an apparently deserted bleak-looking palace. Eventually Mrs Parncutt and the butler Wadman appeared. There had been, it is true, some mix-up about the car – but there was worse to follow. There were no flowers in the sitting-room and no tea, although eventually a nasty little tray with a kitchen teaspoon did arrive. (Pat and Jenny with Michelle had at least the comfort of their own cottage.) I went to my Tower room and saw Greggie on the way. The dogs went crazy with excitement, which gave some life to my grim arrival. They had been hard to handle in my absence, never coming when called, riproaring around the park and chasing everything in sight. After the long-awaited tea I was asked about dinner. I went to bed and something was sent up to me. The following day I left for London to escape the gloom and inhospitality of Blenheim. I should have stayed in London, but my roots had always been in the country so I decided to go to Barbie's that weekend and take another look at Grove Place. It was no good – too much to change and the danger of the roads. I returned to London.

By now I was losing weight, with almost a constant headache, if not a true migraine. I seemed to stagger on with life, and I saw little prospect of finding a house. The property boom of 1972 was at its height, and a new word was constantly being used to me – 'gazumping'. No sooner was a house nearly bought than someone else offered a higher price. By mid-May I made an effort to stay with Loelia Lindsay. It was pointless in my state of health; she was kind but I felt a 'dead duck'. I returned to London to see Dr Goldman but he held out no new hope or ideas.

Robert Heber-Percy meant well by driving me to see a house beyond Salisbury, again a dreadful place; a long way with no potential. I was feeling sick and thus looked at all I saw with a jaundiced eye. We had luncheon with Anne Tree before returning to Faringdon. When I returned to my Tower room at Blenheim, Robert decided something had to be done. He telephoned his friend and house agent, Timothy Tufnell, telling him he must find me a furnished house for a six-month period to which I could move with my maids, Pat, the dogs and all my personal belongings, leaving only my furniture in store at Blenheim to be watched over by Mrs Parncutt and Mr Hoad, the palace carpenter. Timothy was quick in finding me a terrible furnished house called Cranbourne Grange near Windsor and Ascot. It was vast, both in size and price, and hideous to look upon, built in the early days of this century in the worst of pseudo-Victorian style, white with stained-glass windows in the hall and many pinnacles on the roof which, it seemed to me, was constantly being grazed by aeroplanes taking off or landing at London airport. A mere fifty yards of uncut grass separated the house from a busy road nearly opposite Windsor Safari Park.

I agreed to rent the house, provided they fenced the grass leading to this noisy and dangerous road, so anxious was I to leave the gloom of Blenheim, as by now Greggie shopped in Woodstock and did her best to cook meals for me on a gas ring upstairs. There was worse to come when Peggy Munster came over from her house to have a drink one evening. Some spirits were produced by Wadman, but the following morning I was presented with a bill for two bottles of whisky, two of gin and two of vodka.

Not only that, but I was even charged for tonic water and ginger ale!

On 9 June we set off for Cranbourne Grange, having put the Duncans' furniture in store, with mine, at Blenheim. I then borrowed the extra car from the palace for Greggie, Pat, Michelle and the dogs; I drove my own car, taking Jenny with me as I felt far from well. We bade farewell to Blenheim and departed in a cavalcade, which also included Pat's car and a hired van. The weather was colder than winter, so we took thermos flasks of hot tea and sandwiches. When we arrived at the Grange the house was damp, freezing and dirty. No fencing had been carried out – a poor look-out for my dogs. That evening we settled down as best we could. I locked off a huge and dreary drawing-room and a dining-room that appeared only fit for a formidable board-room meeting. This left us with two sitting-rooms, and upstairs I must admit there were plenty of bedrooms, cupboards and large, comfortable bathrooms. But the cold was awful, the so-called central heating did not work and anyway the radiators were inadequate. There was a scarcity of electric fires. The kitchen and many other rooms for washing etc., were plentiful, if grimy. There was a cottage with a strange caretaker-cum-gardener.

That night I was soon in bed. My head felt like breaking with pain. I couldn't even continue scanning *Country Life* in search of some dream house that didn't exist! The following day I attempted some social activities by having dinner with Billy Hamilton and the next day lunching with Mary Anne and Nick Paravicini, who also had a rented house and, like me, were searching for something permanent. Once more I felt a bore and sick in head and body. The following day, Freddie Wilson of John German and Son came to talk about houses. He was a kindly man, not well himself and little help to me then or later. Why I didn't go to London and get better in health instead of remaining at Cranbourne in a horribly and hopelessly depressed state I shall never understand. After Freddie left it was cold, with drizzling rain. It was 13 June, the anniversary of my marriage to Michael. I could scarcely believe how gloriously happy I'd been thirteen years ago. It was only 2 p.m. The dogs clamoured for a walk, but there was no place to walk unless I paced them up and down on leads, almost worse than the animals of the Safari Park across the road. A sudden and total despair overtook me and I decided to take my life.

I had provided for Pat and Jenny and for the dogs. These were the only people that would be saddened by my departure from this world. I went through the baize door to the kitchen. Amongst our mass of cases and boxes I found a bottle of whisky (bought at Blenheim). This I placed in my bedroom, then I searched for Jenny. I made one mistake; instead of telling her I had a migraine I told her I proposed to rest, taking Lindy and Russy with me. Had I said it was a migraine she might have left me to sleep. I went to bed and shed many tears, kissing and fondling my beloved Russy. I believe I left a few instructions. Not being one who drinks, I was certain that a combination of whisky and as many barbiturates as I could swallow, the little yellow Nembutal suiting me best, would undoubtedly do me in, in this way achieving a very cowardly escape from the misery and despair I was now feeling.

It was well calculated and at the time I was determined to succeed. I had never felt this way before. When Michael had died I was far more unhappy, but somehow I was as determined then to pick up my smashed life and have another go at living as I was now determined that there was no future and that I would end everything. This time I was ill, insulted and deeply hurt by various unfortunate events. A type of catabolism overtook my real self. I closed the thin ugly curtains and poured out a glass of whisky. Russy sniffed the air at this unlikely smell. I then opened the bottle of Nembutal and proceeded to swallow down the pills, chased by whisky. I have no idea how many I was able to swallow; I think the strong undiluted spirits probably overcame me before I had taken sufficient pills. It appears that by eight o'clock that evening Jenny came to my room and was horrified by the sight of me, the whisky and spilled Nembutal. When she failed to awake me she telephoned a doctor. He said he was almost retired and didn't take night calls. In desperation she rang Barbie Agar, who quite calmly told her to ring the doctor again, mentioning my name, which she hadn't done before. If that failed she must at once ring 999. On being rung for the second time the doctor said he would come.

All I recall is coming to in an ambulance, bumping through Windsor Great Park. My head was splitting with pain and I felt sick. Jenny was with me. I have no more recollections till I found myself in bed (at what turned out to be the Edward VII Hospital in Windsor), closely observed by a nurse. Then my sister Ann and daughter Sara arrived. I beseeched them to persuade a doctor or nurse to give me something to relieve the pain in my head and after a seeming eternity I was given an injection.

Sometime the following evening a Dr Harris, very Irish and charming, visited me. He said the best idea would be for me to go to his house in Ascot. At this suggestion I jumped out of bed, saying I would be ready in no time; I thought he was asking me to dinner. He laughed and said, 'Not yet. I will send for you.' At this I was very despondent. I tried to explain to him that wherever I was (and I didn't know where that was) I was being treated like a criminal, watched over every minute, sometimes even by a male nurse! He told me not to worry; I would be collected in an ambulance this very evening. On that note he left, saying we would soon meet. Eventually two ambulance men and a private nurse arrived. I was now feeling dreadfully ill once more. I was taken a short distance to a nursing home near the Ascot racecourse, a large villa, not even very secluded for a place containing so many aged nutcases or, as the owner, Dr Storey, would prefer his patients called, psychiatrics.

The first night was pretty grim. I was lifted through the front door, which I discovered later was kept permanently locked. The head nurse was male. His real name was Mr Dadds, commonly called Daddy, or Daddy-O as I called him. I was taken to a small, rather squalid room, where Daddy-O gave me what he said would give me a good night's sleep! Little did they know at this point what was needed to give me a good night's sleep! I tossed and turned, feeling desperate about my plight. The nurse looking after me was, it appears, frightened by the sights and sounds in the place, and she disappeared, never to return. I suddenly found I was named Mrs Spencer, causing me and others great confusion. I believe this was an idea of my sister's or daughter's in case of possible publicity. I was soon moved to a larger room, where the bed was equally hard and my bones seemed to grate against wood, as I was so thin and the mattress so unyielding. Someone engaged a charming young private nurse to be with me during the day, Nurse Edler. I grew very fond of her and as time went on we had many jokes.

The first doctor to visit me was a woman called Dr West. She was nice but very serious, saying, 'You will take a long time to get over this.' She looked rather surprised when I said, 'Balls.' Jenny and Pat had brought me some flowers. Now I began to realize that Jenny had saved my life, for which I was – and am – very grateful. Dr Harris, the old Irish charmer who had got me in here by making me think for a moment he was asking me out to dinner, came to see me, and so did Dr Storey. Then I imagine they discussed the problem of Mrs Spencer, all of them calling me Duchess and then trying to correct themselves. Before long this had become a joke.

I was pretty heavily sedated for a start, nevertheless I complained to my daughter about being put away in such an awful place, saying, 'Everyone but myself is old and crackers.' Nurse Edler was a great solace, and there was an enchanting, cheerful Italian staff nurse who, I slowly gathered, had great experience of psychiatric nursing. I always hoped she would be on night duty, for not only did she rub my back and all other pressure points but she found me cold chicken or anything else in the kitchen when the crazy chef was either asleep or drunk in the dead of night.

They tried many drugs on me, with little success; nearly everything made me shake all over or stutter. I soon insisted that they stop these trial-and-error methods, saying I needed rest and building up with good food, making it clear that this was unobtainable from their kitchen. So my Nurse Edler or Jenny would buy food and the nurse would cook it, usually after the kitchen was vacated by the crazy chef, who called me Me Lady or Your Grace according to his mood and was forever telling me he had once cooked for Sir Winston Churchill.

I was soon up in a dressing-gown and getting to know both patients and staff. From the beginning they did one very sensible thing, however painful it was to my skinny body – I was given an intramuscular injection of Parentrovite each day for two weeks. It is a large injection, two ampoules of vitamins mixed together, the only vitamins that didn't give me a headache. It was hard for the nurse to administer this as when I entered the home I wasn't even six stone in weight. During the first ten days I was pretty low in spirits. Few people knew where I was; even fewer cared. Ivan Moffat sent me a message or two and my daughter made many visits, as always when I'm in trouble. Robert Heber-Percy sent me a telegram saying, 'Cheer up and eat plenty of mashed potatoes.' This was a joke we had during my backgammon contest, for even if I had no wish to eat I could always manage to get down some puréed potatoes.

It was Robert himself who made me turn the corner into wishing to live again, arriving with so many beautiful lilies that they were able to extinguish the smell of the elderly and incontinent, which normally pervaded this nursing home. Then he apparently told a number of people he wanted to marry me. He declared this at a dinner party, which caused Diana Cooper to telephone me saying what lovely news it was, to which I replied, 'What news?' She said, 'I hear you are to marry the "mad boy".' I said I knew of no such news, but nevertheless it gave me the boost I needed; for once I didn't care if the William Hickey column picked up this daydream, which of course they did. Robert and I remain close friends but he would allow nothing, not even me, to disturb in any way his life at Faringdon!

After two weeks I began to take greater interest in the other patients. There was one pathetic man, no more than fifty years old, who hadn't spoken for some five years. He had a private male nurse. His quite young wife visited regularly, although she was working hard to keep him in a private nursing home. I took great trouble with this man. Before I left he actually spoke some words and looked forward to playing croquet with me and our two nurses. He had little idea of how to control his ball or mallet, but if by some lucky chance he struck the ball and came anywhere near a hoop his joy was uncontrollable. It gave me great pleasure to see him make any progress from his illness. Then there was a dotty old lady called Mrs Phillips, who was not too ill. She was just aged and had lost her marbles, as the saying goes. She collected a whole mass of old beads which she called her jewels. This was lucky for me as one day I lost, or couldn't find, an emerald which had come out of its setting. I feared the worst till I remembered Mrs Phillips's mania for beads. I went to her room and discovered my emerald amidst her collection of trash. She had no idea of its value or she would have said so. I just asked her if she would give me the green stone. She at once replied, 'My dear, you can have anything you like.'

In just over two weeks I went to London to have my hair done, my Nurse Edler accompanying me, and after this I improved rapidly. I went for walks up to the paddock in Ascot week, a little fearful that anyone might see me – I don't know why, except that I was ill-clad for such an occasion. Didy Holland-Martin visited me during Ascot week and to my surprise she was all dressed up for the occasion, which was most unlike her usual way of life. She explained that she was taking her daughter, Fiona, to the royal meeting as she was now seventeen. Didy, having gone through many tragedies, was then about to start a long course of study on the Jung system of analytical psychology in Zurich, which she has now completed, enabling her to practise in this country – a far cry from Ascot clothes! During Ascot week each year the doctors at the nursing home gave a drinks party before luncheon on Gold Cup day. Normally they never invited their patients, but I was made the exception to the rule. No attempt was made any longer to call me Mrs Spencer!

One other incident at the nursing home I must report. In the evening, when I most wanted to use what they called the patients' telephone, there was a tall, good-looking but totally crazy woman who hogged the telephone. I enquired why she was so constantly talking and to whom. The funny and gay Italian nurse told me she had done this for years. She was, in fantasy, talking to her husband who, it appeared, had died forty years ago, to which I replied, 'Isn't it lucky I don't do that to my *four* husbands! No one would ever be able to use this telephone at all.' I really believe it was from that moment onwards I had complete freedom.

I soon went back to Cranbourne Grange, where my nurse was staying on for a few days. I frequently returned to visit the staff and inmates of the Ascot home, always entering through the kitchen. I was allowed to take certain patients out, including Mrs Phillips, who escaped one day when shopping in Ascot. Fortunately, she was soon traced and returned to the home. She also came to the ghastly Grange. Here she played happily with Michelle, who was then about five years old. To watch Mrs Phillips with Michelle was a perfect example of second childhood.

There was an old boy they called the Captain. He was a little tricky, but I had promised to take him out in my Mercedes so one day we set off. I suggested we should visit the Safari Park. I forgot to lock the passenger seat door. As everyone knows who has visited the Windsor Safari Park, there are huge iron gates in the lions' enclosure. One group of cars is let through, then the gates are closed for a while before more cars are let through. It was at this moment when, to my horror, the Captain said he was getting out – and did. There were whistles and shrieks from the wardens. As luck would have it, the lions had just been fed! I was therefore able to pull him back into my car. Again, it was fortunate he was a man of light build and in a good humour that day, or the lions would have proved less expensive to feed than usual.

My stay in the Ascot nursing home was fortunately brief, but I remember the alarm I felt when the cleaning maid addressed me as 'Mrs Spencer'. This was the name chosen by Gladys, Duchess of Marlborough, who was still alive at that time but had been incarcerated for ten years in a psychiatric hospital at Northampton. The Marlboroughs would have nothing to do with her and when I asked Bert once, 'Will you take me to visit your step-mother ?', he looked surprised and asked, 'How do you know about her ?' – for a veil of secrecy had fallen over her name and whereabouts. Then he added firmly, 'She's mad. She wouldn't want to see you, or me for that matter.' Finding myself similarly put away and with the same assumed name I began to wonder if Blenheim always had this effect on its Duchesses. These crazy, frightening thoughts did much to speed my recovery.

It was Jenny who first saw an advertisement in *The Times* by Alfred Savill, the estate agents, about a house called Gellibrands. I believe they actually called it a small estate; anyway it was a house and cottage with about thirty acres near Chalfont St Peter in Buckinghamshire. I went to see this place several times, but I was not too happy about its situation – very near Hertfordshire House but not in real country. It was a scheduled house, parts of it being sixteenth century. It needed an enormous amount of money spent on it; it was too suburban, yet nonetheless there was an illusion of real countryside for a short drive gave it a secluded air. There was a dreadful garden crammed with bedding-out plants, nearly all scarlet. The cottage was a modern bungalow. It appeared stark, new and naked to the eye, with no attempt having been made to grow climbing roses or any other creeper. The house had many faults and a long and expensive task lay before me if I bought it, yet I did see a potential. In 1972 it looked very small. Ivan Moffat called it 'the white mouse'. There was yet another drawback: a swimming pool had been sited near the front of the house, too close to the attractive south side so that it ruined that aspect, especially when the terrace was constructed. A pool is a luxury I have never hankered after in our unpredictable English climate, as the heating and general upkeep are expensive and it involves constant work.

My list of necessary changes was endless (many I still hadn't visualized) but when the Agars and I left for Venice on 4 August 1972, Gellibrands was mine for better or worse. Dr Crabb, the previous owner, was a lucky man! Before him, the American novelist Temple Thurston had lived and worked in this house. In some builder's rubble I found a brass plaque on which was inscribed:

> *This part of Gellibrands was built in the*
> *reign of Queen Elizabeth I, 1558–1603. It*
> *was then renovated in the reign of*
> *Queen Elizabeth II in the year 1958.*

The latter half of this statement I find hard to believe. The bungalow needed an extensive addition; a further bedroom and bathroom and (another essential) an ironing and washroom had to be built. If one lives in the country and owns dogs this is a *must*, making it at least possible to clean the mud and rain off them in a utility room such as this.

Pat and Jenny, with their daughter, would be able to move into the bungalow long before my tenancy of the dreadful Grange ran out. I took Robert to see my new acquisition and pointed out all its problems. He told me he was certain Mrs Crabb overheard my remarks. I consider she was entitled to at the price I was forced to pay for a dilapidated house! Poor Gellibrands and poor me, for I bought this house reluctantly for a very large sum of money – £110,000. There appeared to be no other house around and at least it was safe from roads, or so I thought! I had no idea it would take me three years of hard labour, while still suffering from ill-health, before it became habitable.

25

Gellibrands

That summer I went again to Venice, where I met Arne Ekstrone, an intelligent American who took me out for meals at Harry's Bar and with whom I still correspond today. I returned to England dreading the work I had to do on Gellibrands. I had no idea how long the transformation would take, nor how many setbacks there would be. The expense was enormous and was quite a worry as by marrying Bert I had lost my American domicile and my tax position became appalling. At this time I sold Prudence, hoping to use the proceeds in England, but this has so far proved impossible. I could have kept the house but was frightened by the thought of returning to Barbados which held so many happy memories.

From 1972 until 1975 I spent two or three days a week at Gellibrands supervising the rebuilding, returning each night to London absolutely exhausted. Lanning Roper helped me to lay out a small garden and a perfectly proportioned terrace, made of Portland stone slabs. I placed my eighteenth-century lead urns around the swimming pool and garden and a pair of beautiful lead greyhounds on the terrace, and put an attractive weather-vane of an eighteenth-century gilded horse on the roof, all of which came from Hertfordshire House. The interior was more of a problem. At first Angus Menzies helped me until his untimely death following an accident. I found much of my furniture damaged from moving, and also could not accommodate it all. Foolishly I sold much of it at Christie's at a time when prices were low. But at least the Duncans and the dogs were settling in well.

An increasing worry was my health. Felix Mann again tried

to help me with acupuncture but without success and I was often tired, ill and depressed. The deep wounds of the past years were slow to heal. The Colonel (as I called Alex Young) took me to Portugal in April 1973 where I completely collapsed at a dinner party given by Henry Cotton, to everyone's great shock, and remained in bed for the rest of the holiday. Later in the year I went to Biarritz with him and Martin and Loelia Lindsay. Miles Reid also came. I saw and talked to the Duchess of Windsor, now a widow but still as chic as ever, before her long illness confined her to Paris.

During these years I saw much of my nephew, Caspar Fleming. I had known him little until his Eton days; then he used to come over to Hertfordshire House for lunch or to spend the Fourth of June holiday with us. He was alert, lively and full of mischief, indeed often wicked in his own special, intelligent way. In my London flat I had many opportunities to talk to him about his thoughts on life. Despite the fact that all material advantages were in the palm of his hand he was very sceptical about the world we live in. He was devoid of curiosity and seemed to have no wish to live out his natural span. He had travelled extensively in his life, and I asked him once: 'Would you not like to travel again?' He replied, 'I have, but what's the point? The world's no different anywhere else.' At the same time he could be plausible, witty and amusing and sometimes it was hard not to agree with him, particularly then when I was feeling sceptical about so many aspects of today's world. Nothing I nor anyone else might have done could have changed the inevitable course of events. He was to some extent a victim of the 1960s and in 1975 he died by his own choice. I still miss him.

One Saturday I was bashing along the M4 motorway at about 110 miles per hour on my way to Faringdon to stay with Robert, somewhat late for lunch. Unfortunately a police car gonged me and we both pulled up for 'the particulars' to be taken down. While I rummaged in my bag for my licence and insurance policy, Russy sat at my side. But when the officer put his hand in the car to take the documents, suddenly, without so much as a warning growl, Russy bit him savagely on the hand. I visualized a solitary future in Holloway but the officer merely said, 'All my fault. I should never have put my hand in your car. The dog was quite right to guard you and your property.' In a sudden reversal of roles, I found myself tying up his hand with a handkerchief and advising him to go to the nearest hospital for an anti-tetanus shot. No further mention was made of my speeding.

In 1974 I was walking to my aunt Kakoo's house and again Russy came to my rescue. I was trying to cross from Park Lane to Hyde Park to give Russy a walk, but could not get over the road. I asked the commissionaire at Grosvenor House and he suggested I try the underpass. It was a Sunday and so the underpass was very deserted. As we were now safe from traffic I released Russy from his lead. Before I knew what was happening an untidy youth advanced towards me and tried to wrench my bag from me. I clung on to it zealously and at the same time Russy attacked him. At that moment a bowler-hatted gentleman came into sight and the hooligan vanished with torn and blood-stained trousers. The man in the bowler hat wanted to take me to the police station but I dreaded publicity and was in any case far more worried about poor Russy, who had been badly kicked in the fray. I took him to a vet near my aunt's house. The vet feared internal injury and he was right. Russy was obviously in great pain and though for a few weeks he seemed to improve gradually, the damage was too serious for him to recover. With many tears I had to have my brave little friend put to sleep. Later Pat found me two Jack Russell terriers for sale locally. These two brothers, Jack and Russy, live now at Gellibrands, devoted to me but ferocious towards one another, except when united in some mischievous cause.

The rest of 1974 went by with hard work at Gellibrands and more ill-health. The last of many disasters before the house was completed was the flooding of the cellar. Jenny and her mother had to remove all the wine by hand. Most of the labels had come off so now I and my friends have to drink red or white with no further details. Gellibrands became a charming little house, tucked away with no cars or aeroplanes to disturb the peace. It reached a state as near perfection as I could have wished, and from time to time friends came to stay and all was comfortable and attractive. Then, just as I finished my work, a devastating blow was dealt. I discovered that the North Orbital M25 road was coming right through my land. This was thoroughly dis-heartening after three years of work and, worse still, should have been revealed to me before I bought the house. I began to lose interest in the garden and have never settled in properly. Very often when I have been alone there with the dogs I have felt shut up and isolated. With that and my bad health, I spend few weekends there even now.

Towards the end of 1975, my migraines were continuing when a new malady struck. My nose and eyes began to stream constantly. I was living on pain-killing drugs and really felt I must find out what was the matter. After my usual solitary Christmas in London – I've always hated that season since Michael died – my pain and depression grew worse, so I telephoned my daughter Sara. Sara is always wonderful in a crisis, though she soon disappears afterwards. She reunited me with my former doctor, Barry Cooper. He put me on Lythiam for a time and presently I was being observed round the clock by nurses. For three weeks I hardly closed an eye and I experienced many unpleasant side-effects, such as shaking and impediment of speech. For three months after that I seldom dressed but I went on with regular exercises. Only Barry's very heartening evening calls and visits from the Colonel (Alex Young), Ivan Moffat, Deirdre Grantley, my cousin Mary Colquhoun, Diana Cooper and Raimund von Hofmannsthal cheered me up. Otherwise I seemed forgotten or worse still too undependable to bother with. My recovery was slow but June 1976 found me by the swimming pool at Gellibrands enjoying that glorious summer.

I scarcely know any of my neighbours in this suburban area, but two couples are great friends. Mr Burrage is a scrap merchant and he and his wife have been very helpful to me. Sometimes they take me dog-racing in Slough which I much enjoy. Their daughter, Jill, has taught Pat and Jenny's daughter Michelle to be an outstanding rider for her age. My other great friends are a Liberal couple, Leslie and Doreen Darby, who are most hospitable and ready to help me in any way they can, and happy to argue about politics.

One afternoon I invited Doreen Darby over to bathe, but having a bad headache I forgot about this invitation and went to bed for the afternoon. When I heard her car I jumped out of bed and, though not well, insisted on coming down despite Jenny's attempts to prevent me. I remember little more, especially as I was still muzzy from pain-killers. All I know is that I tripped and fell on the stairs, landing unconscious at Jenny's feet. After many dramas and two nights at the local hospital I was taken to the BUPA home in Bryanston Square. Jenny told me later that I had been hard to control when I regained consciousness. She also said, 'You may be thin, but when I carried you upstairs you seemed extraordinarily heavy.' Dead weight is of course always hard to lift. X-rays, examinations and encephalographs followed in London while my foot, damaged in the fall, remained horribly painful and swollen. Even so I spent two weeks in that nursing home. Then I went to Venice with my granddaughter Anabel, travelling first class in the aeroplane and in a wheelchair or on crutches.

Back in London my health soon deteriorated once more. I saw few people and felt sometimes that compared to my past life people must think me dead. However, feeling so deathly ill, I cared nothing about that. My skin began to turn yellow, nurses moved in and my doctor hastened his investigations. At last he began to worry about my gall bladder. I had always thought that something in my body was toxic and that I was being poisoned right through my system. After many tests and discussions I entered the London Clinic for an operation to remove my gall bladder in November 1977. Robert came to stay the night before so that I should not be alone, and the Colonel took me out to lunch and, with his chauffeur Bolton, deposited me in my first-floor room at the clinic. Robert sent masses of books and Barbie had arranged for flowers to be there to take away the clinical look. My gall bladder was removed in an operation that lasted four hours instead of thirty minutes. Afterwards they told me it was not only useless but rotten and septic. The surgeon, Mr Gracey, furthermore informed me that I should have had the operation twenty years earlier.

26

The Clouds of Today

Since my operation I have gradually regained my health. I have suffered no true migraines though under stress or strain I have bad headaches.

I still seem to have many worries, perhaps the most serious one being the motorway which will soon destroy the peace of Gellibrands and the litigation I have had to enter into as a result. The knowledge that all is soon to change at my country house means that I spend more time in London. If I have to sell, then I don't know where I will live. All these problems are unresolved as I write.

London today seems a harsh city, so different from the days of my childhood. True, there is less poverty, but there is more loneliness. The large high-rise blocks of flats contain sadness, a crowded urban solitude. They are incubators of neuroses scarce known in the dirty old streets of former times, despite the comforts of today. Everything seems as stark as the modern street lighting, which offers no pity to those who pass by. I sometimes wonder whether loneliness is not worse than the privy in the back garden.

Ever since Michael's death I have felt desperately lonely and tense, very often ill and feeling myself forgotten. The life I have led since that ghastly Christmas of 1969, followed so soon by my brother's death, has been quite unlike anything I have known before.

A great sadness to me is the way that as mother and daughter Sara and I have grown apart. In some ways she disapproves of me, which makes me unhappy as I don't know why. Sometimes a year can go by with scarcely a talk on the telephone let alone a

meeting. Sara has grown into a woman of considerable capabilities and her education has certainly stood her in good stead.
She married happily and has a son, David, and a daughter,
Anabel, whose wedding took place in May 1979 (Anabel and her
husband now live in Hong Kong). Sara's nature is to work rather
than to play and her life has followed this pattern for many
years. When Edward Heath was Prime Minister she was vice-
chairman of the Conservative Party, but after his government
fell she went to work under the wing of Sir Arnold Weinstock
at the General Electric Company. They make a good working
combination. Sara has other committees and interests and
according to the newspapers I see she is now Chairman of the
National Council of Social Service. She is a good citizen and one
day no doubt she will return to politics, probably ending up a
peeress in her own right or a Dame. I think perhaps that one of
the fundamental differences between us is that I believe life to be a
game and here my darling daughter would not agree. I love and
admire much in her character and wish that we could pull back
from the chasm that separates us.

As I have said I seldom see my sister Ann, especially now that
Caspar is dead. She sold her house in Victoria Square and now
lives at Sevenhampton, near Oxford, where politicians, artists
and writers of consequence gather for the weekend. In London
she stays with Arnold (Lord) Goodman, who has been her close
friend for a number of years. I would love to see more of her,
but when I telephone her she says, 'I'm on the other line. I will
ring you back.' This she never does. Our rare meetings occur
when I go to stay with Robert at Faringdon. Then she comes
over to dine or we visit her at Sevenhampton.

Despite the incident when she sat on me in my early days, my
aunt Kakoo has been one of my greatest friends throughout life.
Now she lives in Wilton Street where I often visit her, and we
talk almost every day on the telephone.

One friend to whom I can always telephone is Diana Cooper,
though I have to choose my time carefully. Since I am inclined
to stay up very late reading, 1.30 or 2 a.m. is about the best
hour to catch Diana in. Her social life remains extraordinarily
active and in the daytime she is out and about in her Mini,
whizzing around London from one party to another, 'doggy' at
her side.

Michael was rather frightened of Diana when he first met her, but when they got to know each other they became great friends and she was a regular and always welcome visitor to Hertfordshire House. Diana has survived many crises, the greatest of all being the loss of her beloved Duff. Now she lives in Little Venice near her son, John Julius, and has created a new and busy life for herself. She has always succeeded in being very 'with it' not only socially but also in the media, helped in this by Nigel Ryan, whom she refers to as her 'last attachment'. In the First World War she took morphine and flew over the trenches with boyfriends, today she talks on Capital Radio and flies Laker to New York. Diana is also wonderfully kind to all friends when they are suffering from ill-health. At a time of deep depression in 1977, I was roused from slumber by a sudden visit from Diana, who came to see me to talk me out of my gloom. She was successful in persuading me to make some effort to clamber back into life.

Diana herself does not give up however depressed she may secretly feel at times. Even now there are light-hearted rumours circulating London about 'The Wedding of the Year'. A close friendship has been forged between Diana and Sir Robert Mayer, the hundred-year-old founder of Youth and Music. Sir Robert has been writing some affectionate letters to Diana and naturally he invited her to his hundredth birthday concert at the Festival Hall. This occasion was not without problems. Diana was standing in the foyer when an attractive young woman came over to talk to her. Being rather short-sighted Diana did not at first recognize that this was none other than the Queen. In a terrible fluster, she realized that she had failed to curtsy and she hurriedly thought of a way to recover the situation. 'I am very sorry, Ma'am,' said Diana, 'but I didn't recognize you without your crown on.' Unfortunately Her Majesty did not seem to find this amusing and the next morning found Diana composing a suitable letter of apology.

My life has changed drastically in the last ten years, but I had many star-spangled years before then, with wonderful sparkling moments. More important I have known true love, contentment and real happiness. I do not share Diana's great wish to be out and about every night, but nevertheless she is an example to us all. For life is a great gift, and life is for living.

There is little else to say – except that one never knows what might be round the next hairpin bend. I keep this in my thoughts as all manner of tricks and twists are played by unseen and unknown powers on us poor mortals.

Index

TENNANT
A select family tree

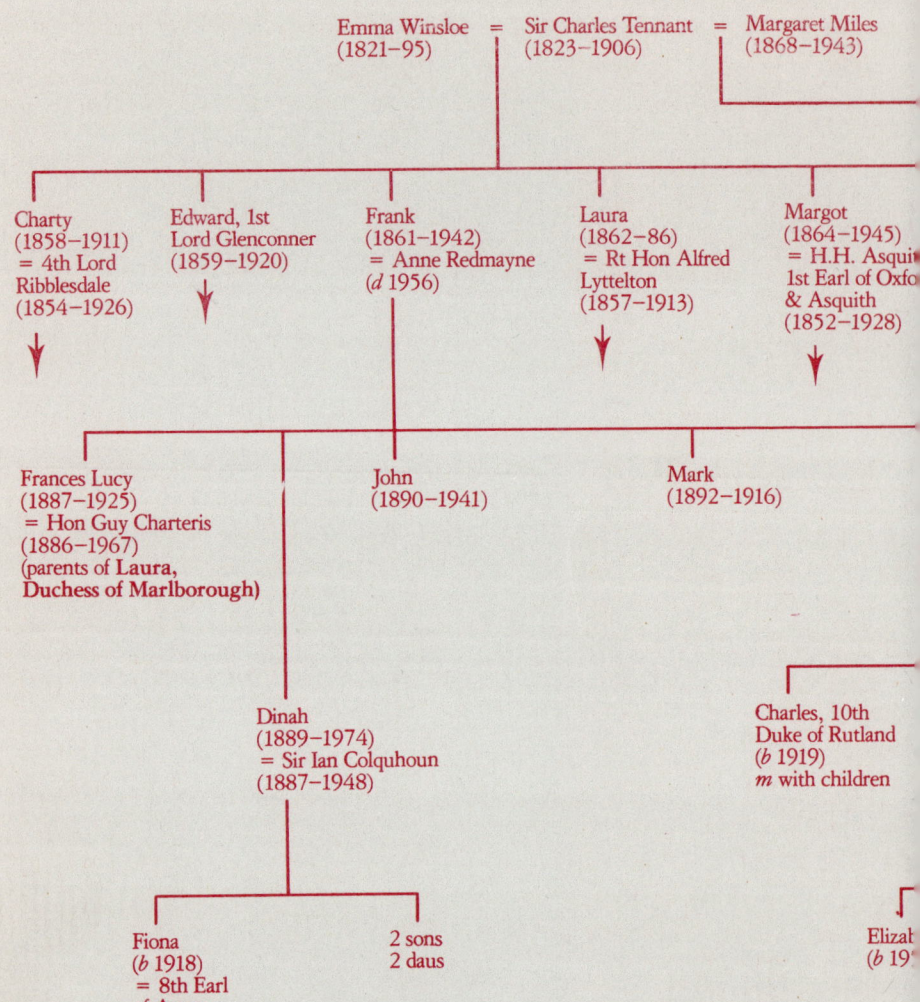

Emma Winsloe (1821–95) = Sir Charles Tennant (1823–1906) = Margaret Miles (1868–1943)

Charty (1858–1911) = 4th Lord Ribblesdale (1854–1926)

Edward, 1st Lord Glenconner (1859–1920)

Frank (1861–1942) = Anne Redmayne (d 1956)

Laura (1862–86) = Rt Hon Alfred Lyttelton (1857–1913)

Margot (1864–1945) = H.H. Asqui 1st Earl of Oxfo & Asquith (1852–1928)

Frances Lucy (1887–1925) = Hon Guy Charteris (1886–1967) (parents of **Laura, Duchess of Marlborough**)

John (1890–1941)

Mark (1892–1916)

Dinah (1889–1974) = Sir Ian Colquhoun (1887–1948)

Charles, 10th Duke of Rutland (b 1919) m with children

Fiona (b 1918) = 8th Earl of Arran (b 1910)

2 sons 2 daus

Elizal (b 19